Advance Praise

"Dr. Mathews has written an extraordinary book on hoarding disorder. In *Recognizing and Treating Hoarding Disorder*, she includes not only what it's like for the person who has it, but what it's like for the family members. She introduces you to what happens in the brain areas that cause this disease and treatments that can work. This hopeful book is a must-read for professionals as well as patients and families who suffer from this disorder."

—**Louann Brizendine, M.D.**, Neuropsychiatrist, Clinical Professor, UCSF, Marc and Lynne Benioff Endowed Professor of Psychiatry

"Too few clinicians can clearly recognize hoarding disorder or know the options available to treat and manage the condition. In this clear and comprehensive book, Dr. Carol Mathews covers all the important bases. Readers will find guidance in identifying hoarding disorder, assessing the condition, and current treatment options and their efficacy. Dr. Mathews takes up other important features of the condition, notably the effect of hoarding behaviors on friends and family members, its presentation in youth, and features of animal hoarding. I highly recommend this book to anyone who wants to understand this condition and how to help those who suffer with it."

—**Michael A. Tompkins, Ph.D.**, ABPP, author of *Digging Out: Helping Your Loved One Manage Clutter, Hoarding, and Compulsive Acquiring* and *Clinician's Guide to Severe Hoarding: A Harm Reduction Approach*

"For people living with HD, 'stuff' is just the tip of the proverbial iceberg. Dr. Carol Mathew's book, *Recognizing and Treating Hoarding Disorder: How Much is Too Much?*, dives beneath the surface to examine the complexities of this often maligned and misunderstood mental health challenge. In a sea of misinformation, stigma, and shame, this book provides the science and sensitivity needed to navigate safely to a life less cluttered."

—**Lee Shuer**, recovering finder/keeper and co-founding member of Mutual Support Consulting, LLC, coauthor of *The Buried in Treasures Workshop Facilitator's Guide* and *WRAP® for Reducing Clutter*

"Dr. Mathews delivers an important book that is a must-read for anyone interested in learning about hoarding disorder. Her work integrates the most contemporary research on epidemiology, etiology, assessment, and treatment of hoarding disorder while also producing a book that is accessible for a broad audience. Information is delivered in a manner that one can see the application readily and use the insights in their own practice or care of individuals struggling with hoarding."

—**Scott Mackin, Ph.D.**, Neuropsychologist, Professor In Residence, Department of Psychiatry, University of California San Francisco

Recognizing and Treating Hoarding Disorder

Recognizing and Treating Hoarding Disorder

How Much Is Too Much?

CAROL A. MATHEWS

W. W. NORTON & COMPANY
Independent Publishers Since 1923

Note to Readers: Standards of clinical practice and protocol change over time, and no technique or recommendation is guaranteed to be safe or effective in all circumstances. This volume is intended as a general information resource for professionals practicing in the field of psychotherapy and mental health; it is not a substitute for appropriate training, peer review, or clinical supervision. Neither the publisher nor the author(s) can guarantee the complete accuracy, efficacy, or appropriateness of any particular recommendation in every respect. As of press time, the URLs displayed in this book link or refer to existing sites. The publisher and author are not responsible for any content that appears on third-party websites.

For information about permission to reproduce selections from this book, write to Permissions, W. W. Norton & Company, Inc., 500 Fifth Avenue, New York, NY 10110

For information about special discounts for bulk purchases, please contact W. W. Norton Special Sales at specialsales@wwnorton.com or 800-233-4830

Manufacturing by Lake Book Manufacturing, Inc.
Book design by Anna Reich
Production manager: Katelyn MacKenzie

ISBN: 978-0-393-71357-2

W. W. Norton & Company, Inc., 500 Fifth Avenue, New York, N.Y. 10110
www.wwnorton.com

W. W. Norton & Company Ltd., 15 Carlisle Street, London W1D 3BS

1 2 3 4 5 6 7 8 9 0

This book is dedicated to all of those who suffer from problematic hoarding, and to their families, friends, and loved ones.

CONTENTS

ACKNOWLEDGMENTS

This work would not have been possible without the scientists and clinicians who have led the way. Many thanks to the thought leaders in this field, and in particular to Randy Frost and Gail Steketee, who are mentors and role models for so many of us. Thanks also to all of my colleagues in the hoarding field, who continuously work to advance scientific knowledge, and to improve the lives and health of those with hoarding disorder. Finally, my deepest heartfelt thanks to Lee Shuer and all of the individuals and families who work so tirelessly to educate the public about hoarding disorder, decrease stigma, and advocate for the rights of people and families who are impacted by hoarding.

Recognizing and Treating Hoarding Disorder

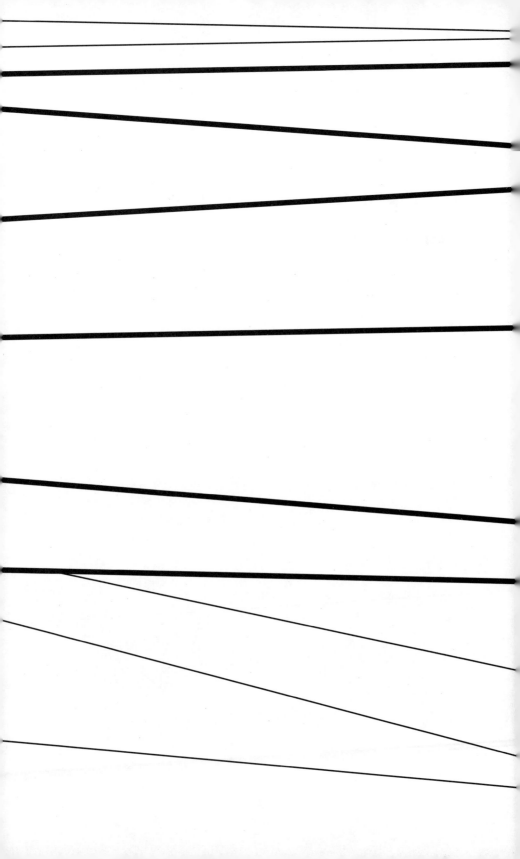

Chapter 1

What Is Hoarding Disorder?

We all have heard the statements, "She's a pack rat" or "He's a hoarder," but how many of us really know what that means? While literary references to hoarding can be found as early as the 14th century, and hoarding behaviors have likely existed since the beginning of humankind, hoarding disorder (HD) was only officially recognized by psychiatrists and other health care professionals as a discrete psychiatric illness in 2013, with the publication of the 5th edition of the *Diagnostic and Statistical Manual of Mental Disorders* (*DSM-5*) by the American Psychiatric Association.

A BRIEF HISTORY OF HOARDING

From the fourth circle of hell in Dante's *Divine Comedy*, circa 1320 A.D., through the Great Depression and World War II, the term *hoarding* referred specifically to the accumulation (and often the hiding) of money or objects of value, and was considered to be a form of greed. In Dante's fourth circle, the Hoarder/Waster was a creature who consisted of two people merged into one: One of whom collected and hoarded coins, which the other then spewed or wasted (Alighieri, 1472/1995r). In the play *Henry VI*, Shakespeare refers to hoarding several times, as in the following speech by King Henry (Shakespeare 1623/1995r):

> **"Didst thou never hear**
> **That things ill got had ever bad success?**
> **And happy always was it for that son**
> **Whose father for his hoarding went to hell?"**

Despite these notable examples, references to hoarding in books and other media were relatively few until the 1930s, when the food and economic scarcity and bank instability resulting from World War I, the Great Depression, and World War II led to the hoarding of gold coins, as well as food and other rations. Hoarding during this time was so prominent that both the Canadian and the U.S. governments banned it (Figure 1.1). Presidents Herbert Hoover and Franklin Delano Roosevelt called out the hoarding of money and rations in their radio addresses—Hoover publicly denounced what he called "traitorous hoarding," saying, "The battlefront today is against the hoarding of currency." Roosevelt went even further by issuing an executive order forbidding hoarding (Hoover, 1934).

Dictionary definitions of hoarding as a general behavior continue to revolve around the accumulation and storage of money or valuables even today. For example, the *Merriam Webster Online Dictionary* (n.d.) defines *hoarding* as: "(1) to accumulate for preservation, future use in a hidden or carefully guarded place, (2) to gather or accumulate, or (3) to keep to oneself" while the *Oxford English Dictionary* (March 11, 2020) defines the verb "hoard" as: "(1) to accumulate (money or valued objects) and hide or store away, (2) to keep in one's mind for future use." However, the behavioral construct of hoarding has evolved over time such that the term now evokes images of large amounts of clutter consisting of a mix of valuable and useless items, often including trash.

The concept and awareness of domestic hoarding—the hoarding of

Figure 1.1: Are You Breaking the Law? Patriotic Canadians Will Not Hoard Food: Canada Food Board sensitive campaign. *Source: Library and Archives Canada/National Archives of Canada fondes/ e01607116. Used with permission.*

objects including trash and broken or otherwise unusable items, rather than money, arose in the mid-20th century, primarily through newspaper reporting, both mainstream and sensationalistic. The most well-known early U.S. media report of domestic hoarding was of the Collyer brothers, who lived in Harlem in the early 1900s. Their strange behaviors, including extreme hoarding, came to public attention through outlets such as *The New York Times*.

The Collyer Brothers

Homer and Langley Collyer were born in 1881 and 1885 respectively, and they lived together for most of their lives in a Harlem brownstone. Although intelligent and well-educated, Homer and Langley were known primarily for their reclusiveness and unusual activities. The brothers kept to themselves, rarely went out of their home, and were generally known as collectors and scavengers.

Although it is not known just how or when their hoarding began, over the course of decades, the Collyer brothers amassed such a volume of items that their home became a warren of pathways and tunnels, with all rooms in the house impacted. They hoarded books, furniture, musical instruments, newspapers, magazines, trash, and many other things (including human organs pickled in jars, inherited from their father who had been a gynecologist).

Because they were rumored to be wealthy and hoarding vast amounts of money and other valuable items, they were the victims of several attempted burglaries. To combat this, they boarded up their doors and windows, further contributing to their image as bizarre recluses. Langley, who studied engineering in college, also set booby traps throughout the rubbish that filled the house from floor to ceiling to prevent intruders from entering their property.

The impact of their hoarding was so great that the Collyer brothers lived for many years without running water or functional electricity, and refused to allow anyone, including plumbers or electricians, into their home. Langley cared for Homer, who had gone blind in 1932, was paralyzed from rheumatism, and never left the house. By the mid-1930s, when the brothers were in their 50s, Langley left the home only late at night, when he would walk for miles, buying food, but also scavenging food and other objects that aroused his interest from trash bins or off the street. Langley brought these materials, including rotting or half eaten food, home on a nightly basis, where it added to the ever-growing collection inside their brownstone.

The extent and nature of the Collyer brothers' hoarding, which was extreme, was well known in the 1930s and 1940s, and received media attention several times, usually when authorities or other officials attempted to enter the home. In fact, clean up and excavation by New York authorities was attempted more than once, always unsuccessfully, as Langley Collyer defended his property from entry by anyone other than himself and his brother.

The story of the Collyer brothers ended tragically in 1947, when an anonymous tipster called the police to report a dead body at the

Collyer home, and a smell of decomposition. The police initially had difficulty entering the home due to the extent of the hoard, which blocked all of the doors and windows. They eventually succeeded by physically breaking in through the front door and moving massive amounts of detritus to create a path into the home.

After several hours of digging through the materials that filled the brownstone wall to wall and floor to ceiling, the police found Homer Collyer's body. He was later declared by the coroner to have died of heart disease and starvation. Langley Collyer was nowhere to be seen, and it was initially thought that he had fled the home. When he did not attend his brother's funeral, however, the police returned to the Collyer brownstone, and continued to search for Langley inside the house.

Several weeks later, after removing more than 19 tons of materials and 86 tons of trash, the body of Langley Collyer was found buried in the hoard. His body was partially eaten by rats, and he appeared to have died several weeks earlier, prior to the estimated date of Homer's death. Langley's decomposing body was actually the source of the smell that led to the previous discovery of Homer's body. The police theorized that Langley had been crawling through one of the many tunnels that he had created through the enormous accumulation of items and rubbish in the home to bring food to his brother when he tripped one of the booby traps he had set, and was crushed by the resulting avalanche of debris.

Although the Collyer brothers case is sensational and extreme, it does serve as a good illustration of hoarding disorder. Homer and Langley collected and kept all sorts of items, including valuables, trash, and outdated food. They fiercely defended their possessions from others, never threw anything away, and felt that all of the items they kept were important, even necessary. For example, when asked why he kept all of the thousands of newspapers that were found throughout the home, including some that were many years old, Langley said that he was "saving newspapers for Homer, so that when he regains his sight he can catch up on the news."

Langley was also an acquirer—on his routine walks around the neighborhood to procure food, he also scavenged for and collected many, if not most, of the other materials that he found along the way, including those abandoned on the street or left in garbage cans. Finally, as is characteristic of many individuals with hoarding disorder, the Collyer brothers had extremely limited insight into their illness and the impact of their behaviors. In other words, they did not recognize that their hoarding was a problem, despite clear objective evidence that they could not function normally within their home and were in clear physical danger from their mounds of materials. As a result of their limited insight, Homer and Langley were profoundly impaired by their disorder, which ultimately led to both of their deaths.

In subsequent decades, several other examples of extreme hoarding also emerged in the media. These cases were of particular interest to the public because, in addition to the sensationalism of their stories, the individuals in question typically moved in prominent social circles early in their lives but became increasingly isolated over time.

Ida Mayfield Wood

An early example of a socialite who suffered from hoarding disorder is Ida Mayfield Wood, who lived from 1838 to 1932. Ida was the wife of Benjamin Wood, who was the publisher of *The New York Daily News* in the late 1800s. Benjamin was a compulsive gambler, whereas Ida was a saver who managed to remain solvent and even wealthy in the face of significant financial losses from her husband's continued gambling. In exchange for providing her with half of his winnings, and for absorbing all of his losses himself, Ida promised not to interfere with or try to stop Benjamin's gambling. This agreement allowed Ida to accumulate a substantial amount of money over time, and perhaps more importantly, to protect it from being lost to her husband's gambling addiction. As was later discovered, over the years, Ida not only hoarded the money she accumulated, she also used some of it to acquire a substantial stockpile of items.

After Benjamin's death in 1900, Ida briefly became the editor and publisher of *The News*, before selling it in 1901. In 1907, Ida moved with her daughter Emma and her sister Mary to the Herald Square Hotel, where the three lived until their deaths 30 years later. Over the next several decades, the three women became progressively withdrawn and cloistered, had little contact with the outside world, and allowed no one, not even hotel staff, to enter their rooms. Emma Wood, Ida's daughter, died in 1928, and in 1931, when Mary became ill, Ida finally called in help. She and her sister were found living in squalor in the hotel suite, which was filled with trash, useless items, and more than $1 million in jewels, cash, and securities. In part because of the publicity that resulted from this discovery, Ida's death in 1932 triggered an avalanche of over 1,000 claimants for her fortune.

The Women of Grey Gardens

After the Collyer brothers, the mother and daughter duo, Edith Ewing Bouvier Beale (known as "Big Edie") and Edith Bouvier Beale (known as "Little Edie"), are perhaps the most well-known individuals with pathological hoarding to come to media attention. Their hoarding symptoms likely began in the early 1930s, although they first came to public attention in the 1960s. The story of the Bouvier Beale women and their mansion, Grey Gardens, has been the topic of multiple books, as well as a documentary, an HBO movie, and a Broadway musical.

Big and Little Edie were the aunt and cousin of Jacqueline Kennedy Onassis, respectively, and moved in the same prominent social circles (Sheehy, 1972). Big Edie, who was born in 1893, briefly pursued a singing career, before marrying Phelan Beale, an attorney in her father's law firm. Little Edie, who was born in 1917, was the oldest of their three children.

In 1923, Phelan Beale Sr. purchased the Grey Garden mansion, which was located in an affluent section of East Hampton, for his family's use. The Beale family lived there from 1923 until 1931, when Phelan and Big Edie separated. After the separation, Big Edie lived at Grey Gardens with the children, receiving child support but not alimony or other financial support from Phelan, who ultimately divorced Big Edie in 1946.

After Phelan abandoned the family, Big Edie's two sons, Phelan Beale Jr. and Bouvier Beale, left the home for school and ultimately for independent lives. Little Edie also left briefly, and lived for a few years in Manhattan, but returned to Grey Gardens in 1952. Big and Little Edie remained together at Grey Gardens for the next 25 years, until Big Edie's death in 1977.

It is not known exactly when or why Big and Little Edie began to hoard. Big Edie was an animal lover who collected cats, and by the 1970s, had over 300 cats and kittens living in Grey Gardens and its environs. Little Edie came back from New York in the 1950s, at her mother's request, specifically to help her care for the animals.

Despite being well known socially, the two women lived on a very limited income for most of their lives. After Phelan left and the child support stopped, neither Big Edie, nor Little Edie, who never married and did not work, had an independent source of income. Big Edie's sons both refused to provide financial support to the women, in the hopes that it would force them to leave Grey Gardens, even to the extent of refusing to pay their property taxes. This approach unfortunately had an unintended outcome. The women, led by Big Edie, refused to leave, and continued to live in ever-increasing poverty and ultimately, in squalor. Their home was filled with animals, old food cans and other containers, old newspapers, and even, as the plumbing and other facilities fell into disrepair, human feces and other waste (Sheehy, 1972).

The extreme hoarding of the Bouvier Beale women rivaled that of the Collyer brothers and is particularly dramatic because it includes animal hoarding, in this case, the hoarding of hundreds of cats. Over time, Big and Little Edie's hoarding led to significant health code violations in their progressively deteriorating home, endangering their health and that of the neighboring villagers. As a result, Big and Little Edie faced eviction several times, and were rescued from this fate at least once by the intervention of Mrs. Onassis and her sister, Lee Radziwill. Big Edie died in 1977, at age 81, of pneumonia. Little Edie left Grey Gardens approximately two years after her mother's death and attempted to start a new life in the theater. She died in 2002 at age 84.

THE EVOLUTION OF HOARDING DISORDER

Although the term was not in use at the time of these extreme case examples, it is clear in retrospect that the Collyer brothers, Ida Mayfield Wood, and the Bouvier Beale women all suffered from what is now known as *hoarding disorder*. As evidenced by the many articles written about the Collyer brothers, Mrs. Wood, and the Bouvier Beale women in the popular press, hoarding cases have appeared in the news media for over 100 years, although the medical literature has been slower to recognize pathological hoarding as a medical or psychiatric problem. In fact, the terms used to describe hoarding symptoms and those who exhibit them demonstrate the evolving conceptualization of hoarding over the years from a somewhat quaint character trait (described using terms such as *squirrel* or *magpie*) to a character flaw (described using terms such as *clutterer* or *pack rat*), to a psychological condition (described using terms such as *disposophobia* or *syllogomania*) (Table 1.1).

Similarly, clinical definitions of what is now formally termed hoarding disorder (HD) have evolved from the 1960s and 1970s, when hoarding was originally described by clinicians as a feature of senility or dementia, to the current conceptualization as a discrete psychiatric disorder that occurs independently of dementia and other neurodegenerative disorders.

The first clear reference in the medical literature to what would now be called hoarding behaviors was in a paper in the *British Medical*

TABLE 1.1: HOARDING DISORDER TERMINOLOGY

Terms used to describe hoarding disorder (left) and terms for people with hoarding disorder (right) in the medical literature and lay press from the 1800s to the present day.

Messy house syndrome	Hoarder
Pathological hoarding	Clutterer
Squalor syndrome	Collector
Self-neglect syndrome	Squirrel
Bowerbird syndrome	Magpie
Collyer brothers syndrome	Accumulator
Domestic hoarding	Pack rat
Diogenes syndrome	Gatherer
Disposophobia	Chronic saver
Syllogomania	Disposophobe
Compulsive hoarding	Finder/Keeper
Senile breakdown syndrome	Compulsive hoarder or acquirer
Chronic disorganization	Organizationally challenged

Journal (*BMJ*) by Macmillan and Shaw in 1966. This paper described 72 community-based older adults who were living in a condition of extreme squalor. In essentially all of these cases, the squalor was found to have occurred secondary to dementia, or senility, as it was called then. The authors termed this phenomenon *senile breakdown syndrome* (Macmillan & Shaw, 1966). Senile breakdown syndrome primarily described symptoms of self-neglect, but the description also included hoarding behaviors, which occurred in 65% of those studied. Interestingly, the authors noted that hoarding behaviors were most prominent in individuals who also had psychotic symptoms such as auditory or visual hallucinations or paranoid delusions. Psychosis is another psychiatric symptom, characteristic of schizophrenia, but also seen in other severe mental illnesses, and in moderate to severe dementia, that, like hoarding, can result in profound functional impairment.

A similar case series of 30 hospitalized elderly patients that was published 10 years later in *The Lancet* also described hoarding behaviors in the context of extreme self-neglect (Clark, Mankikar, & Gray, 1975). In the cases described in this article, the hoarding behaviors were comprised primarily of compulsive hoarding of rubbish, which the authors termed *syllogomania*. Somewhat ironically, the authors named the entire constellation of symptoms seen in these patients Diogenes syndrome, after the 4th century B.C. Greek philosopher Diogenes, who was known for his ascetic lifestyle as well as for his peculiar behaviors (Mark, 2014).

Diogenes is best known as the philosopher who embarked on an ongoing search for an honest man by holding a lantern to the faces of the citizens of Athens. However, he also exhibited other unusual behaviors, and these are likely why the authors of the *BMJ* case series chose the term *Diogenes syndrome* when naming the collection of symptoms that they observed. Diogenes eschewed all material possessions, including housing, and famously lived in a large ceramic jar in the public marketplace. He lived off of the charity of others, and rejected all social norms, urinating, defecating, and even masturbating in public. He claimed that people were trapped in a societal structure that he called a make-believe world, and that for this reason, they were living in a dream state rather than in reality.

Interestingly, half of those with Diogenes syndrome in *The Lancet* (1975) study did not have a known dementia or psychiatric illness, in contrast to the *BMJ* case series. However, they did have signs that neuropsychologists in the late 1990s and early 2000s might recognize as early pre-clinical symptoms of cognitive impairment, such as emotional lability, aggression, dependence, and "distortion of reality," in addition to their hoarding symptoms. This suggests that patients who have symptoms of Diogenes syndrome might actually be at increased risk for developing cognitive impairment, and that hoarding in this context might represent one of the early warning signs of incipient dementia.

Case series of individuals with hoarding symptoms continued to be published for the next 30 years, initially in the setting of dementia and other neurodegenerative disorders and increasingly in the context of psychiatric disorders, including schizophrenia and autism. However, beginning in the early 1980s, symptoms commonly associated with hoarding, including difficulty discarding items and excessive acquisition, were more consistently described in the context of psychiatric illness. In the psychiatric literature, hoarding symptoms were first included in definitions and depictions of obsessive compulsive personality disorder, and later became associated with obsessive compulsive disorder.

The first mention of hoarding behaviors in the *Diagnostic and Statistical Manual for Mental Disorders* came in 1987, with the third edition, revised (*DSM-III-R*), where difficulty discarding worn-out or worthless items was listed as one of the criteria for obsessive compulsive personality disorder, or OCPD. In the theoretical conceptualization of OCPD, the inability to discard unneeded objects was characterized as being primarily a result of indecision, which also manifested as fear of making mistakes, rumination, and procrastination. Excessive acquisition, which is also commonly thought of as a symptom of hoarding disorder, was not a part of the *DSM-III-R* OCPD criteria, and the accumulation of clutter potentially resulted from difficulty discarding was likewise not discussed.

The fourth edition of the *DSM*, the *DSM-IV*, published in 1994, kept the definition of OCPD, including the difficulty discarding criterion, essentially intact, although the description of this aspect of the diagnosis was expanded. Rather than focusing on indecision, the *DSM-IV* noted that individuals with OCPD regarded discarding items as wasteful because they might be needed in the future. For the first time, this edition of the *DSM* also addressed the potential consequences of holding onto unneeded items (i.e., hoarding), suggesting that the volume of material collected could be a source of conflict for the patient and their spouses or roommates. The *DSM-IV* also noted that individuals with OCPD might refer to themselves as or admit to being "pack rats", another indirect reference to the accumulation of clutter that results from hoarding (APA, 1994). In this view of OCPD, the *DSM-IV* thus captured two of what later came to be thought of as the primary symptoms of hoarding disorder: difficulty discarding and the resulting clutter. Somewhat paradoxically, excessive attention to household chores and cleanliness was also described as a component of OCPD, in this case with regard to the criterion describing excessive attention to work and productivity.

Despite being listed as a symptom of OCPD, much of the research that was done on hoarding from the 1980s through the early 2000s was actually conducted in samples of individuals with a different diagnosis, obsessive compulsive disorder, or OCD, rather than in people with OCPD. These early investigations were based on the observation that, in clinical samples at least, individuals with OCD often also exhibited high rates of hoarding behaviors, and focused more on the compulsive aspect of hoarding, excessive (or compulsive) acquisition than on problems with letting go of things.

The association between hoarding and OCD in the literature became so pronounced that, over time, compulsive hoarding came to be seen by many mental health providers as a symptom or subtype of OCD rather than of OCPD. However, it was not until 2013, with the publication of the 5th edition, that the *DSM* listed hoarding behaviors as a possible symptom of OCD. The definition of OCPD in this edition also contains hoarding behaviors as a component of the diagnosis. However, in the *DSM-5*, the OCPD hoarding criterion specifically refers to the hoarding of money and "a miserly spending" style, rather than to the keeping of objects (American Psychiatric Association, 2013).

The *DSM-5* also represents the first time that this fundamental diagnostic guide for psychiatrists and other health care providers formally recognized that hoarding symptoms could occur as a separate, unique, psychiatric illness. In this edition, hoarding symptoms are discussed as occurring *both* as a primary manifestation of hoarding disorder (examined in more detail later in this chapter), *and* as a symptom of OCD. The *DSM-5* also specifically distinguishes between hoarding symptoms that occur within the context of obsessions and compulsions typical of OCD and those that are more characteristic of hoarding disorder.

Although only formally recognized by the *DSM-5* in 2013, pathological hoarding was first conceptualized as a unique and separate syndrome independent of OCD and other psychiatric or neurological illnesses in the early 1990s by Rachel Gross and Randy Frost. Ms. Gross, a psychology student at Smith College, and Dr. Frost, her advisor, conducted a study examining the characteristics of 100 individuals who responded to an advertisement seeking people who considered themselves to be "packrats or chronic savers." They published their findings in 1993 in a seminal article titled, "The hoarding of possessions"(R. O. Frost & Gross, 1993), which was the nidus for the modern era of research on hoarding disorder. This article described pathological hoarding as "the acquisition of, and failure to discard, possessions which appear to be useless or of limited value" (p. 367).

Although Rachel Gross ultimately went on to other things, subsequent work on the theoretical construct of hoarding as a stand-alone syndrome by Dr. Frost and his collaborators, Gail Steketee, Tamara Hartl, and others, form the basis of our current understanding of this illness. Hoarding disorder (HD) is now one of the five disorders listed in the Obsessive Compulsive and Related Disorders (OCRDs) section of the *DSM-5*, along with OCD, body dysmorphic disorder, trichotillomania (hair pulling disorder), and excoriation disorder (skin picking disorder) (American Psychiatric Association, 2013).

DEFINITION OF HOARDING DISORDER

The modern conceptualization of hoarding disorder, as laid out in the *DSM-5*, has not changed substantially from the early definition put forward by Frost and colleagues, with one subtle but important exception. While the 1993 definition focused on both the acquisition of material items and on the failure to discard these items as core elements of the diagnosis, the current definition describes the *accumulation* rather than the *acquisition* of possessions as being key. Excessive acquisition, which was originally characterized by Frost and colleagues as one of the three primary features of hoarding, is no longer thought to be a required element of the diagnosis.

The distinction between *accumulation* of possessions due to difficulty disposing of unneeded or excessive numbers of items and active *acquisition* in the form of excessive buying or collecting is important for the treatment of hoarding disorder in the same way that distinguishing between a symptom of a physical illness and a fundamental feature of that illness is important. For example, while fever and cough are common symptoms of pneumonia, simply treating fever or cough will not effectively treat the underlying cause of the pneumonia. Identifying the source of these symptoms—in this case a specific bacteria or virus—and treating that source, is necessary.

Thus, while the most apparent and easily recognized symptoms of HD are the external manifestations, specifically prominent clutter and excessive accumulation, they are actually secondary rather than primary symptoms. From a clinical and etiological standpoint, the core symptom of HD is neither accumulation nor clutter, but *difficulty discarding,* which then leads to accumulation and clutter, and thus to functional impairment. In order to ultimately understand the underlying causes, identification of the core features of HD, in other words, those aspects of the disorder that come as close as possible to the underlying causes, is necessary.

The current psychiatric criteria for hoarding disorder as defined in the *DSM-5* are listed in Table 1.2. A detailed discussion of the core symptoms and other important characteristics of HD follow.

DIFFICULTY DISCARDING

The first two *DSM-5* criteria for hoarding disorder include persistent difficulty in discarding unneeded items, regardless of their value (Criterion A), that arise from a perceived need to save the items, and accompanied by distress in discarding them (Criterion B). Individuals with HD report being reluctant to part with objects for many reasons, including (1) fears that the item (or the information contained in the item, in the case of papers or other forms of media) will be needed again at some time in the future, either by themselves or by others, (2) sentimental reasons, or (3) belief that the item is or will be needed as a memory aid to remember particular events or people.

TABLE 1.2 DEFINITION OF HOARDING DISORDER ACCORDING TO THE *DIAGNOSTIC AND STATISTICAL MANUAL OF MENTAL DISORDERS*

Primary diagnostic criteria (all criteria must be met):

A. Persistent difficulty in discarding or parting with personal possessions, regardless of their actual value.

B. This difficulty is due to a perceived need to save items and distress associated with discarding them.

C. The difficulty discarding possessions results in the accumulation of possessions that congest and clutter active living areas and substantially compromises their intended use. If living areas are uncluttered, it is only because of the interventions of third parties (e.g., family members, cleaners, authorities).

D. The hoarding causes clinically significant distress or impairment in social, occupational, or other important areas of functioning (including maintaining a safe environment for self and others).

E. The hoarding is not attributable to another medical condition (e.g., brain injury, cerebrovascular disease, Prader-Willi syndrome).

F. The hoarding is not better explained by the symptoms of another mental disorder (e.g., hoarding symptoms in obsessive compulsive disorder, decreased energy in major depressive disorder, delusions in schizophrenia or another psychotic disorder, cognitive deficits in major neurocognitive disorder, restricted interests in autism spectrum disorder).

Specify if:

With excessive acquisition: If difficulty discarding possessions is accompanied by excessive acquisition of items that are not needed or for which there is no available space.

Specify if:

With good or fair insight: The individual recognizes that hoarding-related beliefs and behaviors (pertaining to difficulty discarding items, clutter, or excessive acquisition) are problematic.

With poor insight: The individual is mostly convinced that hoarding-related beliefs and behaviors (pertaining to difficulty discarding items, clutter, or excessive acquisition) are not problematic despite evidence to the contrary.

With absent insight/delusional beliefs: The individual is completely convinced that hoarding-related beliefs and behaviors (pertaining to difficulty discarding items, clutter, or excessive acquisition) are not problematic despite evidence to the contrary.

Source: Reprinted with permission from the Diagnostic and Statistical Manual of Mental Disorders (5th ed.). (Copyright 2013). American Psychiatric Association. All rights reserved.

For many individuals with HD, the thought of discarding items that most people would consider to be not only useless, but actually garbage, such as soiled napkins from a long-ago birthday party, rubber bands, old grocery receipts, or plastic grocery bags can evoke considerable distress. For example, in addition to photos and other more typical mementos, an individual may keep *all* remnants of her child's first birthday party, from the photos to the party favors, and sometimes even to the soiled paper napkins and plates for years or even for decades.

Although the reasons given for saving vary, the most common explanations relate to memory or difficulty in prioritizing or valuing items (R. O. Frost et al., 1998). Someone with hoarding disorder who keeps birthday party leftovers may be afraid that she will forget either the party itself or key aspects of the party, and thus wants or feels that she needs to keep all of the reminders of it as memory aids. Someone else who saves the same items may report difficulty in deciding the relative worth of one item over another, such that the photos of the party and the cake-encrusted plates hold the same value as a reminder of the party. Similarly, individuals who keep all paper bags, plastic bags, and cardboard boxes that enter their homes often realize, intellectually, that they have more of these containers than they will ever use, but are paralyzed by the inability to make decisions regarding how many may be needed, how many might be appropriate to keep, and ultimately, how many to dispose of.

Thus, difficulty discarding can be thought of as being, at its basis, an avoidance behavior. Although many individuals with HD seek help for their problems, the majority of those with HD would feel a great deal of distress if someone were to come and clean out their belongings without their direct oversight, even those things that they objectively recognize as trash. The reasons for this are similar to those that explain the difficulty these individuals experience in trying to discard the items themselves—fear that someone else might throw something away that is or will be needed or is otherwise important.

ACCUMULATION AND CLUTTER

Inability to discard unneeded items, regardless of the means of their accrual, will ultimately lead to accumulation of these items, and from there to clutter, unless someone or something intervenes. In order to meet criteria for hoarding disorder according to the *DSM-5*, the accumulation that results from hoarding symptoms must compromise the intended use of living or work spaces, causing functional impairment unless an outside agency or entity (such as a family member or public health official) has stepped in to remedy the problem (*DSM-5* Criteria C and D). While clutter can be thought of as a collection of things lying about in an untidy mass, and many individuals suffering from hoarding disorder do in fact admit to having cluttered homes, somewhat paradoxically, the presence of clutter in and of itself is not a required feature of HD.

Accumulated items may be organized, tidy, and clean, and still be problematic, if their sheer volume prohibits the normal use of space. For example, a hallway that is full of boxes lining both walls may be impossible to pass through, even if the boxes are neatly labeled and stacked. Similarly, piles of papers and files stored indefinitely on a car seat prohibit the use of that seat for sitting, regardless of how carefully they are organized. Because accumulation of objects is a primary cause of functional impairment in hoarding disorder, the *DSM-5* definition stipulates that if accumulation or clutter are not present in living or workspaces, it is only because of the concerted work or intervention of others such as family members, cleaners, landlords, or other authorities.

Thus, in order to meet criteria for HD, the affected individual must be unable to keep their living spaces clear and usable *without assistance*. It is important to note that, as with all psychiatric disorders, symptoms of HD may improve with treatment or, less often, with time. Individuals with hoarding disorder may make a concerted ongoing effort to declutter and discard items, improving the usability of their living spaces. These individuals meet criteria for lifetime history of hoarding disorder and would be characterized as being in remission or partial remission from their symptoms, depending on the level of impairment related to current or ongoing symptomatology.

IMPAIRMENT

As with all psychiatric disorders, functional impairment or significant distress associated with hoarding symptoms are key components of the illness. Individuals who have mild hoarding behaviors but are not distressed or otherwise impeded by these behaviors do not meet criteria for hoarding disorder. The intent of the impairment criterion is to ensure that the collection or accumulation of items in and of itself is not overpathologized. There are many examples of collectors who have hundreds of thousands of items that have been carefully selected, acquired, and archived. While these items may require large amounts of space to contain, they generally bring joy rather than distress to the individual who owns them.

Similarly, different individuals, families, and cultures have varying levels of acceptance regarding material possessions—in some families or cultures, material goods may be highly prized, while in others, thriftiness or minimalism may be valued.

However, it is important to realize that many people with hoarding disorder will under-report their symptoms, deny distress associated with their hoarding, and minimize the extent to which their hoarding causes problems in their lives. Thus, to differentiate HD from non-pathological hoarding or collecting, and to determine the true impact of hoarding behaviors on affected individuals and their family members, the presence and degree of distress and impairment must be carefully assessed.

For example, distress associated with the thought or action of discarding items, or the inability to discard, is the key feature of HD, rather than distress over the sheer volume of materials owned. Many people whose homes are over-full of materials for non-hoarding reasons (for example, those who are disabled and physically unable to remove unwanted items from their homes) are upset by the problems caused by clutter. In contrast, individuals with HD who lack insight may not exhibit any obvious distress associated with their hoards. They may deny that they have any problems, partly because they have not been asked (or have refused) to declutter their homes or dispose of any of their belongings.

However, they do typically show objective signs of impairment due to their hoarding symptoms (for example, rooms of the house made unusable due to accumulation of items, financial difficulties, fire hazards), despite denying distress associated with it. These individuals would also display high levels of distress, even to the point of requiring psychiatric intervention, if their possessions were removed from their keeping without their permission or knowledge. In assessing potential distress, therefore, it is important to ask about how the person *would* feel in a hypothetical scenario where they were mandated to declutter their homes, and to make decisions about discarding some of their property. Similarly, obtaining objective evidence of functional impairment, in the form of photographs, collateral information from family members, or direct observation, may be required in some cases.

ACQUIRING

Although not a required feature of the disorder, most individuals with HD (80%–90%) will have problems with excessive acquisition at some time in their lives. Acquiring large quantities of unneeded items not only contributes to the accumulation of clutter, it can be impairing in a number of other ways. The most common form of hoarding-related acquiring is excessive or compulsive buying, followed by collection of complimentary items such as flyers, things left on the street or otherwise discarded by others, and items left in dumpsters or recycle bins. Stealing also occasionally occurs in HD, although it is less common.

Individuals with hoarding disorder may purchase large quantities of materials (cans of food, clothing) against future need, or they may buy in excessive numbers for aesthetic or other nonspecific or nonutilitarian purposes (e.g., buying things as potential gifts, but without a specific recipient in mind). Some individuals describe buying objects at thrift stores not because they are attractive or wanted, but because they are *unattractive* or perceived as unwanted—these individuals, who are not psychotic and typically know full well that their actions do not make sense, describe wanting to save the items from a fate of being abandoned, ignored, or unsold. Excessive acquisition can result in rooms full of new, unopened goods, closets full of clothes that are never worn, and food that is purchased, but not used, sitting on a shelf or in the refrigerator until it expires or rots.

Many of those who have prominent symptoms of excessive acquisition feel a thrill when they acquire a new item, describing feeling that they have gotten a bargain, either because they have obtained something without having to pay for it (such as an abandoned chair left near a dumpster), or because they have purchased the item at what they feel is a good sale price (50 pumpkins purchased for 50% off the day after Halloween). However, as with difficulty discarding, excessive acquisition ultimately leads to problems, either due to strain on financial resources or to accumulation of unneeded items for which there is no space.

CLINICAL INSIGHT

Clinical insight is the term used to define an individual's awareness of and understanding regarding their illness and the way in which it affects their interactions in the world. There are multiple ways to define insight, which is described by clinicians as easy to recognize but difficult to characterize. The most common way of categorizing or describing insight is using a simple Likert-type scale, such as that used in the *DSM-5*, which contains a simple rating of good, fair, poor, or absent (delusional). Other clinical terms that can be used to define or describe deficiencies in clinical insight include *anosognosia*, *delusionality*, *overvalued ideation*, and *defensiveness*, all of which have been applied to hoarding disorder. These terms are defined and placed in the context of the more standard, but less informative, Likert scale, in Figure 1.2.

The term most used by physicians for impaired clinical insight is *anosognosia*, which was first described by Joseph Babinski in 1914. In classic anosognosia, damage to the parietal lobe of the brain (as from stroke or traumatic brain injury), causes a deficit in self-awareness such that the affected individuals are completely unaware of a physical disability or deficit that they harbor (e.g., weakness or paralysis on one side of the body). Anosognosia is a common feature of many neurological disorders, including several forms of dementia. Although the term is more often used by neurologists than by mental health practitioners, anosognosia or impaired clinical insight also occurs in many psychiatric illnesses, including schizophrenia, body dysmorphic disorder, and anorexia nervosa. When applied to psychiatric symptoms, the term *anosognosia* is most often used to refer to completely or nearly absent insight.

The American Psychiatric Association defines *overvalued ideation* as a sustained unreasonable belief that is not delusional in quality but is not ordinarily maintained or believed by others in the same community or society. Overvalued ideation can also be thought of as the extent to which an individual recognizes that their beliefs and behaviors are irrational within the context of their social group and cultural norms. People with overvalued ideation can be persuaded, with effort, that their beliefs are not commonly held by others, and may not be rational in nature. A *delusion*, by contrast, is a false belief that is based on an incorrect inference about observable external reality that is firmly held despite evidence to the contrary.

Overvalued ideas can be difficult to differentiate from delusions and can be thought of as occurring midway on a spectrum of insight that ranges from completely rational to delusional. The distinguishing factor between an overvalued idea and a delusion is the intensity with which the idea or belief is held, the strength of the conviction that it is true in the face of contradictory evidence, and the ability to consider an alternative hypothesis (that is, the possibility that the belief or idea may in fact not be true).

Defensiveness is a psychological term that is defined as the need to protect oneself from criticism or the exposure of one's shortcomings to others. Defensiveness can lead to impaired insight when an individual is able to recognize that there is a problem but is unable to acknowledge that the problem is due to their own behaviors, symptoms, or thought patterns. Externalization is a common component of defensiveness and occurs when an affected individual blames external factors (e.g., lack of access to storage, refusal of a landlord to permit stacking of items in a common hallway, economic uncertainty requiring the stockpiling of food) for the observed problems. This externalization then leads to decreased motivation for change, as the problem is perceived to be outside the individual's control.

Individuals with HD have varying levels of insight into the impact of their hoarding; furthermore, the level of insight an individual displays can fluctuate with time, circumstance, and emotional state. Many people with hoarding disorder have intact insight and recognize their difficulty discarding as a problem. These individuals often try to take steps to limit their accumulation, clean out their living spaces, or otherwise manage the adverse effects of their symptoms; however, many with HD have more-limited insight.

Some individuals, particularly those for whom animal hoarding is a component of their illness, have so little insight as to be delusional, firmly denying, despite clear evidence to the contrary, any adverse effects of their hoarding. In extreme cases, individuals with hoarding disorder and anosognosia may not even see their clutter, insisting that the rooms are in fact livable when there is clear evidence of squalor and neglect. This is called clutter blindness, and is an interesting, albeit temporary and easily reversible, form of anosognosia that is discussed in more detail below.

Poor or limited insight is unfortunately a common problem in hoarding disorder. In an internet-based survey of individuals with problematic hoarding and their relatives, over half of the respondents who had hoarding symptoms were classified as having poor or absent insight by their family members (D. F. Tolin, Frost, R.O., Steketee, & Fitch, 2008). Among these individuals, older age and higher levels of difficulty discarding were most predictive of poor insight, while subjective distress about their hoarding symptoms predicted better insight. Sex, race, and degree of clutter were not associated with degree of insight.

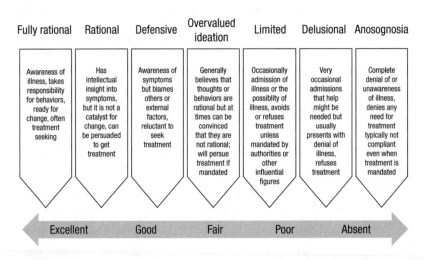

Figure 1.2: Common Conceptualizations and Definitions of Varying Levels of Clinical Insight

CLUTTER BLINDNESS

Clutter blindness, or room blindness as is it is sometimes also called, can be thought of as a form of selective impairment in insight that is specific to hoarding disorder. Clutter blindness refers to the tendency of individuals with HD to block out, forget about, or otherwise mischaracterize the presence of clutter or the state of their homes in their minds, memories, or thoughts. In other words, clutter blindness is the failure to objectively see one's clutter.

Drs. Randy Frost and Gail Steketee describe the cases of several individuals with hoarding disorder and clutter blindness in their book *Stuff: Compulsive Hoarding and the Meaning of Things* (R.O. Frost & Steketee, 2010). The individuals who showed evidence of clutter blindness all had severe hoarding problems. They were asked to first describe or draw their living spaces, and subsequently to allow researchers into their homes for objective assessments of their living spaces and the degree of clutter.

In contrast to what is typically seen when people draw or describe their houses, the individuals who suffered from clutter blindness consistently represented their living spaces as being much smaller and more circumscribed than they actually were. While they accurately represented the amount of space that was available to them, they misinterpreted the causes of the space limitations. For example, when drawing diagrams of their homes, instead of drawing large rooms filled with clutter, these individuals instead drew walls where clutter actually existed, or, in some cases, omitted entire rooms that were full of clutter, suggesting that they saw the home or room as being much smaller than it actually was.

When these same people were asked to look at photographs of their living spaces, or to look at their space in real life with a researcher present, they often did not recognize their own homes. They were shocked (and often upset) by the amount of clutter that they had, and, in some cases, were surprised to find that they had more space than they realized. Frost and Steketee noted that for one of their research participants, "It took me [the researcher] some time to convince her that it was indeed her living room. . . . Somehow, this two dimensional image [the photograph] just didn't match the image she had in her mind" (R.O. Frost & Steketee, 2010, p. 163).

These findings suggest that while people with clutter blindness may know and admit to others that they have problems with hoarding, they do not have an accurate internal visual representation of their living spaces, or of the amount of clutter that they possess. Instead, these individuals unconsciously minimize their hoarding problems when thinking about or describing their homes. It is important to emphasize that this process is entirely unconscious in nature—people who suffer from HD and experience clutter blindness do not *deliberately* misrepresent the state of their homes to themselves or others.

It is also clear that at some unconscious or semiconscious level these individuals are in fact aware of their clutter, stepping over or around the piles on their floors to navigate, for example, despite the fact that they do not consciously recognize the stacks of material objects on a daily basis. Instead, they "see" or interpret the space limitations that they experience as being due to the structural nature of the building itself.

Clutter blindness can create a significant impediment to treatment for individuals who suffer from hoarding disorder. While they may admit to having problems with hoarding, those with clutter blindness, by definition, do not recognize the extent and impact of their hoarding on a day-to-day basis. At worst, this lack of recognition can prevent them from seeking or actively participating in treatment. At best, the volume of the hoard in their homes is not accurately represented to treatment providers, potentially resulting in suboptimal care.

CHURNING

Although it is not listed in the *DSM-5* definition, churning is another common feature of HD. Churning is defined as repeatedly picking up items and putting them down without actually sorting, discarding, or otherwise processing them. Churning typically occurs in individuals with good or fair insight—it is less commonly seen in those with poor insight or those who are delusional, although it can occur in these individuals as well. Churning behaviors represent an attempt—albeit an ineffective attempt—to manage the clutter that accompanies hoarding disorder. Churning is described by those who engage in it as being result of indecision or ambivalence about whether to keep an object or discard it. Paradoxically, although not surprisingly, this symptom of hoarding disorder usually leads to increased, rather than decreased, distress.

WHAT TYPES OF THINGS DO PEOPLE HOARD?

Most people with HD hoard a variety of objects. The items may vary from person to person, but typically include clothes and shoes; containers (paper and plastic bags, boxes, food storage containers); tools and mechanical objects (screws, nails, gears, washers); household objects such as string, rubber bands, and paperclips; household supplies and cleaners; toiletries; photographs and mementos; information storage devices (CDs, DVDs, hard drives); paper (newspapers, bills, magazines, junk mail, flyers); and food, including pet food. In fact, other than rubbish and rotting food, the items that are kept by individuals with HD are not different in content than items in a typical household. The difference is in volume. In most cases, the possessions that are kept are a mix of things, many of which have little or no apparent value, other than to the owner, although useful items and valuables or collectibles such as jewelry, money, or objets d'art can also be mixed in.

SUMMARY

The profound impact of hoarding disorder is embodied in the stories of the Collyer brothers and the Bouvier Beale women—HD is a disease that negatively affects individuals as well as their families, neighborhoods, and the society at large. The remainder of this book details the epidemiology and functional impact of hoarding disorder (Chapter 2) and provides tools for screening and assessment of HD and its comorbid features (Chapters 3 and 4). Special or unusual presentations of hoarding are discussed in Chapter 5 (hoarding behavior in children) and in Chapter 6 (animal hoarding). What is currently known of the neurobiology and etiology of HD is discussed in Chapter 7. Treatment options, including psychopharmacotherapy, psychotherapy, and self-help, are detailed in Chapters 8 through 10. Chapter 11 provides information for clinicians and families regarding the impact of this serious psychiatric illness on families and friends, and it includes effective approaches to take when an individual with HD refuses to seek treatment.

Chapter 2

Epidemiology and Impact of Hoarding Disorder

As mentioned in Chapter 1, hoarding behaviors have existed through-out human history, and in the last decade or so have received increasing attention in the lay press, particularly in the current era of reality TV. Shows like *Hoarders, Hoarding: Buried Alive,* and *Children of Hoarders* have increased awareness, if not understanding, of this common psychiatric illness. Unfortunately, despite the variety of descriptive terms for hoarding behaviors, the sensationalistic reporting of extreme cases, and the recent proliferation of reality TV shows dedicated to hoarding, HD is still a "hidden disease" that continues to be under-recognized by the lay public and underdiagnosed by the health care and scientific communities.

PREVALENCE OF HOARDING DISORDER

Hoarding disorder is one of the most common psychiatric disorders of adulthood, affecting 1 out of every 25 to 50 adults (American Psychiatric Association, 2013). Pooled prevalence estimates conducted in

over 50,000 participants suggest that hoarding disorder has an estimated prevalence of 2.5%, with a possible range of, or confidence inter-
val of 1.7% to 3.6% (Postlethwaite, Kellett, & Mataix-Cols, 2019). The
prevalence is lowest among teenagers and highest among adults over
55, where it has a prevalence of nearly 7% (Cath, Nizar, Boomsma, &
Mathews, 2017; Mathews, 2014) (Figure 2.1).

Hoarding disorder is more common than schizophrenia, eating disorders, obsessive compulsive disorder, and autism spectrum disorders,
each of which affect between 1 in 50 and 1 in 150 people. In individuals
over age 65, HD is more common than lifetime rates of bipolar disorder and panic disorder, each of which affects between 1 in 20 to 1 in 25
adults (National Institutes of Mental Health, 2019). Hoarding has been
reported in all major inhabited continents and in many different coun-
tries and cultures. Although estimates vary somewhat depending on
the study design and method of assessment, lifetime prevalence esti-

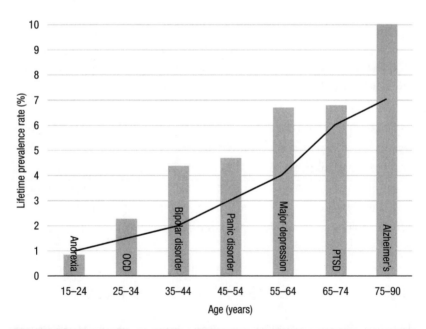

Figure 2.1: Lifetime hoarding disorder prevalence rates by age (black
line). Global lifetime prevalence rates of common psychiatric disorders as
reported by the National Institute of Mental Health are provided as a comparison (bars).

mates for hoarding disorder do not appear to differ greatly by country, ethnicity, or culture.

SEX RATIO

Early clinical studies suggested that hoarding disorder was more prevalent in women than in men, but more recent studies indicate that, in fact, there are no real differences in hoarding disorder rates between the sexes (Postlethwaite et al., 2019). Observed differences in sex ratios between community and clinical samples typically suggest somewhat higher rates of HD among women than among men. However, these differences are likely to be due to referral or ascertainment bias, as women are known to be more likely than men to seek clinical care for psychological symptoms and to participate in clinical research.

Men may also be less likely to report their hoarding symptoms or they may minimize the negative impact of their hoarding behaviors when talking to clinicians or other authorities. Although insight has not been extensively studied, there is some evidence to suggest that men with HD, at least those who participate in clinical research, may have less insight into their symptoms, and thus, less likely to know or admit to having problematic hoarding. For example, a study of over 300 people with hoarding disorder who participated in a clinical trial of group therapy for HD, men were twice as likely to have poor insight into their hoarding as women were (20% of men had poor insight compared to 10% of women) (Archer, 2019).

AGE OF ONSET

Most psychiatric disorders initially manifest in childhood or adolescence, at least for a substantial proportion of individuals, and hoarding is no exception. Early studies (those conducted in the late 1990s and early 2000s) placed the average age of onset of hoarding symptoms sometime between ages 11 and 15. However, estimates in these studies varied widely, in part due to the fact that they all relied on retrospective recall to determine when symptoms began. A meta-analysis that combined data from all studies published before 2019, weighted by sample size, suggests that overall, hoarding symptoms begin around 16 or 17 years of age, but can start as early as age 6 or 7 in some cases (Zaboski et al., 2019).

There is some evidence for two, or even three peak ages of onset for HD—one in childhood (between ages 8–12), one in adolescence or young adulthood (ages 16–22), and one later in life (Steketee, Schmalisch, et al., 2012; Zaboski et al., 2019). Although the relationships are not yet fully elucidated, differences in age of onset of hoarding symptoms may be associated with different clinical features, and with different trajectories and prognoses. For example, individuals with hoarding disorder and OCD tend to exhibit hoarding symptoms approximately 4 years earlier (between 12–13 years of age) than do those without co-occurring OCD (Zaboski et al., 2019). These individuals also tend to have more-severe symptoms and a worse treatment outcome overall than do those who have hoarding disorder but no obsessive compulsive symptoms. Similarly, individuals with a later age of onset may be more likely to have mild cognitive impairment or even dementia (Ayers, Najmi, Mayes, & Dozier, 2015; Dozier, Porter, & Ayers, 2016).

HOARDING TRAJECTORY ACROSS THE LIFE SPAN

There are no longitudinal studies of hoarding symptoms across time, and such studies, although informative, would be quite difficult to conduct, due to the long time lag between reported onset of symptoms (teenage years) and clinical recognition or the development of noticeable impairment (middle to late adulthood). Nevertheless, data from clinical and cross-sectional population-based studies do provide some indication of the trajectory of hoarding symptoms across the life span. Most psychiatric disorders either follow a remitting and relapsing pattern, where symptoms improve and worsen across time (e.g., major depressive disorder, panic disorder) or remain chronic but relatively stable throughout adulthood (as with schizophrenia and OCD).

Hoarding symptoms, in contrast, appear to worsen with age. This pattern is in fact more similar to many neurological disorders such as

Parkinson's disease and dementia than it is to psychiatric illness. The prevalence of clinically significant hoarding increases linearly with every decade of life, beginning at around 1% to 1.5% in adolescence, increasing to 2%–3% in the 30s and 40s, and plateauing at between 6%–7% among adults over age 55 (see Figure 2.1).

It is tempting to explain this increase in prevalence of hoarding disorder with age as the natural consequence of accumulation of material belongings throughout a lifetime. However, a cross-sectional epidemiological study of hoarding symptom patterns among nearly 15,000 individuals ages 15 to 80 indicate that essentially all of the increase in prevalence can be attributed to a steady increase in difficulty discard-

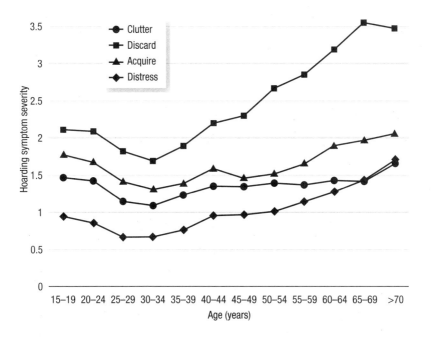

Figure 2.2: Hoarding symptom severity across age groups in a population-based sample of 15,000 twins and their family members from the Netherland Twin Registry. *Source: Cath, D. C., Nizar, K., Boomsma, D., & Mathews, C. A. (2017). Age-specific prevalence of hoarding and obsessive compulsive disorder: A population-based study. Am J Geriatr Psychiatry, 25(3), 245–255. Used with permission.*

ing across the age span, rather than to a substantial increase in clutter over time (Figure 2.2) (Cath, Nizar, Boomsma, & Mathews, 2016). The fact that difficulty discarding is the only symptom that shows a pattern across the life span similar to the pattern seen for HD prevalence rates (e.g., a steady increase in severity, beginning in mid-adulthood) further reinforces the hypothesis that difficulty discarding is in fact a core feature, if not *the* core feature, of hoarding disorder.

PUBLIC HEALTH IMPACT OF HOARDING

Hoarding disorder not only has a profound detrimental impact on individuals; it also affects families, neighborhoods, and society as a whole. As expected, hoarding is associated with increased mental health services utilization and elevated rates of eviction. Somewhat more surprisingly, HD is also associated with a substantial amount of lost work productivity. Individuals with HD report losing, on average, 7 days of work per month, in part, but not entirely, due to the medical or psychiatric illnesses that frequently co-occur with hoarding (D. F. Tolin, Frost, R.O., Steketee, Gray, & Fitch, 2008). Given that an average month has only 20–22 work days in it, this represents a greater than 30% loss in productivity for individuals suffering from HD.

Hoarding disorder leads to impairment through a variety of mechanisms, and it is associated with both increased morbidity and increased mortality. These include the added risks of house fires and accidental falls; problems associated with home deterioration, pest infestation, and other health hazards; and medical illnesses associated with hoarding.

In one study examining the cause of sudden and unnatural deaths that occurred at home, 3% of cases reviewed identified hoarding-related accidents as the cause of death, which is a tremendous cause for concern for families and loved ones of those who suffer from HD (Darke & Duflou, 2017). Additionally, despite the actual cause of death, which in addition to hoarding-related accidents, included more-typical medical and other causes, individuals with HD in this study lost approximately 16 years of life compared to the life expectancy of their age- and sex-matched peers. These individuals also overwhelmingly lived alone, were socially isolated, and had no medical care in the time preceding death, all of which contributed to the increased risk of early death.

Thirteen percent of individuals whose deaths were associated with hoarding in this study died from hypothermia, and in general, hoarding is involved in up to 30% of deaths due to cold exposure (Lane, 2018). Unfortunately, for individuals with severe hoarding disorder, adequate heating may not be safe or even possible, due to high levels of clutter that prevent the use of furnaces or other sources of heat (Darke & Duflou, 2017).

HOUSE FIRES

House fires are also a potential problem in homes impacted by hoarding. Statistics show an average of 7 people per day die in the United States from house fires (NFPA, 2018). Worldwide, firefighters and other professionals respond to over 3 million calls per year; fire is responsible for 20,000 to 60,000 deaths per year (Brushlinsky, 2018; Pappas, 2012). Cooking and heating equipment are the most common sources of fire, although cigarette smoking is the direct cause in approximately 10% of cases (Szlatenyi, 2009).

In hoarding homes, house fires are most commonly caused by papers and other objects being left too close to heating sources or to open stove tops. Using old or unsafe appliances or employing open fires for heating or cooking due to nonworking appliances are responsible for approximately 25% of cases (Szlatenyi, 2009). Although rare, other causes of fires also occur as a result of hoarding behaviors. For example, sunlight hitting stacks of papers through a window in a storage shed has sparked flames in a few reported instances. The sheer volume of materials in hoarding-impacted homes and the flammability of the most commonly hoarded items (papers, clothes, books, and magazines) both contribute to increased fire hazards.

Perhaps more concerning, hoarding behaviors not only increase the risk of fire, they also boost the severity and impact of house fires, substantially increasing the risk of death (Schorow, 2012; Szlatenyi, 2009). Fires in hoarding households spread faster and are more intense than standard house fires. This increased severity is due not only to the buildup of flammable materials in a hoarding household but also to the fact that crowding of materials within a home can cause wind tunnels and otherwise facilitate the rapid spread of a fire that is difficult to contain.

Clutter in homes filled with furniture and other difficult-to-move objects can also impede escape and rescue efforts (Figure 2.3), cause injury from falling materials or collapsing structures, and increase the risk of death by smoke inhalation. Fires in hoarding households require twice as many professional responders, are less likely to be contained to a single room, result in more damage, and are more likely to spread to neighboring homes than are fires in nonhoarding homes. Most significantly, one quarter of *all* reported deaths from house fires are attributable to hoarding (Harris, 2010; Lucini, 2009; Szlatenyi, 2009).

HEALTH HAZARDS

In addition to the increased risk of household fires, hoarding also leads to other health hazards. One of the most commonly reported health hazards in HD is the inability to move safely throughout the home, increasing the risk of falls (Ayers et al., 2015). Many hoarding households have very little accessible floor space—sometimes entire rooms are unusable, and narrow trails through the accumulated clutter are the only available avenues in and out of a room or home. Limited movement due to clutter is a particular risk for elderly individuals, who often have age-related mobility problems, use walkers or other assistive devices, and are more at risk to break a bone or otherwise suffer injury from a fall.

Individuals with HD may not be able to sleep on their beds, use their kitchens or cooktops, or take a bath or shower due to the accumulation of materials on or about these spaces. Up to 50% of individuals with severe hoarding problems have appliances or utilities that are nonfunctional (Szlatenyi, 2009). These individuals may be reluctant to allow landlords, contractors, or others into the home to make the needed repairs, increasing the rate of deterioration of the home and perpetuating the problem (R.O. Frost, Steketee, & Williams, 2000).

Difficulty in finding medications or health care equipment (e.g., finger-stick materials for individuals with diabetes, continuous positive airway pressure or CPAP machines or masks for those with obstructive sleep apnea) in a cluttered home can also contribute to poor health. Similarly, food contamination or rotting due to nonworking refrigerators, or difficulty discarding outdated food, can lead to malnutrition or food poisoning. Large volumes of clutter can encourage high rates of mold, mildew, and dust, which in turn can lead to pest infestation, resulting in health problems such as insect or animal bites—possibly causing infection, allergies, asthma, or other respiratory ailments (Ayers, Iqbal, & Strickland, 2014; Ayers, Ly, et al., 2014).

Figure 2.3: Information sheet regarding hoarding and household fires by the National Fire Protection Association. Used with permission.

MEDICAL ILLNESS ASSOCIATED WITH HOARDING DISORDER

Not only are health hazards that are clearly due to external environmental factors increased among individuals with HD, many other medical conditions are also associated with hoarding. These include elevated rates of obesity, high blood pressure, diabetes, cardiovascular disease, stroke, and emphysema (Ayers, Iqbal, et al., 2014; D. F. Tolin, Frost, R.O., Steketee, Gray, et al., 2008).

Recent work suggests that individuals with hoarding disorder are nearly 20 pounds heavier on average than are those without HD, and they are twice as likely to obese. In fact, over 40% of those with HD are obese, compared to 20% of their age- and sex-matched peers (Nutley et al., 2020). Metabolic and cardiovascular illnesses such as diabetes, stroke, and hypertension also occur more frequently among individuals with hoarding disorder, even when the higher rates of obesity and other relevant demographic and clinical factors are controlled for.

It is possible, and in fact likely, that hoarding itself does not directly cause metabolic or cardiovascular disease, but that factors common to both are responsible. For example, both smoking and depression have been implicated as risk factors for cardiovascular disease. Therefore, if people with HD also smoke more than those without HD, or have higher rates of depression, an association between HD and these cardiovascular diseases might be identified in research studies, even if hoarding is not directly responsible for causing them. For this reason, it is important in such analyses to control for as many factors as possible to identify what behaviors could be responsible for the observed associations.

When lifestyle factors such as age, smoking history, sex, and weight, and mental health conditions such as depression, alcohol use, and anxiety disorders are controlled for, however, the observed relationship between hoarding symptoms and cardiovascular disease persists (Nutley et al., 2020). As expected, when all possible contributors are considered jointly, lifestyle factors have a much stronger relationship to cardiovascular disorders than hoarding symptoms do. However, *even after* controlling for lifestyle factors and mental health conditions, hoarding symptoms still appear to contribute significantly to cardiovascular vulnerability and metabolic disorders such as diabetes. Interestingly, the only hoarding symptom that is *not* associated with cardiovascular disease is clutter, indicating that the increased risk for cardiovascular and metabolic disease is not due to decreased mobility but rather to factors more central to hoarding.

It is not only cardiovascular and metabolic conditions that are elevated with hoarding. Rates of sleep apnea and chronic pain are more than 2.5 times higher among individuals who hoard, even when accounting for differences in age, sex, education, medication status, and body mass index (Nutley et al., 2020). Similarly, although the differences between those with hoarding and those without are not significant after controlling for demographic and other clinical characteristics, half of individuals with HD report having arthritis, while 1 in 4 have asthma or another lung disease.

Importantly, even the presence of subclinical levels of hoarding are associated with increased rates of medical illness. Subclinical symptoms are those that cause some distress or impairment, but do not rise to the level of severity needed to meet diagnostic criteria for current hoarding disorder. In some cases, people with subclinical hoarding may have met full criteria for hoarding disorder at another time in their lives and now only have residual symptoms; some may be developing hoarding disorder; while others may have mild hoarding symptoms that will never develop into HD.

For some conditions, subclinical hoarding symptoms convey essentially the same medical risk as full-blown HD does. Individuals with subclinical hoarding symptoms have similar risks for stroke, cardiovascular disease, diabetes, lung disease, and arthritis as do those with HD. For other medical problems, the risk is elevated, although not quite as high, for those with subclinical hoarding as it is for those with hoarding disorder. For example, in Table 2.1, although the risk of sleep apnea and chronic pain is elevated for those with subclinical hoarding, it is intermediate between those with and those without hoarding disorder.

TABLE 2.1: RATES OF COMMON MEDICAL CONDITIONS AMONG INDI-
VIDUALS WITH HOARDING DISORDER, SUBCLINICAL HOARDING
SYMPTOMS, OR NO HOARDING SYMPTOMS

	Hoarding disorder	Subclinical hoarding	No hoarding
Diabetes	17%	12%	7%
Heart disease	9%	9%	7%
Stroke	4%	4%	2%
Arthritis	50%	46%	39%
Hypertension	42%	36%	32%
Asthma/lung conditions	25%	23%	17%
Allergies	62%	62%	53%
Sleep apnea	33%	23%	16%
Chronic pain	48%	38%	25%
Concussion/ traumatic brain injury	26%	21%	17%

Source: Data from over 18,000 adult participants in the Brain Health Registry (Nutley et al., 2020).

While the rates of all of the medical conditions shown in Table 2.1 are a cause for concern, the high rates of chronic pain and sleep apnea are of particular relevance for clinicians. According to an analysis of over 18,000 adult participants in an online research registry, the Brain Health Registry, nearly half of individuals with hoarding disorder reported experiencing chronic pain, compared to one quarter of adults without hoarding. The Brain Health Registry (BHR) is a website registry for recruitment, assessment, and longitudinal monitoring of adult participants to facilitate neuroscience and brain research.

One-third of the participants with hoarding disorder in the BHR reported having a diagnosis of sleep apnea, compared to one-sixth of those without. These disorders, in addition to being associated with higher rates of medical morbidity and mortality, also contribute greatly to functional impairment, decreased productivity, and decreased quality of life.

RISK TO OTHERS

Hoarding has a profound, negative impact, not only on the person with HD, but also on their family, friends, and neighbors. All individuals living in a hoarding household, including children and dependent elders, are at elevated risk for harm due to the environmental sequelae described in this chapter, including falls, fires, exposure to insects, rodents, and other pests. An estimated 3% of people with hoarding disorder have had a dependent child or elder removed from their home due to safety concerns (D. F. Tolin, Frost, R.O., Steketee, Gray, et al., 2008).

Children living in a hoarding household may not have a clear space in which to do homework, may not be able to invite friends over to play, or may not have a clean and uncluttered place to sleep. If appliances are not functional, children in these homes may not have access to clean clothes, to functional showers, or to unspoiled food. In the worst cases, children may suffer from lice, flea, cockroach, or other pest infestations, or be exposed to rodent urine or feces.

Dependent elders in a hoarding household are arguably at higher risk than are children, as in addition to the risks previously listed, elders are often physically frail and thus may not be able to move safely within the house. The National Adult Protective Services Association (NAPSA) lists hoarding and a number of associated signs and symptoms as cause for concern for potentially vulnerable older adults (Table 2.2). These signs may be indicative in older adults who suffer from hoarding disorder themselves, but symptoms may also occur when a dependent elder lives in the home with a person with HD, such as an adult child or a spouse.

PROTECTION AGAINST DISCRIMINATION

Because HD is a recognized psychiatric illness, individuals who suffer from hoarding disorder are protected from discrimination under both the Americans with Disabilities Act (ADA) and the Fair Housing Act (FHA). The ADA, which became law in 1990, prohibits discrimination against people with disabilities in all aspects of public life (A. N. Network, 2017). This includes employment, education, transportation, and

TABLE 2.2: COMMONLY REPORTED SIGNS OF
NEGLECT OR SELF-NEGLECT AMONG ELDERS

Household characteristics
    A. inadequate heating

    B. plumbing, or electrical service disconnected

    C. pathways unclear due to large amounts of clutter

    D. animal feces in home

    E. extremely dirty or very poorly maintained residence

    F. residence is filled with garbage

    G. challenging to safely exit or enter residence due to hoarding / cluttering

    H. living in squalor, in a dilapidated building, or other hazardous situations

Personal characteristics
    A. lacking fresh food, possessing only spoiled food, or not eating

    B. refusing to allow visitors into residence

    C. dressing inappropriately for existing weather conditions

Source: National Adult Protective Services Organization. Retrieved 10/11/2019.
http://www.napsa-now.org/get-informed/other-safety-concerns-2/

access to places that are open to the public, whether public or private. Disability, for these purposes, is defined as an impairment, whether physical or mental (psychiatric) that substantially limits the activities of daily living in one or more arenas (Weiss & Khan, 2015).

The ADA not only prohibits discrimination, it requires that entities, including employers, schools, places of accommodation such as apartments and hotels, and those who control means of transportation such as trains, buses, and taxis, provide reasonable accommodations and means of access for disabled individuals. Employers with more than 15 employees are subject to the Americans with Disabilities Act and are required to make reasonable accommodations for employees with disabilities, including hoarding disorder, such that they do not experience undue hardship in performing their jobs.

Although most people with hoarding disorder will never need to invoke the ADA, there are exceptions. For example, individuals with HD may exhibit signs of hoarding at their place of employment or may carry bags or boxes of items with them, either for fear of losing the items in the clutter at home or because of a fear that they might be needed during the course of the day. For people like this, a reasonable accommodation may be access to a locker or closet where the items may be stored during the day. Another possibility where the ADA may come into play is when someone with hoarding disorder is engaged in active psychiatric treatment, which is necessary to keep his home sufficiently uncluttered as to be safe. For this person, a reasonable accommodation may be a slight alteration in work hours to allow him to attend his treatment visits regularly.

On the other hand, the Fair Housing Act (FHA) and the Fair Housing Amendments Act (FHAA) are much more likely to be relevant for individuals with hoarding disorder. The FHA, which was signed into law in 1968, protects people from discrimination in buying or renting a home, obtaining a mortgage, and other activities related to housing. The FHAA, which was adopted in 1988, prohibits discrimination in housing sales, rentals, or financing of housing purchases, including discrimination based on disabilities. Although many aspects of potential discrimination in housing are covered under the FHA and the FHAA, the most relevant is eviction or threat of eviction.

Approximately 10% of individuals with HD have been evicted from their homes or have been threatened with eviction due to their hoarding problems (D. F. Tolin, Frost, R.O., Steketee, Gray, et al., 2008). This problem is particularly heightened in urban areas, and especially in big, densely populated cities such as San Francisco, New York, and Boston, where people may not only have limited resources, but they may also have few affordable housing options. For example, in a study undertaken in New York City, which has one of the highest costs of living in the United States, nearly a quarter of individuals seeking assistance from an eviction intervention services center met criteria for hoarding disorder. Of those, one-fifth had been evicted at least once in the past, nearly one-half had previously been involved in legal eviction proceedings, and one-third were currently in legal eviction proceedings (Rodriguez et al., 2012).

The FHA and the FHAA have both been used successfully by individuals with HD and their family members to prevent evictions due to hoarding problems (Weiss & Khan, 2015). The FHA states that individuals with disabilities must be provided with reasonable accommodations and reasonable modifications sufficient to allow them to live in and enjoy their housing. Possible accommodations for hoarding problems may include a stay of eviction for a given period of time to allow a tenant to clean his premises sufficiently enough to ensure safety, or a reduction or elimination of fines or other penalties if a homeowner agrees to enter treatment for hoarding disorder. Provision of additional storage space may also be provided for tenants to allow for effective decluttering without requiring the individual to discard their belongings entirely (Weiss & Khan, 2015).

In adjudicating possible evictions and cleanup requirements, it is crucial that the plans devised to prevent eviction be structured and achievable within a reasonable period of time. According to an analysis by the San Francisco Task Force on Compulsive Hoarding, this may not be as easy as it initially sounds. Landlords and other service providers (including attorneys) report that working with clients who have HD is both time and resource intensive, and is often additionally difficult because of resistance on the part of the tenant or homeowner to engage in the needed cleanup (San Francisco Task Force on Compulsive Hoarding, 2009). To be successful, multiple parties must be involved in working toward an acceptable solution. The team should thus include not only the homeowner or tenant and their landlord but also the appropriate mental health professionals, case managers, attorneys, and possibly community-based hoarding task forces. When other individuals are living in a hoarding home and are therefore at risk, collaboration with community agencies such as child or adult protective services may also be needed. When animals are involved, animal services agencies should also be contacted.

However, the rights of the individual do not take precedence over the rights of the community. Thus, if the safety of a child or vulnerable adult is compromised, or if neighbors or other tenants are experiencing pest infestations as a result of a hoarding home, action must be taken to protect these individuals. Similarly, if an individual with HD is delusional, or refuses the proffered help, it may be necessary to involve a third party to assess capacity (that is, the person's ability to make decisions for themselves), and if needed, to assign someone to act as an intermediary or decision maker. In extreme cases, a conservator may be assigned to make medical, psychiatric, financial, and other decisions; this is especially applicable if the person with hoarding disorder is considered to be at high risk for morbidity or mortality and does not have sufficient insight into their HD to make decisions independently (e.g., is delusional).

As with any psychiatric or medical condition in potentially vulnerable individuals, the goal of intervention is to improve outcomes and to minimize harm while preserving autonomy to the extent possible. Treatment options, including harm reduction approaches that can be implemented when a person with hoarding disorder is refusing or unable to actively participate in treatment, are discussed in Chapters 9–11.

Chapter 3

Assessment of Hoarding Disorder

Hoarding disorder is easy to visually recognize because of the clutter that arises as a result of unchecked accumulation. However, it often goes unrecognized by health care providers who do not typically visit their patients' homes, workplaces, or cars. Individuals with HD will not necessarily bring their symptoms to the attention of their health care providers for a variety of reasons, including shame, poor insight, or simply lack of awareness that there is a name and effective treatment for their symptoms. Thus, it is incumbent on the treatment provider to screen for symptoms of hoarding disorder in order to effectively identify and treat it.

In addition to assessing patients in whom there is a clinical suspicion of hoarding, there are other populations for whom screening is also important. All individuals over the age of 50 should be screened for the presence of clinically significant hoarding symptoms, as should anyone presenting for a psychiatric concern such as depression or anxiety. Because problems with discarding unneeded items appear to increase with age, older individuals should also be periodically reassessed for the presence of problematic clutter and other symptoms of hoarding disorder.

There are many questionnaires and clinical assessments of varying lengths and styles available to evaluate problematic hoarding. These tools have been developed for a variety of needs and settings, and they range from brief screening assessments that are meant to identify potentially problematic hoarding behavior at a population level to in-depth and detailed assessments of safety and potential areas of risk in a known hoarding home. These tools are listed in Table 3.2 and described in detail below.

SCREENING TOOLS

Screening tools are typically used to ascertain potentially at-risk individuals. They are not intended to make a definitive diagnosis of HD, but rather to identify individuals who should undergo further clinical assessment. Screening for hoarding symptoms can be done in the context of a routine yearly medical exam, a medical or psychiatric visit for another problem, or in the context of a health fair or other large-scale public event. As such, these instruments should be brief and targeted to maximize their utility.

If you are a therapist, physician, or other professional who would like to screen for problematic hoarding, you must first decide how much time you have for this endeavor. If you have time for only one or two questions, Table 3.1 provides two questions that can be used as a preliminary screen for potential hoarding disorder in the context of routine clinical care. If the answers to either or both of these questions are "yes," then further assessment is warranted.

If you have time for a few questions, there are a number of good screening measures that are appropriate for use in a clinical setting. These are described next. Note that many of the published screening and other assessment tools described in this chapter are designed to ask only about symptoms that have occurred in the previous week. If you are concerned about hoarding disorder and suspect that the person

TABLE 3.1: BRIEF SCREEN FOR POSSIBLE HOARDING DISORDER

If you have time for only one question, ask this:
Are there any rooms, areas, or appliances in your home that you cannot use because you have too many things covering or filling them?

If you have time for two questions, ask this one also:
Do you have trouble throwing things away, even things that you probably don't need, because you worry that you or someone else might need them in the future?

---

you are evaluating may underrepresent their symptoms, try asking the questions using a lifetime frame. That is, instead of asking about the past week, ask "have you ever experienced the following . . .".

HOARDING RATING SCALE (HRS)

The Hoarding Rating Scale is a brief assessment of hoarding symptoms and their impact that takes less than 5 minutes to administer. It was originally developed by Dr. David Tolin and his colleagues as a clinician-administered instrument (the Hoarding Rating Scale Interview, or HRS-I) that was intended to allow for the assignment of HD diagnoses and to assess severity of symptoms (D. F. Tolin, Frost, R.O., & Steketee, 2010). It has also been adapted for use as a self-report instrument (the Hoarding Rating Scale Self Report, or HRS-SR) that can be completed by patients rather than by clinicians (D. F. Tolin, Frost, R.O., Steketee, Gray, et al., 2008)

Both the interview and self-report forms of the HRS consist of five items, each scored on a scale of 0 to 8. The items assess (a) difficulty using the rooms of the home due to clutter; (b) difficulty in discarding, recycling, giving away, or selling items; (c) problems with excessive collecting or buying; (d) emotional distress because of clutter; (e) impairment associated with discarding or excessive acquisition. Individual symptoms are scored from 0 (no difficulty at all) to 8 (extreme difficulty).

The primary advantage of the HRS is that it is brief and easily understood by both clinicians and patients. There are two ways to score it, one designed to determine the presence and severity of hoarding symptoms, and the other to approximate a *DSM-5* diagnosis of HD. In the first approach, the score for each of the five items is summed to create a total score. The total possible HRS score using this method is between 0 and 40. A total score of 14 or greater indicates clinically significant hoarding symptoms. Scores between 10 and 13 are suggestive of subclinical hoarding symptoms that may need ongoing monitoring.

In the second method, a cutoff score is devised for each question, and subsequently used to assign a likely diagnosis of HD. A score of 4 or higher on both the clutter and difficulty discarding items (the first two questions) plus a score of 4 or higher on either or both of the last two items (emotional distress or impairment) are required, for a minimum total score of 12. The excessive acquisition question, which is not a core feature of the *DSM-5* definition of hoarding disorder, is not used in this method.

In practice, the first approach using the total score is the simplest, and thus the most commonly used. The cutoff score of 14 on the interview version of the HRS was identified from a validation study comparing HRS scores of 73 participants with hoarding disorder, 19 participants with OCD, and 44 control participants with no psychiatric diagnoses. Although the sample was small, the correlation between the scoring of items derived from patient interviews in the clinic and the scoring derived after a visit to the participant's home was very high (80%–95%) as was the consistency of scores across multiple time points, suggesting that this instrument is reliable in multiple settings and across time (D. F. Tolin, Frost, R.O., et al., 2010).

The HRS-SR has been used to assess hoarding symptoms in several large population samples with thousands to tens of thousands of participants (Cath et al., 2016; V. Z. Ivanov et al., 2013). These studies are useful for determining the distribution of hoarding symptoms across individuals from a community rather than from a clinical setting. The results confirm that the HRS can be effectively used as a self-report instrument without clinician administration or oversight. By elucidating the distribution of hoarding symptoms in the general population, and identifying the cutpoint scores that denote the extreme end of the distribution, where hoarding symptoms are most likely to be problematic, these studies also help to substantiate the utility of the HRS as a screening tool for hoarding. However, although clearly useful for screening, the HRS has not yet been validated as a means of assigning *DSM-5* diagnoses of HD, and its specificity and sensitivity for this purpose is unknown.

HOARDING DISORDER DIMENSIONAL SCALE (HD-D)

The Hoarding Disorder Dimensional Scale (Mataix-Cols, Billotti, Fernandez de la Cruz, & Nordsletten, 2012) is one of five brief dimensional assessments that were created by the American Psychiatric Association's Obsessive Compulsive and Related Disorders Task Force during the development of the *DSM-5* (American Psychiatric Association, 2013). The other scales assess severity of OCD, body dysmorphic disorder, trichotillomania (hair-pulling disorder), and excoriation disorder (skin-picking disorder).

The HD-D consists of five questions, each of which assess symptom severity over the preceding week. The first four questions were taken directly from the HRS-SR and assess (1) difficulty discarding items that others would not have trouble with, (2) distress associated with difficulty discarding, (3) impairment due to clutter, and (4) interference with functioning due to clutter. An additional question was added to assess avoidance due to hoarding symptoms, replacing the HRS question that assesses collecting or acquiring. Rather than measuring symptom severity on a 0 to 8 scale, the HD-D uses a scale of 0 (none/no problem) to 4 (extreme), for a total possible score of 20.

The HD-D has good test–retest reliability at 2 weeks, and the items are also internally consistent. As expected, given the high degree of item overlap between the two scales, the HD-D shows strong convergence with the HRS-SR in a community-based sample of over 500 individuals who were recruited through social media, but who did not necessarily have a diagnosis or history of HD (Carey, 2019).

The HD-D was also tested in a subset of 37 individuals with HD and 18 individuals who were collectors but did not have HD as a part of the *DSM-5* field trials that were conducted to validate the *DSM-5* HD diagnostic criteria (Mataix-Cols et al., 2012). A healthy control group was not included in this study. The average HD-D score was 12.6 (±4.6) for those with HD, and 8.7 (±4.7) for those who were collectors. Unfortunately, the confidence intervals for these two participant groups overlapped, making them difficult to distinguish on the basis of HD-D score alone, and no cutoff scores for identifying individuals with potential HD or for differentiating them from collecting have yet been established. Because the HD-D is not widely used, few data are available regarding its utility in nonclinical settings, or among other clinical populations.

CLINICAL INTERVIEW TOOLS

As with screening tools, only a few clinical diagnostic assessments exist for hoarding disorder. Prior to the development of the *DSM-5*, the UCLA Hoarding Severity Scale (Saxena, Ayers, Dozier, & Maidment, 2015) was the only clinical interview available other than the HRS-I, discussed above. Since the publication of the *DSM-5*, hoarding modules have been added to several of the commonly used clinical interview tools, and a stand-alone instrument, the Structured Interview for Hoarding Disorder, has also been published. Each of these is discussed below.

UCLA HOARDING SEVERITY SCALE (UHSS)

The UCLA Hoarding Severity Scale is a brief semistructured clinician-administered questionnaire (Saxena et al., 2015). It consists of 10 items that assess the presence and severity of hoarding-related symptoms that have occurred within the previous week. Each item is scored from 0 to 4, with a maximum score of 40. Scores of 20 or above are generally considered indicative of problematic hoarding.

Like other screening instruments, the UHSS assesses difficulty discarding (anxiety associated with discarding, urges to keep things), clutter (the extent of the home that is affected, embarrassment due to clutter), and excessive acquisition, as well as the effects of these symptoms on daily life (work, daily functioning, relationships). However, unlike most other hoarding screening questionnaires, the UHSS also examines additional symptoms commonly associated with HD, although not part of the formal diagnosis, including perfectionism, procrastination, and indecisiveness.

Although it can be used as a self-report measure, the UHSS was specifically designed to be administered by health care providers in the context of a clinical interview and is most reliable when used in this manner. It aims to assess severity of symptoms and to improve diagnostic accuracy by allowing the person administering it to ask additional questions as needed for clarification, to probe insight, and to assess the degree of potential minimization or exaggeration of symptoms. It has reasonable internal consistency and discriminates well between individuals with HD and healthy age-matched controls (Saxena et al., 2015). It has not yet been tested in additional non-HD clinical populations.

STRUCTURED INTERVIEW FOR HOARDING DISORDER (SIHD)

The Structured Interview for Hoarding Disorder (SIHD) was developed for use in the *DSM-5* field trials for HD. The SIHD is a semistructured interview that assesses the six diagnostic criteria for hoarding disorder as outlined in the *DSM-5* as well as the specifiers (i.e., excessive acquisition and degree of insight) (A. Nordsletten & E., 2013). The SIHD also asks about other relevant diagnoses or conditions that must be ruled out prior to making a diagnosis of HD (hoarding in the context of dementia, autism spectrum disorder, and so forth).

The SIHD takes between 30 and 60 minutes to administer and is best conducted by a clinician or other individual who has been trained in or has experience with the diagnostic criteria for HD. It is intended to be used as a guide when interviewing an individual in whom hoarding disorder is suspected. However, the SIHD can also be used with a reliable informant such as a family member, particularly in cases where poor or absent insight may be a concern.

The SIHD is copyrighted, but the authors have made it freely available for use by clinicians and researchers. The first edition is the most widely used, although a second edition is also available. The second edition of the SIHD contains several useful appendices in addition to the core assessment, including a risk assessment tool and a differential diagnosis checklist (A. Nordsletten & E., 2013).

USING OTHER STRUCTURED OR SEMISTRUCTURED CLINICAL ASSESSMENTS

Modules assessing hoarding disorder are available in the Structured Clinical Interviews for *DSM-5* (SCID-5) (American Psychiatric Association, 2015), the Mini-International Neuropsychiatric Interview for *DSM-5* (MINI-5) (Sheehan et al., 1998). These modules contain interview questions that are based directly on the *DSM-5* diagnostic criteria. However, they have not been formally tested for validity, reliability, or consistency. These modules are likely to be most useful when used in the context of systematically evaluating psychiatric illness more globally, rather than when there is a specific concern for hoarding disorder.

SYMPTOM SEVERITY MEASURES

Most of the screening measures discussed in this chapter can also be used to assess hoarding symptom severity. For example, the HRS-SR and the UHSS, both of which have severity ratings for each symptom that can be summed to create a global or total hoarding symptom score, can be used to assess hoarding severity and track how it changes over time or with treatment. However, the most widely used, and arguably the most clinically useful measure for assessing hoarding symptom severity is the Saving Inventory-Revised.

SAVING INVENTORY-REVISED (SI-R)

Developed by Drs. Randy Frost, Gail Steketee, and Jessica Grisham, the Saving-Inventory is a self-report measure that assesses multiple aspects of hoarding symptoms. Although originally somewhat longer, the most recent and most widely used version of this questionnaire, the Saving Inventory-Revised (SI-R), consists of 23 questions. Each question is scored on a scale of 0 (no problem/not at all) to 4 (extreme problem), for a total possible score of 92 (R. O. Frost, Steketee, & Grisham, 2004).

Questions can be grouped into three subscales that assess the three primary components of hoarding: clutter, difficulty discarding/saving, and excessive acquisition. Impairment and distress are also evaluated by specific questions for each of these three symptom categories. The SI-R requires approximately 10 minutes to complete.

While commonly used as a screening and diagnostic tool, the SI-R is most useful as a measure of symptom severity. In fact, it is the instrument of choice for this purpose in most clinical studies of hoarding disorder. This is because it contains a broad assortment of questions related to hoarding symptoms, and is relatively normally distributed in the general population, with a wide range of possible scores, making it sensitive to change over time or with treatment.

The *sensitivity* of the SI-R, that is, its ability to accurately capture problematic hoarding symptoms, is very high, around 98% (Kellman-McFarlane et al., 2019; D. F. Tolin, Meunier, Frost, R.O., & Steketee, 2011). The discriminant validity of the SI-R, that is, the likelihood that it will correctly differentiate hoarding symptoms from other clinical symptoms such as OCD, is also high (around 93%). However, its specificity, the ability to correctly identify someone who *does not* have hoarding disorder, although still fairly good, is somewhat lower (approximately 80%). Like most self-report measures, if used in isolation, the SI-R has the potential to misclassify individuals, typically those who have high levels of clutter for nonhoarding-related reasons, or those who live with individuals with HD.

The original validation studies in the early 2000s suggested that an SI-R total score of 41 or above is indicative of clinically significant hoarding symptoms (Steketee & Frost, R.O., 2014a). A more recent study in 2019 using a large, diverse sample of individuals with HD (N = 541) and two comparison groups, healthy population controls (N = 319), and clinical controls with non-HD diagnoses (N = 256), indicates that the optimal cutoff for determining HD diagnoses varies with age (Kellman-McFarlane et al., 2019). In this study, the optimal cutoff SI-R total score was 43 for individuals aged 40 and under, 39 for those between the ages of 40 and 60, and 33 for those ages 60 and over.

Most individuals who meet criteria for HD have SI-R scores between 60 and 80. Subscale scores, while potentially informative, are primarily used for hoarding-related research, and are not commonly used in clinical settings. This is in part because the discriminant validity of the subscale scores varies across settings, but is typically lower than that of the total score, and in part because the subscales do not consistently fit the data for all populations, including older adults and some psychiatric populations (Ayers, Dozier, & Mayes, 2017; Lee et al., 2016).

ASSESSING CLUTTER

Another way to assess for possible hoarding disorder is to probe for the presence of clutter. Although excessive or problematic clutter can occur with other medical or psychiatric conditions (depression, physical disability), clutter is an obvious physical manifestation of HD and is the most straightforward to objectively measure. There are two commonly used tools available to assess clutter due to hoarding, the Clutter Image Rating Scale (CIR) and the Clutter-Hoarding Scale. The CIR is discussed below. The C-HS is designed to assess functional impairment related to hoarding and is discussed later in this chapter.

CLUTTER IMAGE RATING SCALE (CIR)

The Clutter Image Rating Scale is a visual way to quantify the degree of clutter in a person's home (R. O. Frost, Steketee, G., Tolin, D.F., Renaud, S., 2008). The CIR consists of nine images depicting varying amounts of clutter for a bedroom, a living room, and a kitchen. The images are scored from 1 (no clutter, very neat room) to 9 (room completely filled with a disorganized pile of materials, where furniture and appliances are not visible). The CIR is easy to use and takes only a few minutes to administer. It can be completed by a person with HD, by a family member, or by a clinician or other professional, either in a clinical setting or at home.

The correlations, or degree of agreement, between patient CIR scores and clinician ratings are reasonably high when both the patient and the clinician perform the assessment in the patient's home, and range between 74% (scores for the bedroom) and 94% (for the total composite scores) (R. O. Frost, Steketee, G., Tolin, D.F., Renaud, S., 2008). Correlations between scores when the CIR is completed by a patient at a clinic and clinician ratings assessed at a home visit are somewhat lower, as expected, ranging from 69% for the bedroom to 81% for the living room. The correlation between clinician ratings at a home visit and patient ratings when completed in the clinic is 78% for the composite score of all three rooms. Reliability and validity of the CIR are similar between adults in midlife and older adults (Dozier & Ayers, 2015).

There are two caveats to be aware of when using the CIR. The first is that although the scale can assess the degree of clutter that is present in a person's home, it does not determine who is responsible for that clutter. Scores on the CIR will be high for individuals who live with roommates or spouses who have hoarding disorder, whether or not the person completing the CIR has HD themselves or not. While this may seem like an obvious point, it is important to ask about the source of the clutter directly, especially if the CIR is the only instrument being used for assessment of HD.

The second is that individuals who have HD but who are not messy will not relate to the images in the CIR and thus their scores may not reflect the volume of material in their homes. These individuals typically have stacks rather than piles of materials; their possessions are aligned against walls and on tables and surfaces (including beds). They may have limited access to furniture or appliances and may have narrow pathways providing access to various areas of their homes. However, for these individuals, the floors can be seen, if only in a limited fashion, and thus the photos in the CIR do not feel appropriate to measure the state of their homes. These individuals may under-represent the volume of accumulated material in their home because it isn't cluttered, or they may be unable or unwilling to complete the CIR because they cannot relate to the photos.

FUNCTIONAL IMPAIRMENT MEASURES

Several measures have been developed to assess functional impairment and safety concerns that may arise due to hoarding. These include the Activities of Daily Living in Hoarding scale, the Clutter Hoarding Scale, the Home Environment Index, the Uniform Inspection Checklist, and the HOMES Multi-Disciplinary Hoarding Risk Assessment.

ACTIVITIES OF DAILY LIVING FOR HOARDING SCALE (ADL-H)

The Activities of Daily Living for Hoarding Disorder is a 15 item scale that assesses the functional impact that hoarding and the resulting clutter have on essential life activities (R. O. Frost, Hristova, Steketee, & Tolin, 2013). These items ask about difficulties that hoarding may cause in an individual's ability to care for themselves on a daily basis, which is also known as their activities of daily living. The ADL-H assesses important functional domains such as preparing food, using appliances, moving around the house, doing laundry, and finding important things such as bills or financial documents. Each item is rated on a scale of 1 (can do it easily) to 5 (unable to do).

The ADL-H has high internal consistency (91%), meaning that the items within a subscale all relate appropriately to one another and reasonable test–retest reliability, meaning that the results of the scale are consistent when readministered to the same individual across a period of a few weeks (Frost et al., 2013). Like the other assessments discussed here, it accurately distinguishes between hoarding and nonhoarding samples (it has good discriminant validity). It correlates reasonably well with the common hoarding severity measures as well.

The ADL-H is scored somewhat differently than the other assessments discussed here. Either the entire ADL-H score can be calculated, or, because each item examines a different aspect of functional impairment due to hoarding, the items can be examined separately. The ADL-H also differs in that not all questions or sections are applicable to all people or situations. For example, some people may not have stairs or a porch, and thus questions about the amount of clutter in these areas will not apply. Thus, to create a global score for the ADL-H, the scores for each question that are relevant to a particular individual are summed, leaving out those that do not apply, and the total is divided by the total number of questions answered, resulting in a possible range of 1–5.

There are two supplements to the ADL-H, one that assesses living conditions and one that assesses safety. The living condition items ask about problems in the home such as structural damage due to hoarding, presence of rotten food, insects, human or animal urine or feces, and nonworking plumbing or heating. The safety items ask about fire hazards, sanitation, difficulty with emergency personnel entering due to clutter, blocked exits, safety on stairs, and clutter in outside areas such as porches. All of the living condition and safety questions are assessed on a scale from 1 (not at all) to 5 (severe).

CLUTTER HOARDING SCALE

The Clutter Hoarding Scale (C-HS) was developed by the Institute for Challenging Disorganization, and the instrument is intended for use by professional organizers and related professionals (The Institute for

Challenging Disorganization, 2011). The C-HS is not intended to be used as a diagnostic or screening tool, but rather as a way to assess the functionality of a home, including potential safety concerns. It is primarily intended for use by professionals who are coming in to assess a home and/or to work to help declutter a home. The C-HS consists of a five-by-five matrix, with five levels of impairment, and five types of assessments. The impairment levels range from level I-low (normal household environment, no concerns) to level V-severe (unsafe, do not work alone in the home due to safety concerns). The assessment categories include structure and zoning, animals and pests, household functions, health and safety, and personal protective equipment needs for anyone entering the home to assess or declutter.

Although the C-HS is not likely to be used by clinicians on a regular basis, it is nevertheless an important tool to be aware of, as it outlines in great detail the types of health and safety concerns that may afflict individuals suffering from hoarding disorder. The C-HS also provides information about specific areas of potential concern that can be addressed in a clinical interview by clinicians or other care providers with individuals with known HD.

HOME ENVIRONMENT INDEX (HEI)

The Home Environment Index is similar to the ADL-H in structure, but it differs somewhat in content (G. Steketee, Frost, R.O., 2013). The HEI was specifically designed to identify squalor and unsanitary living conditions that can occur as a result of moderate to severe HD (Rasmussen, Steketee, Frost, Tolin, & Brown, 2013). It consists of 15 items that assess common safety and sanitation problems. These include fire hazards; moldy or rotten food; mildew or mold in the home; human or animal waste; insect infestation; dirty or contaminated surfaces, clothing, dishes, linens; odors in the home; and standing water. Each item is scored on a scale of 0 (none) to 3 (high risk, large volume of dirty items).

In a study of nearly 800 individuals with self-identified HD, higher scores on the HEI were most strongly correlated with hoarding severity scores, as expected. However, they were also correlated with higher levels of anxiety, depression, and stress, albeit to a lesser degree. The authors of this study hypothesized that, in addition to hoarding symptoms, negative emotion (or affect) in general may be correlated with higher levels of squalor among individuals with HD, regardless of the type of negative emotion expressed.

The HEI has good internal consistency as a questionnaire (Rasmussen et al., 2013). However, no cutoff scores have been determined that would indicate the levels of squalor that would require intervention by public health or other professional agencies. Despite this, the information contained in each item is valuable in and of itself for determining potential areas of concern regarding safety and self-care.

UNIFORM INSPECTION CHECKLIST (UIC)

The Uniform Inspection Checklist was developed by Marnie Matthews, in collaboration with members of an online organization called The Clutter Movement (thecluttermovement.com). The UIC is copyrighted, but the authors have made it freely available for use through their website. It is intended to assess, in a consistent and objective fashion, whether a residence meets the minimum safety and sanitation standards required by public health agencies and other inspectors.

The UIC consists of both a quick-reference version, for use as an initial assessment of the home, and a longer version, which provides a more thorough and detailed evaluation of the home. The quick-reference version and the long version should be used in sequence. The UIC provides helpful information to both the resident and the inspector about the intended use of the instrument (for instance, assessing safety and potential hazards and not housekeeping).

The UIC quick reference is intended to be used by a variety of individuals, including those with HD, their family members, professional organizers, and inspection or governmental agencies. This version consists of three sections, a harm reduction section, a primary inspection section, and a general health and safety section. Each item is scored as pass/fail. An area for notes detailing specifics is also provided for each item.

The harm reduction section assesses whether or not key areas of the home, such as exits or egresses, smoke detectors, doors, appliances, and emergency pull cords are unobstructed (e.g., completely clear of items) or obstructed. This section represents the most immediate dangers to the resident. The primary inspection target section assesses the accessibility of specific areas, that is, whether an inspector or other person can easily reach the area or item in question. This section assesses windows, electrical panels and outlets, heat sources, plumbing fixtures, sinks, bathtubs, and showers. The final section addresses general health and safety. This section assesses whether sinks are functional and reasonably clean, if kitchens have sufficient space for food preparation, and notes the presence of excess paper, rotten food, insects, pet waste, and garbage.

In contrast, the long version, which is based on the inspection checklist used by Housing and Urban Development (HUD), should not be used by or shared with residents. The harm reduction and general health and safety sections of the long version are similar to those contained in the quick reference. Section 2, which assesses primary inspection targets, is much more extensive, however, and addresses each room separately. In addition to a pass/fail option, the priority with which the hazard must be addressed is also noted (e.g., immediate, or within 30 days).

HEALTH, OBSTACLES, MENTAL HEALTH, ENDANGERMENT, STRUCTURE AND SAFETY (HOMES)

The HOMES is a multimodal assessment that measures potential hoarding-related problems with *H*ealth, *O*bstacles, *M*ental Health, *E*ndangerment, and *S*tructure and Safety (Bratiotis, Sorrentino Schmalisch, & Steketee, 2011). It is a relatively brief initial assessment, containing 24 questions, scored as present/absent, regarding health or safety hazards that can be seen in hoarding homes. A person's ability to sleep in their bed, access their toilet, prepare food, and locate medications or medical equipment are asked about, in addition to their ability to use the bathtub, shower, stove, refrigerator, or sink. The presence of insects or rodents, spoiled or rotten food, garbage, human or animal waste, or mold or chronic dampness are also determined. In addition, elements critical to structural safety are asked about, including unstable floorboards or stairs; the presence of flammable items next to heating units; unstable piles of materials; blocked exits, vents, or heating units; leaking roofs or walls; exposed electrical wires; and storage of hazardous or flammable materials.

Unlike the other instruments described in this section, the HOMES also assesses insight (the Mental Health section of the instrument), the capacity of the individual in question to address any safety or health concerns (including their awareness, physical or psychological ability to clear clutter or accept intervention, and their willingness to accept intervention or assistance), any potential risk of eviction, condemnation, or potential safety risks to other people or pets living in the home.

ASSESSING BELIEFS AND INSIGHT

Several other aspects of hoarding disorder that are not core to the diagnosis but do impact daily functioning and treatment prognosis may also be of interest to health care providers. These include degree of insight, particularly with regard to the presence and impact of hoarding symptoms, and belief systems (cognitions) around hoarding and reasons for hoarding. There are two primary tools that can be used to assess insight or other cognitive aspects of hoarding behaviors. They are the Saving Cognitions Inventory and the Brown Assessment of Beliefs Scale.

SAVING COGNITIONS INVENTORY (SCI)

The Saving Cognitions Inventory (Steketee, Frost, & Kyrios, 2003) assesses four aspects (of thoughts or beliefs related to hoarding in four subscales: emotional attachment to items, need for control over one's belongings, feelings of responsibility for items, and memory concerns.

The SCI contains 24 items, each of which are scored from 1 (not at all) to 7 (very much).

The emotional attachment subscale, as the name suggests, assesses personal attachment to items. This subscale includes statements such as, "Throwing away this possession is like throwing away a part of me," "I love my belongings the way I love some people," and "This possession provides me with emotional comfort." The control subscale asks about the perceived need to control one's belongings and includes items such as, "I like to maintain sole control over my things," and "No one has the right to touch my possessions."

The responsibility subscale assesses feelings of responsibility for the usefulness and preservation of items. Sample items on this subscale include statements such as the following: "Throwing this away means wasting a valuable opportunity," "I am responsible for the well-being of this item," and "If this possession may be of use to someone else, I am responsible for saving it for them." Finally, the memory subscale assesses the degree to which an individual uses personal items as memory aids. This subscale includes items such as, "Saving this item means I don't have to rely on my memory," and "If I discard this without extracting all the important information from it, I will lose something."

The SCI is not useful for identifying individuals with potential hoarding, for determining whether someone meets diagnostic criteria for hoarding disorder, or for assessing safety or functional impairment. Instead, it is intended to provide a snapshot of the emotions and beliefs that the individual holds about their possessions, which may be useful either for helping family members to understand the belief systems underlying hoarding behaviors, or for psychotherapeutic treatment.

BROWN ASSESSMENT OF BELIEFS SCALE (BABS)

The Brown Assessment of Beliefs Scale (Eisen et al., 1998) was developed in 1998 by researchers who were interested in measuring insight among individuals with obsessive compulsive or psychotic symptoms such as those commonly seen in schizophrenia. It is a clinician-

TABLE 3.2: HOARDING ASSESSMENT TOOLS

Instrument	Administration time	Format	Screen
HRS	3 min	Self-report or clinical interview	✔
HD-D	3 min	Self-report	✔
UHSS	10 min	Clinical interview	✔
SI-R	10 min	Self-report	✔
SIHD	30–60 min	Clinical interview	
CIR	5 min	Self-report or in-home assessment	
C-HS	15–30 mins	In-home assessment	
ADL-H	5–10 min	Self-report or clinician assessment	
HOMES	15 min	In-home assessment	
HEI	5 min	Self-report or in-home assessment	
UIC Quick Reference	30 min	In-home assessment	
UIC Long Form	60 min	In-home assessment	
SCI	10 min	Self-report	
BABS	30–60 min	Clinician interview	

Diagnosis	Symptom severity	Clutter	Safety	Cognitions/ insight
	✔			
	✔			
✔	✔			
✔	✔			
✔				
		✔		
		✔	✔	
	✔	✔	✔	
		✔	✔	
		✔	✔	
			✔	
			✔	
				✔
				✔

administered interview that is intended to provide a dimensional, rather than a dichotomous (e.g., present vs. absent) assessment of an individual's beliefs and their insight into their symptoms.

The BABS consists of seven items. These items assess (a) conviction, (b) perception of others' views of the individual's beliefs, (c) explanation of differing views that others may hold, (d) fixity of ideas, (e) attempt to disprove the belief or idea, (f) ability to assign a psychological/psychiatric cause to the belief or idea, and(g) ideas or delusions of reference. The first six items are scored on a scale of 0 to 4, with 4 representing more-severe symptoms/lower insight for each item. The seventh item, ideas and delusions of reference, is not included in the total score.

The BABS is not specific to any particular diagnosis. Instead, it was designed to be used for a variety of psychiatric conditions. Although it is not always intuitive in its administration, the BABS contains detailed instructions regarding administration and scoring, including how to score different beliefs that underlie the same illness (e.g., two separate obsessions in OCD), or beliefs associated with two separate illnesses (e.g., body-related beliefs stemming from body dysmorphic disorder and beliefs about worthlessness stemming from depression). Example beliefs or fears from a variety of disorders are also provided, although unfortunately, hoarding disorder is not one of them.

Chapter 4

Differential Diagnosis and Co-Occurring Psychiatric Disorders

While HD is a distinct neuropsychiatric disorder, hoarding and behaviors that mimic hoarding also occur in a variety of other neurological or psychiatric illnesses. Hoarding and similar behaviors are common symptoms in many of the dementias and have also been reported in schizophrenia, autism, developmental delay, and obsessive compulsive disorder. Distinguishing when hoarding behaviors are a secondary manifestation of another underlying illness and when they a primary manifestation of hoarding disorder is important both for prognosis and for treatment planning.

Complicating matters further, even when hoarding disorder is the primary diagnosis, most individuals will have at least one additional co-occurring psychiatric disorder, and many will have two or more. Awareness of these comorbidities is important because they are often the reason that patients with HD come to clinical attention, and their co-occurrence can impact the recognition, course, prognosis, and treatment of hoarding.

This chapter discusses the differential diagnosis of hoarding disorder, the differentiation of hoarding from other similar behaviors such as collectionism and punding, and the psychiatric disorders that commonly co-occur with primary hoarding disorder.

COLLECTING IN NORMAL DEVELOPMENT

Collecting is a common and developmentally normal aspect of human life and behavior. Most children between the ages of 4 and 18 collect at least one type of object, and many have multiple different collections, from rocks to stamps to baseball cards to stuffed animals. The extent of collecting behaviors typically decrease as children grow and develop, but collecting is also fairly common in adults.

The prevalence of active collecting in the general population is estimated to be about 70% in children, 30% in adults, and 15% in older adults (Nordsletten, Fernandez de la Cruz, Billotti, & Mataix-Cols, 2013). The prevalence of extreme collectors—those who have rooms full of collected objects—is unknown, but is thought to occur in less than 5% of the population.

Whereas children can and do collect all sorts of things, collecting in adults tends to be narrowly focused on one or a few types of objects, and follows thematic areas often enough that specific types of collecting have individual names (e.g., *philately*, the collection and study of postage stamps).

COLLECTIONISM VERSUS HOARDING

Pathological hoarding behaviors such as those that occur in HD are often confused with the behaviors seen in collectionism. The National Library of Medicine defines *collectionism* in its Medical Subject Headings or MeSH terms as the "excessive or pathological tendency to save and collect possessions," but it is actually clinically distinct from hoarding, and usually is not problematic. Most mental health professionals would not see collectionism as pathological in nature, but would define it as the acquisition and retention of large numbers of specific objects, typically for pleasure. Although there is some overlap with hoarding behaviors, in that the objects are actively collected and can occupy large amounts of space, collectionism is a potentially extreme behavior, but not necessarily a disorder.

When it is pronounced, collectionism in an adult can lead to excessive volumes of acquired possessions, which may initially be difficult to differentiate from hoarding disorder. Collectionism and hoarding can be distinguished from one another by several key features that are discussed in detail below and outlined in Table 4.1.

For collectors, acquisition, even when high volume, tends to be planned and specific to the collection. Items that will add to the collection, but only such items, are actively sought out and obtained. These additions are often carefully curated and displayed. In contrast, for individuals with hoarding disorder, acquisition is often impulsive rather than planned, and many types of things are included. With HD the acquisition itself is the primary goal, and subsequent display of the acquired item is not a focus. Individuals with collectionism will often look at, hold, and show their acquisitions off. Individuals with hoarding disorder will not think much about their items once they have been procured, unless someone threatens to discard them.

Hoarding and collectionism also differ in how the owner of a particular object views it, and the importance or value it is given in the context of their other belongings. In hoarding, an individual item is not put into a larger context but tends to be valued for itself only, independent of the larger mass of items. In contrast, in collecting, and particularly in extreme collecting, both the individual items and their context in the collection as a whole are valued (A. E. Nordsletten & Mataix-Cols, 2012).

PANIC BUYING VERSUS HOARDING

As evidenced during the 2020 COVID-19 pandemic, panic buying or acquiring can also be confused with hoarding disorder. As the name implies, panic buying involves buying large quantities of goods, usually household supplies or food, in preparation for a real or anticipated

TABLE 4.1: FEATURES DIFFERENTIATING HOARDING FROM
SIMILAR BEHAVIORS SUCH AS COLLECTIONISM AND PUNDING

	Collectionism	Hoarding	Panic Buying or Acquiring
Deliberation	Present. Specific items are actively sought and acquired to add to or complement a collection.	Absent. Items are typically acquired impulsively, without regard to what is already owned.	Mixed. Acquisition is planned, but impulsive purchases also occur
Focus of acquisition	Narrow. Most collectors focus on or collect only one or a few types of objects (e.g., stamps, cars, baseball cards).	Broad. Literally anything can be an item of interest, and there is no particular focus or theme to the pattern of acquisitions.	Items thought to be needed in a crisis (e.g., toilet paper, gasoline, food, etc.), or expected to be in short supply
Context/ valuation	Objects are valued not only for themselves, but also in the context of their place in the larger collection.	Objects are valued only for themselves. There is little to no thought of how they would fit into the owner's belongings.	High. Items are primarily of value for their perceived practical use.
Level of organization/ display	High. Objects are often displayed in special cases, cabinets or rooms. If not displayed, they are still carefully organized and stored.	Little to none. Objects are added to the owner's hoard of belongings in no particular order, fashion, or display.	Mixed. Items are typically not displayed, but are often organized so that they can be used when needed.
Distress related to discarding	Present. Objects are highly valued by the owner, and are not readily discarded, although they may be deliber-ately sold or traded.	Present. Objects are felt to be of potential future value, and thus are not easily discarded.	High initially, decreasing following the occurrence (or avoidance) of the anticipated disaster. Items are deliberately acquired to prevent shortage. Once the anticipated threat has passed, unneeded items may be easily discarded.

Punding	Hoarding in OCD	Collecting in Dementia
Absent. Behavior is automatic in nature, and patients often do not seem to be aware that they are engaging in the behavior.	Present. Specific items are searched out and kept, often to protect them or their owner from feared harm.	Absent. Items are typically acquired impulsively, without regard to what is already owned.
Broad. Although anything can be collected, the focus is usually on sorting and arranging rather than collecting.	Narrow. Focus is on items or belongings that are part of an obsessional fear. Although the types of items that are hoarded may vary, there is usually a common theme surrounding their collection or retention.	Narrow. Focus is often on one or a few types of items, usually objectively useless items, or even trash.
None. Individuals are not even aware of their behaviors, and objects do not have value to the owner.	Objects are not valued for themselves. Rather, they are kept in an attempt prevent an obsessional fear from coming true or for compulsive reasons such as to prevent feelings of incompleteness.	None. Items, once acquired, do not appear to have value and are typically ignored by the owner, unless someone attempts to discard them.
Mixed. Items are repeatedly sorted, organized and re-sorted, but with no apparent theme or structure.	Little to none. Items, once acquired, are typically ignored unless someone attempts to dispose of them.	None. Items, once acquired, are randomly or haphazardly left or piled, often in a corner or on the floor.
Mixed. If objects are discarded while the owner is sorting or organizing, distress is high. Distress is absent if objects are discarded at other times.	Present. Objects are kept for obsessional reasons, and any attempt to discard or dispose of them creates substantial distress.	Present. Although a rationale is often not given for keeping the item, collected objects are not easily discarded.

disaster or crisis (such as a hurricane or pandemic). Panic acquiring is similar to panic buying, but involves the acquisition of free things, either through giveaways, services such as food pantries, or occasionally through scavenging. Although less common, panic buying can also occur when the prices are expected to rise or supply shortages are predicted for a specific product or commodity (such as chocolate or coffee). Panic buying is distinguished from hoarding in several ways. First, despite the fact that it is excessive in nature and tends to have an impulsive quality, panic buying generally tends to be targeted to items that might be needed during the feared or impending disaster, or to common household items that might be difficult to acquire in the middle of a crisis. Toilet paper and bottled water are two commonly acquired items in all types of expected or feared disasters. Gasoline, propane, and canned or dried food are commonly acquired articles when a hurricane or tornado is anticipated. During the early days of the COVID-19 pandemic, hand sanitizer, household cleansers, and germicidal disposable wipes were bought in large quantities by panicked shoppers, in addition to bottled water and toilet paper, emptying store shelves of these items.

The items acquired in preparation for a disaster are typically stored and organized for easy access rather than forgotten about once purchased. Items are highly valued leading up to and during the crisis, but are often easily given away, used, sold, or otherwise disposed of once the danger has passed.

PUNDING VERSUS HOARDING

Punding is another behavior that can be confused with pathological hoarding. The term *punding* was first coined in the 1960s by the Swedish psychiatrist, Gösta Rylander, to describe a type of repetitive and seemingly purposeless behaviors that he observed among individuals who were chronically using amphetamines or other stimulants (Rylander, 1972). Punding is defined as a series of complex, repetitive, prolonged, and compulsive routine or mechanical behaviors that serve no clear purpose. These behaviors include compulsive collecting, arranging, and rearranging of specific objects; repeatedly assembling and disassembling objects; and systematic sorting and re-sorting behaviors.

Punding is now best known as a symptom of Parkinson's disease, but it can also be found in other disorders such as autism and dementia, as well as in the chronic stimulant abuse described by Rylander. It is thought to be secondary to dopamine dysregulation, specifically the presence of elevated levels of exogenous dopamine such as are seen in amphetamine intoxication or following dopamine replacement therapy for Parkinson's (A. H. Evans et al., 2004; Lim et al., 2009).

At first glance, punding behaviors can appear to be similar to those seen in hoarding. From an observational standpoint, some of the key differences between punding and hoarding behaviors lie in the repetitive and almost stereotyped nature of punding, which is not seen in hoarding, and the single-minded persistence with which the behaviors are carried out. As has been noted previously, difficulty discarding, rather than collecting or excessive acquisition, is the core element of hoarding disorder, even though collecting, acquisition, sorting, and churning may also be manifest as secondary symptoms of hoarding in a given individual.

Most individuals with punding behaviors will find it difficult to stop once they have begun, even when it is for a good reason. For example, Dr. Rylander described a burglar who began punding during a robbery and could not stop, despite fears that he would be caught red-handed in the middle of the theft. Individuals with punding will typically not have any awareness that they are behaving in a compulsive manner, making the task of interrupting their repetitive behaviors more difficult.

HOARDING IN OBSESSIVE COMPULSIVE DISORDER

Because hoarding has for several decades been described and studied primarily in the context of obsessive compulsive disorder, it can be difficult to distinguish between hoarding obsessions or compulsions, and hoarding behaviors that are characteristic of a primary hoarding disorder. Differentiating these disorders is complicated by the fact that HD co-occurs with OCD in up to 40% of cases, according to some studies (Pertusa et al., 2008).

In fact, hoarding-related obsessions and compulsions can be distinguished by a number of factors, including what type of objects are hoarded, the reasons an individual gives for hoarding a particular item, and the presence of other obsessional symptoms in relation to the hoarding behaviors or hoarded objects.

While the volume of accumulated clutter due to hoarding often does not differ between individuals with HD and those with hoarding-related OCD symptoms, the content of the hoarded items does. People with HD and those with OCD-related hoarding obsessions and compulsions both report hoarding common items such as mail, receipts, old medication bottles and other containers, old clothes, and old food. However, those with hoarding-related OCD also report hoarding unusual items, typically bodily waste or other fluids such as feces, saliva, urine, fingernail clippings, or rotten food (Pertusa et al., 2008).

In addition to collecting or keeping bizarre items, those with OCD-related hoarding also give unusual reasons (e.g., obsessional reasons) for keeping their hoarded items. As discussed in Chapter 1, individuals with HD have fairly ordinary reasons for keeping items, reasons that most people can relate to, at least on the surface, even when the results are extreme. For example, someone with hoarding disorder will say a particular item needs to be kept for sentimental reasons or because it may be needed by themselves or someone else in the future.

In contrast, someone with OCD-related hoarding may keep fingernail clippings because of feelings of incompleteness when discarding them. Another person may keep urine or anything that might contain saliva (e.g., toothbrushes, water used to rinse the mouth after brushing teeth, dental floss) because of fears that their DNA will be stolen. A third might only be able to discard items on certain days or dates, or might not be able to discard items of a particular color because of fears that something bad might happen.

For most individuals with OCD-related hoarding behaviors, these symptoms are ego-dystonic. That is, the individuals not only know that their fears and behaviors are irrational, they also find them to be distressing and in conflict with their own belief systems (e.g., ego-alien). In contrast, individuals with HD may find their symptoms distressing, but they are not ego-dystonic. Instead, those with HD will say that even though they recognize that their behaviors are excessive, they do not necessarily feel that they are irrational.

Finally, those with OCD-related hoarding will often have other obsessions and compulsions related to the hoarding behaviors. These could include obsessions about what would happen if an item were discarded (e.g., obsessions related to catastrophic fears or magical thinking), as well as compulsions such as repeated checking of items, or the need to memorize or repeatedly read and re-read information in newspapers and magazines). Those with HD rarely check their possessions, and if they do, the checking behaviors are mild and self-limited. Howard Hughes—the entrepreneur, Hollywood playboy, aviator, and inventor— is a well-known example of someone who suffered from OCD-related hoarding. His symptoms, and his story, are recounted in the following section.

Howard Hughes, Obsessive Compulsive Disorder, and Hoarding

As a public figure in the early to mid-20th century, Howard Hughes was famous for many things, among them his lifelong fears and phobias. These fears started in childhood, initiated perhaps, at least in part, by his mother's health-related anxieties. Although there was no evidence that he was particularly sickly, as a child, Hughes was prevented from participating in many normal childhood activities, including camps, school sports, and at times, even from attending school, due to his mother's obsessive fears regarding his health. Hughes resented and resisted the restrictions imposed on him by his mother for much of his childhood, but as a teenager, he began to develop his own germ phobias and health-related fears. For most of his life, Howard Hughes spent a substantial amount of time worrying about acquiring a variety of illnesses, primarily, but not exclusively, infections. As an adult, Hughes kept a doctor on retainer and called on him for advice, examination, and treatment at all hours of the day and night for both real and imagined illnesses.

Hughes's fears impacted his life in many ways, and he took great precautions with his health. Ironically, and consistent with the nature of obsessional fears, which are by definition not logical, Hughes's fears of illness did not stop him from pursuing a variety of reckless and risk-taking behaviors. Even as a teenager, Hughes had a reputation as a ladies' man, and actively pursued several women simultaneously throughout most of his life. He was also a thrill-seeker, with a love for fast cars and airplanes. Hughes's risky lifestyle included multiple promiscuous sexual encounters as well as driving and flying under dangerous conditions, which ultimately lead to a number of serious real-life injuries and illnesses, including numerous head traumas from driving and flying accidents, and tertiary syphilis from his sexual encounters. Although these injuries and illnesses did not cause his obsessive compulsive thoughts and behaviors, they did undoubtedly exacerbate his psychiatric symptoms, which progressed from anxiety to paranoia to psychosis over his lifetime.

In his 20s, Hughes's fears and obsessions expanded from fear of illness into full-blown paranoia, including a severe, generalized fear of contamination. He spent a great deal of time, energy, and money in the effort to avoid or prevent exposure to germs and other potential contaminants. He washed his hands until they bled, and on more than one occasion came out of the bathroom in a club, restaurant, or other public place with his shirt soaking from his excessive washing. When queried about the reason, he explained that something had gotten on his shirt, typically a stain, or a spot of blood from his aggressive handwashing, and he had to clean it off.

Hughes was notoriously unaware of, or perhaps uninterested in, the social mores of the time, and was more than willing to appear in public soaking wet rather than suffer from a possible contaminant on his clothing. He was also willing to do anything necessary to avoid touching surfaces that he suspected were contaminated, using towels to open doors, and, if clean towels were unavailable, waiting in public bathrooms after washing his hands, sometimes for hours, until someone else came in or out in order to avoid having to touch the door handles.

All of these symptoms are characteristic of classic OCD. However, because Howard Hughes was both rich and powerful, his obsessive compulsive symptoms not only controlled his life, they also controlled the lives of people around him. Hughes lived in a time when OCD was not yet recognized or understood, even by psychiatrists. He was wealthy, powerful, and strong-willed, and for these reasons, the world around him typically bent to his wishes. This was to his detriment rather than to his advantage in the end. Although Hughes had essentially limitless resources, his riches did not help him to understand or find ways to effectively manage his symptoms. Instead, his wealth provided him with the means to indulge his fears and obsessions, ultimately intensifying them.

Hughes's symptoms worsened throughout his life and ultimately became completely disabling. In addition to his ongoing contamination obsessions, health-related fears, and associated compulsions, over time he developed first generalized paranoia, unrelated to his OCD, and subsequently OCD-related hoarding symptoms. Hughes's paranoia caused him to hire armies of men to provide constant surveillance, first on the many women (most of them Hollywood starlets), with whom he was involved, and subsequently on anyone else he felt he needed to keep tabs on, such as business rivals and government officials who he felt might be monitoring or interfering with his business.

Hughes's hoarding symptoms were primarily related to his contamination fears, although in some instances, his paranoid fears also manifested in hoarding behaviors. Hughes owned several homes and had multiple offices, but he also rented several hotel suites for his personal use. He had thousands of Kleenex tissue boxes stacked in corners of every hotel room, house, and in the trunk of every car that he regularly used. Hughes kept the tissues for a specific compulsive purpose—they were to be used as barriers to prevent contact with doorknobs and other surfaces. Hughes not only used the tissues to open all doors and clean off all surfaces prop to use himself, he also directed his staff to use them for this purpose. Hughes wrote out numerous pages of specific instructions regarding when and how his staff were to use the tissues (typically six to eight at a time, stacked together) to open doors, wipe off surfaces, answer the telephone, and so forth.

In addition to tissue boxes, Hughes had thousands of legal pads upon which he wrote endless notes, littering his many hotel rooms and houses. He repeatedly stacked the pads and boxes, sometimes in a precise formation and sometimes haphazardly. He kept literally millions of documents, including all of the notes that he wrote over the years to his staff, compatriots, and lovers; he stored decades' worth of surveillance documents and records of telephone conversations in locked file cabinets and boxes. Because of his ongoing health concerns (and also because of legitimate medical problems caused by his multiple injuries and illnesses), Hughes also had boxes upon boxes of medications, which were administered in a compulsive fashion, As he insisted that the doses be precisely measured, to the tenth of a milliliter and administered within a second of the prescribed time.

In his later years, Hughes was prescribed opiates, sedatives, and stimulants, initially for pain from his multiple injuries. He came to take, on a daily basis, doses that were many times above the safe upper limits of these drugs. Although the original underlying cause of his psychiatric symptoms was obsessive compulsive disorder, all of the medical complications that Hughes experienced, along with their treatments, which were in themselves dangerous, undoubtedly contributed to his increasing psychiatric instability through the course of his life.

Over the decades, Hughes became increasingly reclusive and progressively psychiatrically impaired. Addicted to opiates and sedatives and controlled by his obsessive fears, his staff shamelessly took advantage of his deteriorating mental state. In the last decade or two of his life, Hughes spent the majority of his time lying naked on a filthy, battered recliner in a locked and darkened room, watching hour after hour of movies. No one was allowed into the room, even to clean it, as he was terrified of contamination from the outside. Hughes's fingernails and toenails grew exceedingly long, as did his hair, and he stopped bathing entirely. He wrote pages of notes dictating exactly how his food was to be prepared to avoid contamination, and he compulsively checked to make sure that his instructions were precisely followed, even to the exact shape and size of the portions served to him. Despite this obsessive preparation, in his last years, Hughes nearly stopped eating entirely. He died at age 70, from kidney failure brought on by severe malnutrition. He weighed 93 pounds at his death.

COLLECTIONISM, HOARDING, AND DEMENTIA

As discussed earlier in this chapter, collectionism is not typically a pathological behavior. There is one important exception, however: Individuals with dementia can exhibit hoarding, collecting behaviors, or both hoarding and collecting behaviors (Anderson, Damasio, & Damasio, 2005). Collecting behaviors in dementia are very different in nature from the behaviors seen in those who collect for pleasure. Individuals with Alzheimer's disease, behavioral variant frontotemporal dementia, and several other forms of dementia, will sometimes actively collect unusual (typically useless) objects, such as cigarette butts, dirty pizza boxes, or plastic soda bottles.

As with HD, individuals with dementia-related collecting or hoarding may refuse to allow their collected objects to be discarded. However, for these individuals, the actual act of obtaining the item appears to be the driving factor. The object itself is of little or no interest and there is no expressed concern that the item is needed or might be needed in the future. In fact, most of the time, the collected items are completely ignored once obtained. Collectionism and hoarding in the context of dementia typically develop later in the course of illness, although these behaviors can upon occasion be among the first indications of incipient cognitive impairment.

DEMENTIA AND MILD COGNITIVE IMPAIRMENT

Dementia is defined as a progressive deterioration or worsening of in cognitive functioning, including, but not limited to, memory, attention, language, problem-solving, judgement, and social abilities, such that the loss of such skills impairs everyday functioning. *Mild cognitive impairment* is a somewhat more amorphous term that is typically defined as decline in cognitive function that is intermediate between the level of change that is typically expected for a particular age and the more severe impairments seen in dementia. There are several types of mild cognitive impairment (MCI), but most of the time the term MCI refers to memory changes that are subtle enough that they do not lead to clear impairment, although they can be detected with formal testing.

There are few data for the rate of dementia amongst individuals with hoarding disorder. However, there is some indication that rates of both dementia and MCI are higher in people with HD compared to rates in the general population. Part of the problem in establishing the prevalence of co-occurring HD and dementia is that both disorders affect fewer than 5% of individuals younger than 65. In determining the expected frequency of co-occurrence between these disorders, it is important to first know the prevalence of each disorder separately. As discussed in Chapter 2, HD occurs in between 2%–4% of the population, with rates of 6%–7% among those over age 55.

Estimated prevalence rates for dementia have been calculated by pooling data from multiple population-based studies in Europe among individuals ages 65 and older. These studies give overall rates of 6.4% for dementia (all causes), 4.4% for Alzheimer's disease, and 1.6% for vascular dementias (van der Flier & Scheltens, 2005). The prevalence of dementia among people younger than age 65 is much lower (less than 1% for all types of dementia). For all age groups, including the younger ages, dementia rates essentially double every 5 years, reaching nearly 30% at ages 90 and older.

In general, women are more likely to have dementia than are men, although prevalence rates between men and women are similar from age 65 through the mid-70s, when the rates in women begin to increase faster than the rates in men (van der Flier & Scheltens, 2005). Studies in the United States show similar patterns, with rates of dementia among individuals older than 70 around 15%, increasing from approximately 5% in the 7th decade of life, to 24% in the 8th, and more than 35% in those ages 90 and over (Plassman et al., 2007).

WHEN TO SUSPECT DEMENTIA IN A PATIENT WITH HOARDING

As discussed, rates of hoarding behaviors are elevated among patients with dementia, and rates of dementia are elevated among patients with hoarding disorder. This does not mean, however, that all people with HD have or will develop dementia. In fact, most people with HD will never develop dementia.

So how do you determine when to further evaluate someone for dementia when they present in your office with hoarding symptoms? Unfortunately, there are no prospective studies that can provide definitive answers to this question. Fortunately, cross-sectional studies of older adults living in squalor and population-based studies examining the co-occurrence of dementia and HD do provide some hints. The sections below outline some of the potential signs to look for if dementia is suspected.

First, Think About Age. Both the age of the patient at the time of assessment and the reported age of onset of hoarding symptoms is relevant when screening for possible dementia. As with the nonhoarding population, older individuals with hoarding have a higher risk of dementia than do younger individuals. Thus, suspicion for dementia should be much higher for an 80-year-old who presents with hoarding symptoms than for a 50-year-old. As with any patient, a reasonable rule of thumb regarding screening for mild cognitive impairment or dementia in those with hoarding disorder is to screen people who are age 65 or older, as this is when prevalence rates of dementia begin to climb more dramatically.

Age of onset of hoarding symptoms is a less sensitive indicator of risk for dementia than age at assessment, but it may be more specific. If there are consistent reports that hoarding behaviors did not begin until later in life (that is, over the age of 50), then suspicion for dementia is higher. In contrast, an earlier age of onset of hoarding does not completely eliminate risk for dementia, and these patients should still be screened routinely when they reach age 65. Although somewhat lower than those whose hoarding began after age 50, dementia rates are still elevated among individuals with earlier ages of hoarding onset compared to the general population.

Second, Look for Squalor. Contrary to popular depictions in the media, hoarding and squalor are not synonymous. In fact, most people with hoarding disorder do not live in squalor, and most people who live in squalor do not meet criteria for primary hoarding disorder (Snowdon, Halliday, & Hunt, 2013). There are many reasons individuals live in squalor, which is defined by the presence of dirt, filth, and neglect rather than by accumulation of items. In addition to hoarding disorder, these reasons might include dementia, alcoholism, or other substance abuse, psychosis, physical illness or physical disability, and severe personality disorders (including obsessive compulsive personality disorder) (Snowdon & Halliday, 2011). However, dementia or other forms of executive dysfunction, including alcohol-related brain dysfunction, are among the most common causes of severe squalor, especially in older adults.

Third, Look for Collectionism. Adults who are lifelong collectors do not appear to be at higher risk for dementia, at least as far as we know (A. E. Nordsletten & Mataix-Cols, 2012). However, individuals who begin to collect unusual objects, particularly those who collect or keep food, cigarette butts, or other items that appear to others to be trash, may be showing signs of incipient dementia. In addition, collectionism due to dementia or organic brain injury differs from both hoarding and collecting in that it appears to be purposeless rather than goal directed. Difficulty discarding is not a typical feature of collectionism in dementia. Although interrupting the act of collecting may be difficult, discarding the objects at a later time is typically not a problem.

Fourth, Look for Objective Reports of Memory Problems. Many individuals with hoarding disorder will report that they have memory problems, or that they are not confident in their memories. However, as will be discussed in Chapter 7, the majority of those with HD do not show objective evidence of memory impairment. Thus, patient report of memory impairment is not a reliable metric when assessing for potential dementia. This is where obtaining collateral information from friends and family can be helpful. Objective reports of problems with memory, in particular, notable worsening of memory across time, may indicate incipient dementia. If a spouse or other loved one reports that a patient with hoarding disorder has begun to lose their way in familiar neighborhoods, forget common words or well-known names, or loses their car, keys, or other important items with increasing frequency, this is a cause for concern. Note that a change in memory or functioning is the key here, not chronic disorganization, which is characteristic of people with HD, and not necessarily indicative of dementia.

Fifth, Look for Psychosis. Several studies of older adults suggest that psychotic symptoms are associated with higher rates of dementia among individuals with hoarding behaviors (Halliday, Banerjee, Philpot, & Macdonald, 2000; Snowdon & Halliday, 2011). In the Brain Health Registry, the population-based online survey of medical and neuropsychiatric conditions among adults that was described in Chapter 2, individuals with hoarding and dementia had a nearly threefold increase in self-reported diagnoses of psychosis. Similarly, in a study of over 400 nursing home residents and 177 community-dwelling seniors who attended a day care/senior center, hoarding behaviors were associated with both dementia and hallucinations/delusions (Marx & Cohen-Mansfield, 2003).

RISK FACTORS FOR DEMENTIA IN INDIVIDUALS DISPLAYING HOARDING SYMPTOMS

- age older than 65
- hoarding symptoms began after age 50
- squalor present
- collectionism, particularly of odd items, rather than difficulty discarding
- objective evidence (not subjective report) of memory problems
- psychosis present

**TABLE 4.2: BRIEF SCREENING TOOLS FOR DEMENTIA
AND MILD COGNITIVE IMPAIRMENT**

	Time to administer	Number of items	Format
Mini Mental State Exam (MMSE)	7 to 8 min	30	Paper and pencil
Montreal Cognitive Assessment (MoCA)	8 to 10 min	12	Paper and pencil
Verbal Fluency Test	1 to 2 min	1	verbal
Mini Cognitive Assessment Instrument (MCAI or Mini-Cog)	2 to 5 min	3	Paper and pencil, verbal
Sweet 16	2 to 4 min	12	verbal
General Practitioner Assessment of Cognition (GPCOG)	2 to 5 min	12	Paper and pencil, verbal
Memory Impairment Screen	2 to 5 min	6	Paper, verbal

WHAT DOESN'T NECESSARILY PREDICT DEMENTIA AMONG PEOPLE WITH HOARDING DISORDER?

There are many characteristics and conditions that are seen both in patients with mild cognitive impairment and in those with HD, yet are not necessarily predictive of either. These include depression, disorganization, and anxiety. These symptoms are known to be higher among people with dementia or mild cognitive impairment (MCI), and among

Cutoff scores indicating possible cognitive impairment	How to administer/where to obtain
19–23 (MCI) ≤18 (likely dementia)	Copyrighted Obtain from PAR Inc. https://www.parinc.com/
≤25 ≤24 if fewer than 12 years of education	https://www.mocatest.org/
<15 if ≥8th grade education <12 if 1–7 years of education <9 if no formal education	Ask the patient to name as many animals as they can in one minute. Give one point per animal, repeats are not given points.
<3	www.alz.org Search for cognitive assessment tools
<16	(Fong et al., 2011)
≤7 on part 1, ≤10 on Part 2	www.alz.org Search for cognitive assessment tools
≤4	www.alz.org Search for cognitive assessment tools

people with hoarding disorder. They are not specific for either, nor are they sensitive to distinguishing one condition from the other.

WHAT TO DO WHEN YOU SUSPECT DEMENTIA

Many people with hoarding disorder exhibit symptoms of executive dysfunction, including problems with organization, concentration, and categorization (Mackin, Arean, Delucchi, & Mathews, 2011; Mackin et al., 2016). Some individuals with HD also report problems with memory, attention, or decision making. Although hoarding disorder is associated with changes in specific neurocognitive domains, these changes do not typically rise to the level of clinical impairment, nor do they indicate incipient dementia. The neurocognitive features of hoarding disorder are discussed in more detail in Chapter 7.

If dementia or MCI is suspected in a particular individual with hoarding disorder, the first step is to do a brief cognitive screen. These screens are standard in many psychiatric, neurological, or general geriatric practices. They are relatively brief in nature and generally do not require extensive training to administer (Simmons, Hartmann, & Dejoseph, 2011). Screening measures for suspected dementia are outlined in Table 4.2. They include the Mini Mental State Exam (MMSE), the Montreal Cognitive Assessment (MoCA), the Verbal Fluency Test, the Mini Cognitive Assessment Instrument (MCAI or Mini-Cog), and the Sweet 16. If any of these screens are positive, consider referring the patient for a full neuropsychological assessment.

CO-OCCURRING PSYCHIATRIC DISORDERS

In addition to being associated with multiple medical conditions (discussed in Chapter 2), HD is also highly comorbid with a number of psychiatric disorders. Although the reported rates of specific psychiatric comorbidities in HD varies, studies are fairly consistent in their estimates of the proportion of individuals with HD who have at least one additional psychiatric condition. Most studies report that between 60% and 65% of individuals with HD will have one or more additional psychiatric disorders, although rates as high as 90% have been reported (Archer, 2019; Ayers, Dozier, Pittman, Mayes, & Twamley, 2018; Chakraborty et al., 2012; R. O. Frost, Steketee, & Tolin, 2011; A. E. Nordsletten, Reichenberg, et al., 2013; Torres et al., 2012). The psychiatric illnesses that are most commonly seen in people with hoarding disorder, and their prevalence rates in the both general population and in those with HD, are discussed next.

DEPRESSION

Mood disorders affect approximately 21% of adults at some point during their lifetimes (National Institute of Mental Health, 2019). Major depressive disorder (MDD) is by far the most common, accounting for all but 1%–2% of the mood disorders (Hasin et al., 2018). Women are twice as likely as men to experience MDD, and younger adults (under age 30) are 3 times as likely as older adults to have a major depressive episode in any given year. Non-White individuals have lower rates of MDD than do White individuals (Hasin et al., 2018).

Reported rates of major depressive disorder among individuals with HD range from just over general population rates (26%) (A. E. Nordsletten et al., 2018; A. E. Nordsletten, Reichenberg, et al., 2013) to nearly twice the expected population rate (48%–51%) (Ayers, Dozier, Pittman, et al., 2018; R. O. Frost et al., 2011). In all studies that examine rates of co-occurring psychiatric illnesses in HD, depression is the most commonly reported psychiatric comorbidity. The presence of depression is also associated with an increased risk of additional comorbid psychiatric disorders—in one study of over 300 individuals with HD who were assessed for a variety of psychiatric illnesses, 35% met criteria for major depressive disorder. Of those, 60% had depression alone, while 40% had additional psychiatric disorders (Archer, 2019).

Depression is not only prevalent in the general population, it is also the leading cause of disability worldwide, according to the World Health Organization. As discussed in Chapter 2, individuals with HD have high rates of disability even in the absence of other comorbid psychiatric disorders. For those who also have depression, disability rates are even higher, with quality of life and social and occupational impairment also reduced (Archer, 2019; Saxena et al., 2011).

ANXIETY

If depression is the leading cause of disability worldwide, anxiety is right behind in its global impact. According to the Global Burden of Disease Collaborative Network, anxiety disorders collectively contribute to between 300 and 600 years of healthy life lost to disability per 100,000 people (G. B. o. D. C. Network, 2018). The impact of this loss of years of life and productivity is highest among those ages 50–69, in other words, during the time of life when hoarding is most prevalent, and when rates of hoarding disorder are increasing rapidly.

In any given year, nearly 20% of adults will experience an anxiety disorder. Over 30% of adults will experience one or more anxiety disorders in their lifetimes. Rates of anxiety disorders among individuals with HD are even higher. Studies estimate that lifetime rates of anxiety range from 37% to over 50% among those with hoarding (Archer, 2019; R. O. Frost et al., 2011; A. E. Nordsletten, Reichenberg, et al., 2013).

The anxiety disorders most commonly seen in adults include generalized anxiety disorder (GAD), panic disorder, agoraphobia, and social anxiety disorder (also called social phobia). These are also common in people with hoarding. GAD affects between 15% to 25% of individuals with HD, agoraphobia affects 12%–16%, and social anxiety disorder affects between 7% and 24% (Archer, 2019; Ayers, Dozier, Pittman, et al., 2018; R. O. Frost et al., 2011; A. E. Nordsletten et al., 2018; A. E. Nordsletten, Reichenberg, et al., 2013).

As is the case for depression, among individuals with HD, the presence of an anxiety disorder also increases the risk of additional psychiatric comorbidities. In the study by Archer and colleagues described above, more than 80% of individuals with three or more psychiatric comorbidities had at least one anxiety disorder, and 45% of individuals with two psychiatric comorbidities had at least one anxiety disorder (Archer, 2019). Among the anxiety disorders, agoraphobia and GAD were the most likely to co-occur with other psychiatric illnesses. In contrast, social anxiety disorder most commonly presented as the only psychiatric illness among people with hoarding, and was less frequently seen in the context of other anxiety or mood disorders.

Screening for Anxiety and Depression. There are two simple tools that can be easily used in a variety of clinical and other settings to screen for depression and anxiety. These are the Patient Health Questionnaire 9 for depression, or the PHQ-9, and the Generalized Anxiety

Disorder 7-item scale, or GAD-7 for anxiety (Spitzer et al., 1994). Both of these instruments are freely available for general use. No permissions are required to reproduce, translate, display, or distribute either the PHQ-9 or the GAD-7. The PHQ-9 and the GAD-7 are reproduced below in Tables 4.3 and 4.4.

Both the PHQ-9 and the GAD-7 ask about symptoms that the patient has experienced in the preceding two weeks. The PHQ-9 scores each of the nine *DSM* criteria for major depression on a scale of 0 (not at all) to 3 (nearly every day). The GAD-7 has a similar structure, and asks about seven common symptoms of anxiety, again on a 0 (not at all) to 3 (nearly every day) scale. For both instruments, scoring is divided into four groups. Scores of 5 or less indicates no or minimal depressive or anxiety symptoms. Scores between 6–10 indicate moderate depression or anxiety. Scores of 11–15 indicate moderately severe depression or anxiety, and scores above 15 indicate severe depression or anxiety. The GAD-7 asks an additional question that is not included in the scoring. This question asks about impairment: "If you checked off any of the problems listed above, how difficult have these problems made it for you to do your work, take care of things at home, or get along with other people?" Answers range from "not at all" to "extremely difficult." Anyone who marks "somewhat difficult" or higher should be further screened, regardless of their GAD-7 total score.

TRAUMA AND POSTTRAUMATIC STRESS DISORDER

Trauma has long been hypothesized to play a role in the development of hoarding behaviors. A relationship between traumatic life events and the development of hoarding is in some ways intuitive, and many people, both lay and professional, have gone further, and have argued that trauma in fact causes hoarding. For example, take an article that appeared in the online version of the popular science magazine *Psychology Today* in 2013. This article was titled "Hoarding as a Reaction to Trauma," and subtitled "Filling the Emotional Hole with 'Stuff'." The author posited that hoarding arises from an "obsessive need to collect and keep material objects," which in turn serves "as a coping mechanism for grief or posttraumatic stress" (Muller, 2013).

TABLE 4.3: THE PATIENT HEALTH QUESTIONNAIRE 9 (PHQ-9)

During the last two weeks, how often have you been bothered by the following problems?	Not at all	Several days	More than half the days	Nearly every day
1. Little interest or pleasure in doing things	0	1	2	3
2. Feeling down, depressed, or hopeless	0	1	2	3
3. Trouble falling or staying asleep, or sleeping too much	0	1	2	3
4. Feeling tired or having little energy	0	1	2	3
5. Poor appetite or overeating	0	1	2	3
6. Feeling bad about yourself, that you are a failure or have let yourself or your family down	0	1	2	3
7. Trouble concentrating on things such as reading the newspaper or watching television	0	1	2	3
8. Moving or speaking so slowly that other people could have noticed? Or the opposite, being so fidgety or restless that you have been moving around a lot more than usual	0	1	2	3
9. Thoughts that you would be better off dead or thoughts of hurting yourself in some way	0	1	2	3
Total for each column=	____	+____	+____	+____
	Total score=_____			

Source: From Spitzer, R. L., Williams, J. B., Kroenke, K., Linzer, M., deGruy, F. V., 3rd, Hahn, S. R., . . . Johnson, J. G. (1994). Utility of a new procedure for diagnosing mental disorders in primary care: The PRIME-MD 1000 study. JAMA, 272(22), 1749–1756.

TABLE 4.4: THE GENERAL ANXIETY DISORDER
7-ITEM QUESTIONNAIRE (GAD-7)

During the last two weeks, how often have you been bothered by the following problems?	Not at all	Several days	More than half the days	Nearly every day
1. Feeling nervous, anxious, or on edge	0	1	2	3
2. Not being able to stop or control worrying	0	1	2	3
3. Worrying too much about different things	0	1	2	3
4. Trouble relaxing	0	1	2	3
5. Being so restless that it is hard to sit still	0	1	2	3
6. Becoming easily annoyed or irritable	0	1	2	3
7. Feeling afraid as if something awful might happen	0	1	2	3
Total for each column=	____	+____	+____	+____
	Total score=_____			

Source: From Spitzer, R. L., Williams, J. B., Kroenke, K., Linzer, M., deGruy, F. V., 3rd, Hahn, S. R., . . . Johnson, J. G. (1994). Utility of a new procedure for diagnosing mental disorders in primary care: The PRIME-MD 1000 study. JAMA, 272(22), 1749–1756.

This hypothesis makes sense, at least superficially, based on observations of in whom and at what time of life hoarding manifests. As discussed in Chapter 2, while hoarding symptoms typically begin in adolescence, they do not become clinically apparent until midlife or later. This is also a time of life when losses, including traumatic losses, start to become more common. People lose loved ones, including parents and spouses, to death and divorce; children grow up and leave home; and jobs are lost or left.

But what is the evidence that trauma causes hoarding? Remarkably little, as it turns out. However, before discussing the data regarding trauma and hoarding, and the potential relationships between these, it is important to define the relevant terms. First, it is critical to distinguish between a traumatic event and an adverse life event, as these are clinically quite different. Second, it is important to differentiate association or correlation from causation.

Trauma Versus Adversity. The *DSM-5* definition of a *traumatic event* is one that may result in death, serious injury, or sexual violence, or involves the threat of one of these. In contrast, an *adverse life event*, also referred to as a *psychosocial stressor*, is an event that potentially increases stress and decreases function but does not rise to the level of severity that defines a traumatic event. Examples of traumatic events include natural disasters such as wildfires, earthquakes and hurricanes, serious car accidents, exposure to war or other life threatening conflicts, and sexual or physical assault or abuse. Examples of adverse life events include the death of a loved one, divorce, job loss, and bankruptcy or other financial stressors. Of course, there are many events or exposures that fall into a gray area between adversity and trauma. Similarly, for some people, particularly those who have a previous history of repeated exposures, some forms of adversity may be experienced as trauma, and have the same negative impacts.

Association, Correlation, and Causation. When two variables or characteristics occur together in the same individual(s) more often than would be expected by chance, these characteristics or variables are said to be *associated*. When rates or occurrences of the two variables covary (e.g., increase or decrease) either together or in opposition to one another, they are said to be correlated.

There are many examples of association or correlation without causation both in science and in the world at large. Two famous examples, one of association, and one of correlation, include (a) belonging to a particular national or ethnic group (for example, being Italian) and eating food associated with that group (in this case, Italian food) and (b) taking hormone replacement therapy and having coronary artery disease.

In the case of the former example, while it is true that many Italian people do eat Italian food (that is, there is an association between these two things), it is clearly incorrect to assume either that being Italian causes the eating of Italian food, or conversely, that eating Italian food means that one is of Italian origin. In other words, being Italian does not cause one to eat Italian food. This is an example of association without causation.

The latter case is a good example of correlation without causation. Observational studies in the late 1980s and early 1990s indicated that women who took hormone replacement therapy (HRT) for menopause had much higher rates of coronary heart disease than those who did not. This observation was published in a famous article in 1991 (Stampfer & Colditz, 1991), and led to hundreds of thousands of women being taken off of estrogen prescriptions by their gynecologists and primary care doctors. However, later studies that actually randomized women in menopause to either receiving HRT or receiving placebo and followed them over a number of years found either no increased risk or a small increased risk of cardiac disease (Lawlor, Davey Smith, & Ebrahim, 2004).

In this case example, the correlations between HRT and coronary artery disease seen in the early studies were probably due to unrecognized baseline differences between the two groups of women. Although speculative, it is possible for example that women who sought out HRT in these studies were more likely, for other reasons, to have underlying medical problems, and thus more likely to visit their doctors. It is also possible that these women were more likely to be screened for cardiovascular disease by their doctors precisely because they were asking for a prescription than those women who were not.

The terms *causation* or *causative*, on the other hand, are used when there is clear evidence that Variable 1 is responsible for the occurrence of, or *causes*, Variable 2. There are many clear examples of causation, both in the medical literature, and in life in general. For example, it is an undisputed fact that sex between a man and a woman causes pregnancy. This is not to say that every instance of sex results in pregnancy, or that heterosexual sex is the only way to cause a pregnancy. However, pregnancy is clearly one outcome of sex.

One of the most commonly cited examples of causation in the medical literature is the relationship between smoking and lung cancer. This relationship began as an observed association, and over time, a multitude of studies, both epidemiological and experimental, have repeatedly shown that there are thousands of toxins in the smoke that is created from burning tobacco, and that inhaling this smoke directly leads to the development of many kinds of cancers, including lung cancer (Services., 2014).

So what is the relationship between adversity, trauma, and hoarding? There is some evidence that people with HD have higher rates of adverse life events than others, although the data regarding this potential relationship are not entirely consistent. Some studies suggest higher rates of what could be called everyday adversity, experiences such as divorce, the death of a loved one, or job loss, among individuals with hoarding disorder, while others suggest that a history of adverse experiences in childhood and early adulthood is associated with increased likelihood and severity of hoarding symptoms among individuals with OCD (Chou, Mackin, Delucchi, & Mathews, 2018; Cromer, 2007; Grisham, Frost, Steketee, Kim, & Hood, 2006; Hartl, Duffany, Allen, Steketee, & Frost, 2005).

One internet-based study of individuals who self-reported significant hoarding symptoms described high rates of many types of adversity, including employment or financial problems, interpersonal violence, loss of or change in relationships, and loss of or damage to possessions (D. F. Tolin, Meunier, Frost, & Steketee, 2010). As expected, many of these adverse events occurred after the onset of hoarding symptoms and may in fact have been a direct result of hoarding. However, in some instances, the events were reported to occur at the time of hoarding symptom onset. In particular, loss of or changes in relationships and interpersonal violence occurred at high rates (e.g., were reported by

20% or more participants), at the time of hoarding symptom onset (D. F. Tolin, Meunier, et al., 2010).

In contrast, other studies do not find an association between adversity and hoarding. In particular, material deprivation and impoverishment during childhood does not appear to be more common among individuals with HD than among those without (Ayers, Saxena, Golshan, & Wetherell, 2009; R. O. Frost & Gross, 1993; Landau et al., 2011). When events that are more traditionally considered by clinicians to be traumatic events rather than adverse life events (e.g., sexual, physical, or emotional abuse; living through war or a natural disaster) are examined, a few studies suggest individuals with hoarding disorder report experiencing higher numbers of traumas (including physical or sexual mishandling or forced behaviors, exposure to natural disasters, and crime related events) compared to controls (Chou, Mackin, et al., 2018; Hartl et al., 2005; Landau et al., 2011).

However, although rates of adversity and perhaps trauma appear to be elevated among individuals with hoarding disorder, this does not indicate causation. In fact, it is not currently known whether either deprivation or adversity actually causes or contributes to the progression of hoarding disorder. HD is strongly biological in etiology, but environmental factors also clearly play a role in its development. What those factors may be is at this point unknown. The neurobiology and etiology of HD is further discussed in Chapter 7.

POSTTRAUMATIC STRESS DISORDER

If rates of trauma are higher among people with hoarding disorder, it would stand to reason that rates of posttraumatic stress disorder, or PTSD, are also higher than would be expected among the general population. Lifetime rates of PTSD are approximately 7% in the United States, and are typically more than twice as high in women than in men (National Institutes of Mental Health, 2019). Nearly 40% of those exposed to trauma will develop PTSD (Santiago et al., 2013).

Interestingly, rates of posttraumatic stress disorder (PTSD) are not clearly elevated among individuals with hoarding disorder, despite potentially higher rates of adverse childhood events. Lifetime prevalence estimates for PTSD range from 7% to nearly 20% in studies of individuals with HD (Archer, 2019; Ayers, Dozier, Pittman, et al., 2018; Chakraborty et al., 2012; R. O. Frost et al., 2011; Landau et al., 2011; A. E. Nordsletten et al., 2018; A. E. Nordsletten, Reichenberg, et al., 2013). On first look, the reported prevalence rates seem to indicate that PTSD rates are higher among people with HD than they are in the general population. Across all studies, the rates of PTSD are around 15%, which is twice the lifetime population prevalence rate.

However, the story changes somewhat when PTSD rates in those with hoarding disorder are directly compared to PTSD rates in controls within the same study, rather than just to the general population rates. Multiple studies have shown no differences in PTSD rates between individuals with HD and age- and sex-matched control participants (R. O. Frost et al., 2011; Hartl et al., 2005; Landau et al., 2011; A. E. Nordsletten, Reichenberg, et al., 2013). So what accounts for the apparent disparity in findings—do people with HD have more PTSD than the general population or not? Why are PTSD rates in HD higher than the reported population prevalences but not elevated when directly compared to a control group?

The most likely answer is that rates of PTSD *are* probably higher among individuals with HD than they are in the general population in the United States, taken as a whole, but they are not all that much higher. Many variables come into play when determining whether a group is disproportionately affected by a particular condition or disorder, and individuals with HD as a group differ from the general population in multiple ways. For example, as discussed in Chapter 2, hoarding disorder increases in prevalence with age, and older adults are twice or three times as likely to suffer from hoarding than are younger individuals. Older adults are also more likely to have been exposed to trauma in their lives than younger adults, just by virtue of having lived longer and experienced more. However, there are other possible reasons for the discrepant results between studies. For example, studies with small sample sizes can provide misleading information about disease prevalence, as the accuracy of the prevalence estimates is lower. Until more research is available, clinicians should be aware of the possibility that people with HD may be at higher risk for trauma and perhaps also for PTSD.

ALCOHOL AND DRUG ABUSE

Substance abuse, which includes both misuse of alcohol and illicit drug use, is a major health problem in the United States. Approximately 7% of Americans ages 25 and older meet diagnostic criteria for alcohol dependence or abuse in any given year, 2% to 3% meet criteria for drug abuse or dependence, and nearly 5% meet criteria for both. However, only 1.5% receive treatment for these problems (Administration, 2014). These numbers, including the low proportion of individuals with substance abuse problems who have received treatment, have remained remarkably stable for the last decade or so.

It may seem that people with HD are at increased risk for all of the psychiatric disorders, and thus also must have dramatically increased rates of substance abuse. As discussed in this chapter, rates of mood and anxiety disorders are clearly increased among individuals with hoarding disorder, and rates of PTSD are also possibly higher. All of these disorders are associated with an increased risk of substance abuse or misuse.

Despite the relationships between HD, depression, and anxiety, rates of substance abuse do not appear to be greatly elevated among individuals with HD, at least on initial investigation. Alcohol and drug abuse rates among individuals with hoarding range from 2% to 12%, depending on the study and definitions used, and most studies report rates that are similar to those of the general population of 2%–5% (Archer, 2019; Chakraborty et al., 2012; R. O. Frost et al., 2011; A. E. Nordsletten et al., 2018; A. E. Nordsletten, Reichenberg, et al., 2013).

However, as with the other psychiatric illnesses discussed in this chapter, when assessing the prevalence of substance abuse among individuals with hoarding, it is important to recognize that comparing rates to a general population-based estimate may lead to inaccurate interpretations. This is because risk factors that predispose to substance abuse independent of hoarding symptoms may differ between the general population and individuals with hoarding disorder. These include, among other characteristics, age and sex.

Thus, comparing rates of alcohol and drug abuse between individuals with HD and a matched group of individuals without HD is the best approach. If such comparison groups are not available, the next best method is to compare rates among individuals with HD to publicly available population-based data for the most comparable group possible. In the case of hoarding, this would be middle-aged to older individuals.

Fortunately, several studies that examine rates of substance abuse in hoarding disorder do include control groups. These studies have compared rates of either alcohol use disorder or drug use disorder or both between individuals with HD or those with OCD and clinically significant hoarding symptoms to those with OCD but no hoarding (Frost et al., 2011; Torres et al., 2012; Wheaton, Timpano, Lasalle-Ricci, & Murphy, 2008), or to matched community controls (Nordsletten, Reichenberg, et al., 2013; Samuels et al., 2008).

Unfortunately, the findings from these studies are mixed. While some studies indicate that there are increased rates of both alcohol use disorder and drug use disorder among individuals with hoarding, others show no differences between those with hoarding and those without. This inconsistency does not appear to depend on whether co-occurring OCD was examined. Two of the three studies that looked at hoarding in the context of OCD found no increased rates of either alcohol or substance abuse among those with hoarding symptoms (Frost et al., 2011; Torres et al., 2012). These studies cited rates of 2% and 4% for substance use disorder and 2% and 8% for alcohol use disorder, respectively.

In contrast, a third study reported rates of substance abuse that were more than 2 times higher among individuals who had both OCD and hoarding disorder than among individuals with OCD who did not have HD (Wheaton et al., 2008). Rates of substance abuse in this study were 26% among those with OCD and hoarding, and 10% in those with OCD only. Alcohol abuse was present in 33% of the sample of those with OCD plus hoarding, compared to 25% of controls with OCD only. It is important to note that this study examined lifetime rates of alcohol and substance abuse rather than rates of current alcohol or substance abuse.

The two population-based studies that examine substance misuse and hoarding are also discrepant from one another. The first study, published in 2008, compared current and lifetime rates of alcohol use disorder among 27 individuals with pathological hoarding symptoms and 708 without hoarding. This study found much higher rates of lifetime alcohol use disorders among those with hoarding compared to those without (52% vs. 20%), and higher, but not significantly higher, rates of current alcohol use disorder (11% vs. 5%) between those with hoarding and those without (Samuels et al., 2008).

The second study, published in 2013, compared 19 individuals who met the *DSM-5* criteria for hoarding disorder to over 1,300 individuals who screened negative for HD (screen controls), and 80 individuals who underwent comprehensive diagnostic interviews and did not meet criteria for HD (interviewed control group). In this sample, rates of current illicit drug use were 26% among those with HD, compared to 23% in the interviewed control group, and 13% in the screen controls. Rates of hazardous alcohol use were 26% among those with HD, 27% for the interviewed control group, and 20% in the screen controls.

Part of the difficulty in interpreting these data, taken as a whole, are the low rates of individuals in the HD groups. Small sample sizes, as discussed above, can lead to inaccurate estimates, due to the natural fluctuation that occurs when adding even one or two individuals to the sample who just happen to have the diagnosis in question. Similarly, self-report data, such as are collected in a screening approach, may under-identify individuals who would actually meet criteria for a substance use disorder, due to under-reporting of either symptoms or impairment. Thus, whenever possible, studies that include clinical interviews should be used in favor of self-report or screen data.

Taken together, these results, although somewhat complicated to interpret, suggest that at any given point in time, individuals who suffer from hoarding disorder are probably not more likely than their peers to suffer from either alcohol or drug abuse. However, over the course of their entire lifetimes, individuals with HD may be slightly more likely to experience problematic substance use than are their age-matched peers. Most importantly, these studies suggest that a substantial subset (up to 25%) of individuals with HD will also have problems with substance abuse. Thus, independent of the question as to whether rates of these disorders are higher in HD than in the general population, it is clear that ongoing screening for these disorders, and providing treatment options for them when they are identified, is an important part of appropriate clinical care.

SUICIDAL THOUGHTS AND BEHAVIORS IN HD

Suicidality is not technically a psychiatric illness, but it is a common, and potentially lethal, symptom of many psychiatric (and medical) disorders, and as such, is worth discussion. Suicide is the 10th leading cause of death in the United States, and rates are highest among middle-aged adults and older adults (American Foundation for Suicide Prevention, 2019). According to the American Foundation for Suicide Prevention, nearly 1% of Americans age 18 and older have attempted suicide at least once in their lifetimes. Psychiatric illness, substance abuse or misuse, and socioeconomic stressors, all of which are prevalent among individuals with hoarding disorder, contribute to an increased risk of suicide.

Only a few studies have assessed for the presence and frequency of suicidal thoughts and behaviors among individuals with HD. Alarmingly, all of these studies indicate that rates of both current suicidal thoughts or behaviors and the prevalence of lifetime suicide attempts are high among individuals with hoarding. The percentage of individuals with HD who have had at least one suicide attempt in their lifetimes rages from 13% to 38%, while the percent of individuals with active suicidal thoughts at the time of interview ranged between 10% and 20% (Archer, 2019; Chakraborty et al., 2012; Torres et al., 2012).

Psychiatric comorbidity is a strong predictor of suicidality among those with hoarding. However, hoarding symptom severity also independently predicts suicidality. In assessing the relationships between hoarding, psychiatric illness, and suicidality in a study of over 300 people with HD who were participating in a clinical treatment trial, Archer and colleagues found that psychiatric comorbidity and hoarding severity each increased the risk of suicidality through two means, which are shown in Figure 4.1. First, both psychiatric illness and more severe hoarding symptoms contribute *directly* to suicidality. In other words, having co-occurring psychiatric problems in addition to having hoarding disorder directly increases the risk that someone will have suicidal

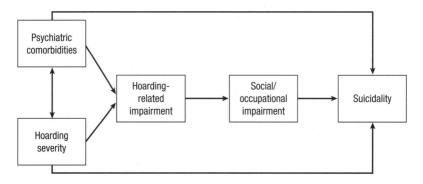

Figure 4.1: Path From Psychiatric Illness and Hoarding Severity to Increased Risk of Suicidality Among Individuals With Hoarding Disorder. The width of the arrow indicates the relative contribution of each of the steps in the path, such that hoarding severity has a stronger relationship with hoarding-related impairment than do psychiatric comorbidities, and psychiatric comorbidities contribute more to suicidality directly than does hoarding severity, although both factors contribute to suicidality through both direct and indirect paths. *Source: Adapted from Archer, C. A., Moran, K., Garza, K., Zakrzewski, J., Martin, A., Chou, C.-Y., Uhm, S.Y., Chan, J., Gause, M., Salazar, M., Plumadore, J., Smith, L.C., Komaiko, K., Howell, G., Vigil, O., Bain, D., Stark, S., Mackin, R.S., Eckfield, M., Vega, E., Tsoh, J.Y., Delucchi, K.L., Mathews, C.A. (2019). Relationship between symptom severity, psychiatric comorbidity, social/occupational impairment, and suicidality in hoarding disorder.* J Obsessive Compuls Relat Disord, 21, *158–164.*

thoughts or behaviors. Similarly, the worse an individual's hoarding symptoms are, the more likely that person is to feel suicidal.

Second, psychiatric comorbidity and hoarding severity both contribute *indirectly* to an increased risk of suicidality through their contributions to social or occupational impairment. As discussed in Chapter 1, hoarding leads to indecision about what to discard, and thus to clutter, and in these ways, it causes functional impairment. In particular, mounting clutter leads to difficulty with completing activities of daily living, due to the inability to use parts of the home or workplace, inability to find needed objects, or inability to move about the home or workplace safely.

The consequences of hoarding, which often results in unsanitary or unhealthy living and suboptimal working conditions, also lead to social or occupational impairment, including social isolation, dissolution of relationships, and loss of employment. Individuals with hoarding are reluctant to invite their friends and family members into their homes, or their loved ones refuse to visit. Medical and psychiatric illnesses result in lost work days, which leads to economic instability. In turn, these problems can lead to hopelessness and, from there, to suicidality.

SUMMARY

As discussed in this chapter, hoarding disorder rarely exists independent of other psychiatric problems. Co-occurring psychiatric illness is the rule, rather than the exception, occurring in over 60% of individuals with HD. People who hoard are at highest risk for anxiety and depression, and should be screened for these disorders at initial evaluation, and yearly thereafter. Assessment for other psychiatric illnesses may also be warranted, and screening for suicidal thoughts and behaviors should also be conducted periodically, particularly if warning signs or acute triggers, such as divorce or job loss, are present.

Chapter 5

Hoarding Behaviors in Children

As almost any parent can attest, children are collectors, and many, if not most, have difficulty throwing or giving away their collected items. This is especially true for young children. Children keep rocks and sticks, notes and old homework, broken toys and torn stuffed animals, and anything else that strikes their fancy. For the most part, this is developmentally normal behavior, and is in many ways adaptive. But when does hoarding and collecting in children become problematic or concerning?

HOARDING BEHAVIORS IN EARLY DEVELOPMENT

Very young children normally exhibit a range of ritualistic and compulsive behaviors. These include the insistence on doing things in the same or in a particular way, ordering, arranging, and lining things up, having strong preferences for particular foods or insisting on eating foods in a particular order or style, and having strong preferences for (or against) wearing particular items or types of clothing. These behaviors begin between ages 1 and 2, and typically resolve or significantly diminish by age 5.

The collecting and keeping of items is also developmentally normal in young children. Although strong attachments to one or a few favored objects (e.g., "lovies") begins early, usually around 1 year of age, other collecting behaviors begin a bit later, typically between ages 2 and 3 (D. W. Evans et al., 1997). Children of this age like to find and keep things that their parents might wish they wouldn't (like bottlecaps, leaves, sticks, and rocks), and take great pleasure in their discoveries. In addition, they sometimes have a hard time giving things up, such as outgrown toys and clothes that no longer fit, as well as other things, including what can feel to parents like every single scrap of paper brought home from preschool.

This need to keep things typically peaks around age 3, and continues into the kindergarten and first grade years, when it starts to taper off. As many as 60% of children ages 2 to 6 years old will have at least moderate hoarding behaviors, and in this age group, such behaviors are developmentally normal (Leckman & Bloch, 2008). After age 6, the prevalence of noticeable but not necessarily impairing hoarding behaviors in typically developing children decreases to about 10%, where it stays fairly stable through adolescence (Alvarenga et al., 2015; Burton et al., 2016; Ivanov et al., 2013).

Although no formal studies of problematic hoarding or hoarding disorder in younger children have been conducted, epidemiologic studies suggest that the prevalence of hoarding disorder is only approximately 2% in adolescents and in adults under the age of 55. Given this relatively low prevalence rate, and the fact that the estimated mean age of onset of hoarding symptoms is between ages 14–19 in the absence of OCD (Zaboski et al., 2019), it stands to reason that hoarding and keeping symptoms must diminish in frequency during adolescence and early adulthood, at least in the majority of people.

DIFFERENTIATING NORMAL KEEPING FROM PATHOLOGICAL HOARDING

So how does one differentiate "normal" keeping behaviors from pathological hoarding behaviors in children and adolescents? Does hoarding disorder even exist in children prior to adolescence? Unfortunately, hoarding behaviors in children have not been well-studied, particularly from a clinical standpoint. However, there is some evidence to suggest that hoarding disorder probably does occur as a distinct illness in children (Morris, Jaffee, Goodwin, & Franklin, 2016). Perhaps more importantly, hoarding symptoms also occur at elevated rates in a variety of childhood neuropsychiatric and neurodevelopmental disorders, including intellectual disability, autism spectrum disorders, learning disorders, attention deficit hyperactivity disorder (ADHD), and pediatric obsessive compulsive disorder (Morris et al., 2016).

Figure 5.1: Example of Normal Collecting Behaviors in Childhood. Note that, despite the messiness of the dresser's surface, the contents (toys, books, school papers) are within normal parameters and are not indicative of hoarding. *Photo credit: C. A. Mathews*

The first step in deciding whether a child has pathological hoarding behaviors is to rule out collectionism, as is demonstrated in Figure 5.1. Collecting is a fundamental activity of childhood, and children find value in many objects that adults would consider useless. As is true in adults, the active collection of particular types of objects, even if those objects are rocks or bottlecaps, does not represent pathology in children. Similarly, keeping behavior, in and of itself, is not abnormal in children. Many children will choose to keep old school notes or homework, or stuffed animals or toys, or even clothes that have been outgrown, for sentimental reasons or because they believe that they might need the notes in the future or might want to play with a particular toy again. As children get older, they typically become more willing to discard items from their childhood, with the exception of toys or other things to which they have been highly attached (e.g., a beloved stuffed animal) or which represent a particular success or epoch in their life.

There are some types of hoarding or keeping behaviors that are clearly abnormal in childhood, however. For example, the hoarding of garbage or food other than candy is not usual in typically developing children and can be a warning sign that something is amiss with the child, either psychologically or developmentally. Collecting things like cigarette butts, used wads of gum, or items from public garbage cans (with some exceptions, such as recyclables) is also not typical.

Similarly, even for kids who tend to be keepers, the quantity of material is usually minimal to moderate, whereas children at risk for hoarding disorder will have excessive quantities of material, to the point that functioning can be impaired. As the cleanliness and amount of clutter in a household is typically under the control of parents or guardians, problematic clutter in children is usually confined to their bedrooms. Children with pathological hoarding will have bedrooms full of stuff, such that their beds, closets, dressers, and even floors are nearly or completely unusable and will exhibit strong resistance to having their bedrooms cleaned out or decluttered. Children with hoarding problems will also be abnormally attached to items that other children may discard easily, such as toilet paper or paper towel rolls, paper crowns from a birthday party, old and crumbling leaves, and even garbage. They may also store and hide food in their rooms, including half eaten sandwiches, fruit, bread, and sweets.

ASSESSMENT OF HOARDING IN CHILDREN

As noted, the first thing to recognize when assessing for potential hoarding disorder in children is that the majority of hoarding behaviors do not represent pathology. However, if the child is collecting or insisting on keeping large quantities of materials, or collects and keeps half-eaten food or garbage, or if the keeping or acquisition behaviors are impairing or unusually persistent, formal assessment is warranted.

Many questionnaires aimed at assessing pediatric OCD contain a few items related to hoarding. These include the Children's Yale Brown Obsessive Compulsive Scale (C-YBOCS) (Scahill et al., 1997), the Obsessive Compulsive Inventory, Child Version (OCI-CV) (Foa et al., 2010), and the Toronto Obsessive Compulsive Rating Scale (TOCS) (L. S. Park et al., 2016), among others. There are also two hoarding specific scales that have been used to assess hoarding behaviors in children, the Hoarding Rating Scale, which was discussed in Chapter 3, and the Children's Saving Inventory. All of these measures are described below.

CHILDREN'S YALE-BROWN OBSESSIVE COMPULSIVE SCALE

The C-YBOCS symptom checklist, in addition to assessing standard obsessions and compulsions such as fears of contamination and excessive handwashing, also contains two hoarding-related questions. The first one asks about whether the child has either difficulty throwing things away or has excessive saving behaviors, while the second is more general and asks about other unspecified hoarding or saving compulsions. Both items are scored as present or absent. A positive answer on either of these two questions should be followed up with additional screening questions.

Although the C-YBOCS can provide information about whether hoarding symptoms might be present in a given child, assessing the functional impact of hoarding symptoms identified by the C-YBOCS can be somewhat problematic. Because the severity portion of the C-YBOCS is primarily aimed at assessing obsessive compulsive symptoms globally, rather than assessing any specific symptoms, including hoarding symptoms individually, the severity and time spent on all of the obsessive and compulsive symptoms that were endorsed on the C-YBOCS are assessed jointly in one global severity score. Although the severity scale can be modified by the user to assess hoarding symptoms alone, the severity and functional impact of the C-YBOCS hoarding symptoms are not typically calculated independently, and the questions are written with more classic obsessions and compulsions rather than with saving and discarding behaviors in mind.

THE OBSESSIVE COMPULSIVE INVENTORY, CHILD VERSION

The OCI-CV is a 21-item questionnaire that includes three hoarding-related questions. Two questions address collecting (collecting so much that it gets in the way and collecting unneeded things), and one addresses difficulty discarding (not throwing things away for fear of needing them later). Each item is scored as "never," "sometimes," or "always." Although there are no scoring algorithms that specifically address hoarding questions for the OCI-CV, a score of "always" on two or more of these items should be followed up with a more in-depth assessment. A score of "always" on one item only or scores of "sometimes" on the items is somewhat more ambiguous and may represent more typical collecting or keeping behaviors.

TORONTO OBSESSIVE COMPULSIVE RATING SCALE

The TOCS is a 21-item scale that asks a child or their parents to compare themselves or their child to other children of the same age on a variety of obsessive compulsive symptoms (L. S. Park et al., 2016). The ratings on each question range from −3 (far less often than other children) through 0 (average amount of time) to +3 (far more often than other children). The TOCS includes two hoarding-related questions: collecting useless objects and difficulty throwing things away.

The hoarding questions on the C-YBOCS and the OCI-CV have been studied primarily in the context of children with OCD; there are no data available on hoarding symptoms in a general population of children using these instruments. In contrast, the psychometric properties of the hoarding questions on the TOCS have been assessed in over 16,000 children and adolescents, including both those with obsessive compulsive symptoms and those without (Burton et al., 2016). The internal consistency of the overall TOCS was very high (94%), and acceptable for the hoarding symptoms (82%). Hoarding symptoms were fairly normally distributed in this population, suggesting that the items captured the full range of symptom profiles among the children assessed.

THE HOARDING RATING SCALE
SELF REPORT (HRS-SR)

Described more fully in Chapter 3, the HRS-SR has also been used to assess hoarding behaviors in adolescents ages 15 and older (V. Z. Ivanov et al., 2013; V. Z. Ivanov, Mataix-Cols, D., Serlachius, E., Brander, G. Elmquist, A., Enander, J., Rück, C., 2019). However, this instrument was not designed for use in children, and has not been validated for use in either adolescents or in children. The wording and language are fairly sophisticated, and the questions are aimed at adults who have control over all of the space in their home, and over their finances. Thus, although the HRS-SR has many advantages, it is not currently recommended for use in children or adolescents.

Only one clinical assessment tool has been developed to formally assess a wide variety of hoarding behaviors in children. This tool, the Children's Saving Inventory (CSI) (Storch, Muroff, et al., 2011), is directly modeled after the Saving Inventory, Revised (SI-R) (R. O. Frost et al., 2004).

CHILDREN'S SAVING INVENTORY

Like the SI-R, the CSI contains 23 questions, each scored on a scale of 0 (not at all/none) to 4 (extreme/completely). The CSI assesses clutter, difficulty discarding, acquisition, and distress/impairment, and is designed to be completed by parents about their child. In addition to asking about the child's urges to acquire or save, and their control over these urges, the CSI also assesses the degree of the child's attachment to their possessions, as well as the functional impact of that attachment on the child and on their family. More recently, a 15-item version of the CSI has been developed that eliminates the acquisition questions, as they are not part of the *DSM* diagnostic criteria for hoarding disorder (Soreni et al., 2018).

The psychometric properties of the original 23-item CSI were evaluated in over 300 children with OCD between the ages of 8 and 17 in two separate studies (Soreni et al., 2018; Storch, Muroff, et al., 2011). These studies showed that the CSI had strong internal consistency and 1-week test–retest reliability. It also had good convergent validity with the hoarding questions on the C-YBOCS and good discriminant validity with nonhoarding obsessive compulsive symptoms on the OCI-CV. The 15-item version also had good validity and reliability in children with OCD (Soreni et al., 2018). Unfortunately, however, neither version of the CSI has been tested in children without OCD.

HOARDING SYMPTOMS IN OTHER DISORDERS OF CHILDHOOD

While the prevalence of hoarding disorder alone is probably fairly rare in children, the prevalence of hoarding symptoms in children with some other neuropsychiatric disorders is clearly elevated. These include autism spectrum disorders, genetic disorders such as Prader-Willi and Williams syndromes, attention deficit hyperactivity disorder, and of course, obsessive compulsive disorder (Morris et al., 2016).

AUTISM SPECTRUM DISORDERS

Children with autism spectrum disorders (ASD) are known to have high rates of comorbid psychiatric conditions, including OCD, anxiety disorders, and ADHD (Lai, Lombardo, & Baron-Cohen, 2014). Recent studies indicate that they also have a much higher than expected rate of hoarding. Approximately half of children with ASD will have collecting or storing behaviors that exceed what is expected based on their developmental age (Greaves, Prince, Evans, & Charman, 2006). Between one quarter and one third of children with ASD have clinically significant moderate to severe hoarding symptoms, with high rates of clutter, difficulty discarding items, and excessive acquisition. Approximately 7% will have severe or extreme, clearly functionally impairing hoarding behaviors (La Buissonniere-Ariza et al., 2018).

Interestingly, the strongest predictors of hoarding behaviors in ASD are not the restricted repetitive behaviors that are among the core features of an ASD diagnosis. Instead, ADHD symptoms, anxiety symptoms, and ASD-associated problems with social interactions are linked to increased rate and severity of hoarding behaviors. Multiple studies have shown that girls with ASD are more likely to have problematic hoarding than are boys (Burton et al., 2016; La Buissonniere-Ariza et al., 2018; Scahill et al., 2014; Storch et al., 2016).

NEURODEVELOPMENTAL GENETIC DISORDERS

Hoarding behaviors are also common in children and adolescents with neurodevelopmental genetic disorders, particularly those associated with intellectual disability. Nearly 40% of children with Prader-Willi syndrome (PWS) have hoarding behaviors, according to one longitudinal study; another study found that approximately 80% of children with Prader-Willi collect or store objects (potentially including food hoarding, which has long been known to be a feature of PWS) (E. Dykens & Shah, 2003; E. M. Dykens, Leckman, & Cassidy, 1996; Greaves et al., 2006). Individuals with Williams syndrome and Down syndrome also exhibit hoarding behaviors, although at somewhat lower rates than those with PWS (Royston et al., 2018). Rates of hoarding symptoms in other neurodevelopmental disorders have not been formally evaluated. Given the high levels of hoarding behaviors seen in the few that have been studied, children with any form of genetically determined neurodevelopmental disorder, particularly if intellectual disability is a part of the picture, should be assessed for problematic hoarding.

OBSESSIVE COMPULSIVE DISORDER

Hoarding symptoms in children have been the most studied in the context of pediatric OCD. Although a few studies report comorbidity rates as high as 50%, most suggest that between 20%–25% of children with OCD will also have hoarding symptoms (Mataix-Cols, Nakatani, Micali, & Heyman, 2008; J. Samuels et al., 2014; Storch et al., 2007). As with ASD, hoarding symptoms are more common in girls with OCD than in boys (J. Samuels et al., 2014).

Hoarding tends to begin early in this group (between 7–8 years of age), and earlier age of OCD symptom onset is itself a risk factor for the development of hoarding behaviors. Children with OCD plus hoarding have an average age of OCD onset symptoms around 6.6 years, while those who have OCD but no hoarding symptoms have an average age of onset of OCD a year or more later (around age 9 or so) (J. Samuels et al., 2014). Poor insight, indecisiveness, difficulty starting or completing tasks, pervasive slowness, and magical thinking are all risk factors for the development of hoarding among children with OCD (Mataix-Cols et al., 2008; J. Samuels et al., 2014; Storch et al., 2007).

Children with OCD who also have hoarding symptoms respond to standard treatments for OCD, including cognitive behavioral therapy (Morris et al., 2016; Storch, Rahman, et al., 2011). However, these children also tend to have higher rates of psychiatric comorbidities than those without hoarding symptoms, particularly anxiety disorders, and possibly also ADHD (Burton et al., 2016; Frank et al., 2014; J. M. Park et al., 2016; J. Samuels et al., 2014). They may also have a longer duration of illness and possibly poorer treatment outcomes, particularly if the hoarding symptoms go unrecognized or are not actively addressed (Mataix-Cols et al., 2008; Morris et al., 2016). Thus, assessing (and regularly reassessing) for hoarding symptoms in children with OCD is an important component of care.

ATTENTION DEFICIT HYPERACTIVITY DISORDER

Studies in both adults and children have reported increased rates of co-occurring hoarding disorder and ADHD (Fullana et al., 2013; Hartl et al., 2005; Sheppard et al., 2010). Of the three types of ADHD symptoms (inattention, hyperactivity, and impulsivity) (American Psychiatric Association, 2013), inattention has been most consistently identified as being associated with HD, although some studies suggest that all three symptom types may be elevated (Frost, Steketee, & Tolin, 2011; Fullana et al., 2013; Tolin & Villavicencio, 2011).

Clinical and population-based studies suggest that the direction of association between ADHD and hoarding goes both ways. That is, rates of ADHD are elevated in children with hoarding, *and* rates of hoarding are elevated among children with ADHD (Burton et al., 2016; Hacker et al., 2016). Up to 30% of children with ADHD who are referred for assessment or treatment will have clinically significant hoarding behaviors (Hacker et al., 2016).

Co-occurring ADHD is also seen in adults with HD, although rates vary widely among studies, ranging from as low as 2.5% to as high as 28% (Archer, 2019; R. O. Frost et al., 2011; Fullana et al., 2013; Grisham, Brown, Savage, Steketee, & Barlow, 2007; Hartl et al., 2005). These variations in reported rates are most likely due to differences in the types of sample and study methods used between the studies. A population-based study of nearly 3,000 adults conducted in 2013 provides the most reliable estimate, due to its large sample size and rigorous methods. The results of this study indicate that adults with hoarding disorder have a threefold higher likelihood of having had ADHD when they were children, particularly the inattentive subtype of ADHD (9%), compared to their age-matched peers (3%) (Fullana et al., 2013). To put these numbers in context, the current data suggest that although ADHD rates are higher among people with problematic hoarding than among those without hoarding, the overall risk of ADHD is fairly low. In general, adults with HD are at higher risk for depression and anxiety disorders, which both occur in over 25% of people with hoarding, than they are for ADHD.

Despite the variability in reported rates of co-occurring ADHD and HD, studies have consistently demonstrated that inattentive symptoms are highly correlated with hoarding disorder. In particular, inattentive symptoms are associated with difficulty discarding (which is the core feature of hoarding disorder) as well as with overall hoarding symptom severity. Individuals who exhibit hyperactive and impulsive symptoms, in contrast, are more likely to have problematic acquiring or to experience distress due to their hoarding (Burton et al., 2016; Frost et al., 2011; Fullana et al., 2013; Hacker et al., 2016; Sheppard et al., 2010; D. F. Tolin & Villavicencio, 2011).

Children who have hoarding and ADHD also have more oppositional symptoms than do children who have ADHD but no hoarding, at least according to the only study to examine oppositionality among children who hoard (Hacker et al., 2016). Although intriguing, this result has not yet been replicated, and if true, the cause of this relationship is not known. One possibility that has been put forward is that presence of inattention plus hyperactivity plus impulsivity (e.g., combined type ADHD) may contribute to an increased risk of developing hoarding behaviors, which then contribute to higher rates of disruptive behaviors (Hacker et al., 2016). As the combined type of ADHD is itself associated with high rates of oppositional behaviors (American Psychiatric

Association, 2013), it is not yet entirely clear if this observed association is in fact driven by or mediated through hoarding behaviors.

The complex relationship between OCD, ADHD, and hoarding is not yet well understood. Some studies indicate that as many as 40% of individuals with both OCD and hoarding will have had ADHD as children (Burton et al., 2016; Sheppard et al., 2010; Torres et al., 2016). Others indicate that OCD symptoms do not contribute to the high rates of ADHD symptoms that are seen among individuals with hoarding (D. F. Tolin & Villavicencio, 2011; R.O. Frost et al., 2011). However, both OCD and ADHD are much more common in children and adolescents than hoarding symptoms are, and are more likely to be problematic. Unless there is a high suspicion for hoarding, assessment and treatment planning for children should focus on the primary presenting problems.

HOARDING IN THE CONTEXT OF ABUSE, NEGLECT, OR TRAUMA

Individuals with hoarding disorder sometimes anecdotally report that their hoarding behaviors began after a trauma or significant adverse life event (Grisham et al., 2006). Small studies have examined the rates of adverse life events using retrospective recall, where participants with HD are asked to think back over the course of their lives and try to remember whether they experienced specific types of events, and if so, when they occurred. The results of these studies have been mixed, with some showing an increase in reported rates of adversity or trauma (Chou, Mackin, et al., 2018; Cromer, 2007; Grisham et al., 2006; Hartl et al., 2005) and others showing no relationship between trauma and hoarding (Ayers et al., 2009).

Part of the problem is that the observed relationship between childhood adversity and hoarding disorder in adulthood is based entirely on retrospective recall (in other words, memory). To date, there are no longitudinal studies prospectively following those children who may be at risk for hoarding into adulthood, most importantly in their 40s and

50s, when hoarding most often develops. Instead, adults with hoarding disorder are interviewed and asked about their past histories, including, or sometimes with a particular focus on, childhood traumas. In some cases, they are asked specifically to recall triggering or anchoring events that may have occurred when their hoarding symptoms were thought to begin, or when they worsened.

Although these methods are the best that are currently available, they also are likely to lead to biased outcomes. It is human nature, when asked to think about when a particular problem started, to also try to identify potential causes of that problem. This tendency is especially pronounced when the actual causes of the problem or disorder are unknown. Thus, when people are asked to think about trauma and childhood adversity in the context of a study about hoarding, people with hoarding may think harder about the question, or may place more relevance on a particular event than someone else with a similar life history but who does not have hoarding behaviors would. This difference between how people think about their pasts is known as recall bias, and in this example, would result in a false positive association between trauma and hoarding disorder. The only way to definitively determine the relationships between hoarding and life events is to prospectively follow people from childhood through adulthood, assessing them on a regular recurring basis.

There is one type of hoarding behavior that has been consistently associated with childhood adversity, however, and that is food hoarding. Children who have been maltreated, neglected or abused, or who have suffered severe deprivation, either material or emotional, have been repeatedly observed to hoard food (Perry, 2013). Commonly hoarded food items include the usual foods that appeal to kids, that is, cereals, cookies, candies, fruit, and single serve wrapped items such as cheese sticks and crackers. Other food-related hoarding behaviors seen in neglected or abused children include consistently saving and hiding a portion of a meal in case of later need. These behaviors can persist for years after the child has been removed from the abusive or neglectful situation and placed in a nurturing environment with plenty of free access to food (Casey, 2012). Thus, persistent food hoarding can act as a warning sign to alert clinicians and other professionals to the possible presence of neglect or abuse in an at-risk child.

HOW STABLE IS HOARDING IN CHILDHOOD?

Only one prospective study has been conducted examining the longitudinal course of hoarding behaviors in childhood or adolescence (V. Z. Ivanov, Mataix-Cols, D., Serlachius, E., Brander, G. Elmquist, A., Enander, J., Rück, C., 2019). In this study, Swedish teenagers who screened positive for hoarding symptoms during an epidemiological survey of adolescent twins at age 15 were reassessed several years later. Of the 79 children who originally screened positive for hoarding, 42 agreed to participate in formal clinical interviews an average of 3 years later, along with 33 of their 67 co-twins and 49 screen negative controls.

This study found a number of interesting things, many of them unexpected, about the trajectory of hoarding in adolescence. First, fewer than half of the teenagers who met cutoff criteria for significant hoarding symptoms at age 15 continued to have problems with hoarding several years later. Only 20 of the 42 who were interviewed later endorsed difficulties with discarding items, and only 17 endorsed feeling a need to save items and distress associated with discarding them.

Second, none of the children met criterion C of the *DSM-5* diagnostic criteria for hoarding disorder, that is, the presence of excessive clutter that compromises the use of living or other spaces. The authors of this study went so far as to physically travel to the homes of the participants in this study to assess their rooms and the level of clutter in them. They found more clutter on average in the bedrooms of adolescents who reported difficulty discarding than in those who did not, but these levels were moderate at most, and were not deemed to be impairing.

Third, approximately 13% of children who screened negative for hoarding at age 15 endorsed difficulty and distress associated with discarding their belongings at reassessment several years later. These results, in addition to the finding that over half of the children who screened positive for hoarding at age 15 no longer met criteria for hoarding at the second assessment, indicate that hoarding behaviors are not stable across childhood, as they are in adulthood, but rather may be episodic in nature. This is consistent with what other clinicians and researchers, including those who treat hoarding in childhood, have suggested (Storch, Rahman, et al., 2011).

These results also indicate that the instrument originally used to screen for clinically significant hoarding symptoms in this study, the HRS-SR, although useful in adults, may not be reliable for the identification of hoarding disorder in children and adolescence, or for predicting which children will go on to develop hoarding disorder. Instead, the HRS-SR, and indeed, all of the clinical instruments that have thus far been used to assess hoarding behaviors in children, may actually be documenting developmentally normal hoarding-like behaviors rather than identifying abnormal childhood behaviors that are precursors to later psychopathology.

THE ROLE OF PARENTAL ACCOMMODATION

Parental accommodation is a term that is frequently used by clinicians to describe a pattern of overprotective behaviors that are intended to shield a child from distress. As most parents would argue, protecting a child from distressing or frightening situations is normal under many, even most, circumstances. However, there are times when such protection backfires and unintended negative consequences result. For example, when a child has a fear or behavior that may become impairing (e.g., a phobia of dogs or the dentist or vaccines) it is appropriate for the parent to help the child to face down their fear, rather than accommodating it.

Parental accommodation is known to play a role in the maintenance and in some cases, the worsening, of symptoms of obsessive compulsive disorder, other anxiety disorders, and disruptive behavior disorders (Thompson-Hollands, Kerns, Pincus, & Comer, 2014). It has been theorized that parental accommodation may also play a role in the maintenance of hoarding behaviors in children and adolescents. Paradoxically, the opposite has also been theorized, that is, that as many parents play an active role in limiting the amount of clutter that is present in a child's bedroom, they may also minimize the negative effects of potential hoarding symptoms (Frank et al., 2014; Storch, Rahman, et al., 2011).

However, the most recent data available suggest that neither of these scenarios is actually the case. As expected, the parents of twins who had high levels of hoarding behaviors in the longitudinal study conducted in Sweden by Ivanov and colleagues did report elevated levels of accommodation by parents of their children's hoarding symptoms. However, the level of accommodation was actually quite low overall, and there was no elevation in reported family burden due to hoarding symptoms. Perhaps more tellingly, the adolescents themselves did not report that their parents actively prevented the accumulation of clutter in their rooms. Instead, they appeared to have as much control over their own rooms and belongings as did their nonhoarding co-twins and control participants (V. Z. Ivanov, Mataix-Cols, D., Serlachius, E., Brander, G. Elmquist, A., Enander, J., Rück, C., 2019). These findings reinforce the idea that, throughout childhood and early adolescence, some degree of keeping behaviors and clutter are developmentally normal. Unless hoarding behaviors are extreme, the items collected are very unusual, or there are other reasons to suspect psychiatric illness, clinicians and parents can be reassured that the presence of these behaviors do not necessarily predict future problems.

WHAT SYMPTOMS MIGHT PREDICT MORE WORRISOME HOARDING BEHAVIORS IN CHILDHOOD?

A great deal is still unknown about the prevalence, meaning, and predictive value of hoarding behaviors in children and adolescents. Similarly, despite consistent retrospective studies indicating that symptoms of hoarding disorder begin in childhood, it appears to be likely that true clinically impairing hoarding disorder as defined by the *DSM-5* is actually rare in childhood. Nevertheless, it is clear that at least a small proportion of children will develop clinically significant problematic hoarding behaviors. For this reason, it is still useful to identify potential risk factors or clinical correlates of hoarding in childhood.

As discussed in this chapter, the presence of other psychiatric disorders of childhood, particularly autism, ADHD, and OCD, increases the risk of problematic hoarding. Unfortunately, while the risk for hoarding among children with these disorders is clearly increased, the relative increase in risk is still unknown. If pathological hoarding is suspected, the presence of other pertinent signs and symptoms may help to raise (or lower) the index of suspicion. These include not only the level of distress evinced by the child when seemingly useless items are discarded, but also the types and variety of items that are kept and the reasons given for keeping.

Children with problematic hoarding symptoms tend to have difficulty discarding a larger variety of items than do children who do not have such symptoms. In addition to the typical schoolbooks, letters, and tickets that most children resist disposing of, those with problematic hoarding also tend to have difficulty giving up things typical children will not. These include old or expired food items, used food wrappers, cardboard boxes, old receipts, plastic bags, fabric or string or thread, and even old makeup. Similarly, children with problematic hoarding differ in their explanation of why they save.

Like their nonhoarding peers, the two most common reasons children with pathological hoarding behaviors give for saving are (a) the item has sentimental value and (b) the item may be useful or needed in the future. However, children who have problematic hoarding are twice as likely to report feeling that a particular item may be needed or useful in the future, and somewhat less likely to report that they want to keep it for sentimental reasons when compared with children who do not hoard. Perhaps more importantly, children who hoard tend to give both answers, rather than one or the other, as their reasons for their need to save.

SUMMARY

While an emerging field of research, very little is known about hoarding behaviors in children. Encouragingly for parents and health care providers, the preponderance of the data collected to date suggests that the majority of hoarding behaviors in children are developmentally normal in nature. They also appear to be episodic, for many, if not most. However, children who routinely show extreme levels of distress when items with little clear sentimental value are discarded or who have persistent food hoarding are among those who may benefit from additional evaluation.

Chapter 6

Animal Hoarding

Most mental health professionals consider animal hoarding to be a special manifestation of hoarding disorder, and a majority of people who hoard animals also hoard objects. Due to the nature of their illness, which typically includes insight so poor as to be delusional, individuals who exhibit signs and symptoms of animal hoarding rarely come to the attention of mental health professionals. Instead, animal hoarding may only come to light because a neighbor, veterinarian, or other concerned individual has contacted the authorities reporting potential animal cruelty.

DEFINITION OF ANIMAL HOARDING

Animal hoarding first appeared in the public health literature in the early 1980s, and was subsequently described in the veterinary, legal, medical, and psychological literature later that decade. Animal hoarding has variously been called zoophilia, multiple-animal ownership, and animal collecting—the term *animal hoarding* came into use in 1999, coined by the Hoarding of Animals Research Consortium (HARC). HARC is a group of researchers, who, between 1998 and 2007, worked to define and better understand the phenomenon of animal hoarding. HARC consists of veterinarians, social workers, and psychologists, led by Gary Patronek, a veterinary epidemiologist.

As a group, the HARC researchers have guided the conceptualization of animal hoarding as a psychiatric illness and, in order to better understand its etiology and clinical presentation, have compared it to both object hoarding and to other forms of animal neglect and cruelty. Although reference is made to animal hoarding in the *DSM-5*, the diagnostic criteria for animal hoarding as laid out by HARC are the most widely used for the identification and quantification of this disorder, particularly by law enforcement officers, animal protection agencies, and veterinarians.

The four criteria for animal hoarding as defined by HARC include

- having more than the typical number of companion animals,
- failing to provide even the minimal standards of care, including nutrition, sanitation, shelter, and veterinary care, with neglect often resulting in illness or in death of the animals from starvation, infection, or untreated medical conditions or injuries,
- denial of the inability to provide adequate care for the animals, and the impact of this inability on the animals, household, and human occupants,
- persistence in accumulating and controlling animals, despite the failure to maintain adequate standards of care for them (Petronek, 1999).

In contrast, the American Psychiatric Association (APA) does not include animal hoarding as a separate diagnosis, but instead conceptualizes it as a special manifestation of hoarding disorder. The *DSM-5* definition incorporates many aspects of the HARC criteria, and characterizes animal hoarding as the presence of a large number of animals, accompanied by the failure to provide the minimal standards of nutrition, sanitation, and veterinary care, plus the failure to act on the resulting deteriorating conditions of the animals and their surrounding environment. The *DSM-5* also identifies two characteristics that differentiate more typical (object) HD from animal hoarding. These include much poorer insight (reaching delusional levels in many cases), and an increased presence of unsanitary (as opposed to unsafe and/or merely cluttered) conditions that occur as a result of keeping large volumes of animals. However, no mention is made of ongoing (persistent) accumulation of animals, which is a core feature of the HARC diagnosis.

DIFFERENTIATING ANIMAL HOARDING FROM ANIMAL CRUELTY AND OTHER FORMS OF NEGLECT

Animal hoarding, by definition, leads to neglect, illness, and often the premature death of the animals involved, and thus, is considered a form of animal cruelty by many law enforcement and animal welfare agencies. Animal cruelty is defined by the *National Incident Based Reporting System* (NIBRS), the Department of Justice's user manual for crime definition and reporting, as "intentionally, knowingly, or recklessly taking an action that mistreats or kills any animal without just cause, such as torturing, tormenting, mutilation, maiming, poisoning, or abandonment" (p. 1).

On the surface, the NIBRS definition appears to exclude animal hoarding, as it specifies knowledge or intent to cause harm as a component of animal cruelty. However, included in the definition are gross neglect, which include failure of "duty to provide care, e.g., food, shelter, water, care if sick or injured," in other words, neglect (p. 1). Agencies are instructed to identify the type of activity (simple/gross neglect, organized abuse, intentional abuse, torture, or animal sexual abuse) when reporting animal cruelty cases.

Under both the HARC and *DSM-5* definitions, individuals who hoard animals do not knowingly or willingly cause harm to animals in their keeping, and do not meet strict criteria for animal cruelty for this reason. Instead, they do not appear to recognize or comprehend the damage that they are causing by their inability to maintain the animals in a safe and healthy environment.

Similarly, individuals who hoard animals do not meet the strict definition of recklessness, in that, rather than acting without caring about the consequences of their actions, they universally express love and concern for the animals and often believe that they are actually providing adequate care for their animals, despite clear evidence of neglect. Instead, these individuals exhibit poor insight about their ability to provide appropriate care, often to the point of being delusional. Nevertheless, individuals who hoard animals can be prosecuted for animal cruelty under the current regulations, and often are, especially if their cases are brought to the attention of agencies or law enforcement officers who are unfamiliar with the concept of hoarding as a psychiatric or psychological problem.

Although a serious problem when it does occur, animal hoarding is rare, and most cases of animal abuse or neglect are not due to hoarding. Many instances of neglect occur because the animal owner person is overwhelmed or compromised in some way, due to health problems, financial stressors, or emotional or social difficulties. Similarly, animal abuse does exist, and differs from animal hoarding in important ways. Distinguishing between people who suffer from animal hoarding, those who do not hoard but instead are unable to effectively care for their animals (compromised or overwhelmed caregivers), and those who are actually abusing or exploiting animals can be complicated, but is critical for public health officials and mental health providers who encounter or suspect cases of animal neglect. Differences between these groups are detailed in Table 6.1.

EPIDEMIOLOGY OF ANIMAL HOARDING

Although the exact prevalence is unknown, animal hoarding appears to be much less common than object hoarding. There are approximately 2,000 to 3,000 new reported cases of animal hoarding per year in the

TABLE 6.1: DISTINCTIONS BETWEEN ANIMAL HOARDING, OVERWHELMED CAREGIVING, AND ANIMAL EXPLOITATION

	Animal hoarding	Compromised or overwhelmed animal caregiver	Animal exploitation
Awareness of animal care problems	Unaware	Aware, but minimizes	Aware
Shows concern for animals	Yes	Yes	No
Willing to cooperate with authorities	No	Yes	No
Motivation for keeping animals	Need to "rescue" or otherwise care for animals	Strong attachment to/ love for animals	Control, monetary gain
Risk of recidivism once intervention is initiated	Nearly 100%	Low	Variable, depending on perceived benefit/ risk
Other characteristics	Very poor insight, often delusional in belief that they are helping rather than neglecting animals under their care	Gradual deterioration in ability to care for animals due to economic, medical, social, or domestic circumstances	Lack of empathy for the animals under their control, often display characteristics of psychopathy, lack of remorse or guilt

United States, which represents less than 0.001% of the U.S. population. However, there is general agreement that animal hoarding cases are consistently under-reported and thus underestimated. The public health department in Massachusetts, which conducted a survey of reported cases of hoarding in that state in the late 1990s, reported that approximately one third of reported object hoarding cases also involved animal hoarding.

Although it is not clear whether those numbers are generalizable, they can be used to provide a rough estimate of the likely prevalence of animal hoarding in the United States. Thus, assuming that Massachusetts data are similar to what would be found throughout the U.S. (that is, one third of people with HD also hoard animals), and using the lower bound of the HD population prevalence estimates (2%), the estimated prevalence of animal hoarding in the United States would be approximately 0.6%. The majority of individuals who come to attention are women (73%–90%), although, as population-based studies have not yet been conducted, it is not known whether women are more likely to have problems with animal hoarding or whether they are simply more likely to come to attention.

ANIMAL HOARDING IN THE MEDIA

As with HD, animal hoarding first came to public attention through the media. Animal hoarding is less well understood as a phenomenon, and it is less common than hoarding disorder. However, the obvious manifestations of this illness, make for compelling reading in some media markets. This is especially for true animal hoarding cases that involve exotic animals such as tigers or other large predators or very large numbers of animals (usually in the hundreds), or when extreme squalor, severe neglect, or multiple animal deaths are involved.

Mary Chantrell

One of the earliest known cases of animal hoarding, and one of the first to be reported in the media, was a woman named Mary Chantrell, who lived in England in the 1800s. As initially reported by the Luton *Illustrated Police News* in 1855, and subsequently recounted in multiple additional newspapers, Mrs. Chantrell and her husband were recipients of multiple complaints and legal actions over the course of 40 years as a result of their animal hoarding, which are depicted in Figure 6.1a and 6.1b. Over this time, the Chantrells, but particularly Mary, were repeatedly convicted of "keeping cats in a state of starvation," collecting large numbers of cats and dogs, and neglecting them, including "150 [live] cats, and about 50 dead ones, some dried up, some putrefying, and several dead dogs in the same state."

Mrs. Chantrell was an artist who met her future husband, Robert Chantrell, a wealthy architect who was 40 years older than she, at the London Society for the Arts in 1846, where, at age 14, she was receiving an award for her artwork. Over the years, Robert and Mary developed a close relationship, with Robert—who was married and had a family—first taking on the role of guardian, and later the role of lover to young Mary. Robert's first wife died in 1863, and he married Mary in 1867.

Throughout her life, Mrs. Chantrell had an interest in sketching animals, particularly cats, and she was known for keeping a large number of cats at her home, purportedly as models for her drawings. The first report of problems came in 1855, when Robert Chantrell was called before the courts for having between 100 and 200 cats, many of which were dead. In response to the charges, he claimed that the animals were models for Mary's artwork, and Mary was fined £5 for starving the animals. Over the following two decades, Mary and Robert were in and out of the courts many times for charges related to cruelty to animals.

Although Mary saw herself as an animal rescuer, stating that she had established an asylum for cats when she saw some lying dead on the beach, she was clearly unable to care for them (or, as later became apparent, for herself) appropriately. Both Mary and her husband (until his death in 1872) lived in a progressive state of squalor, in part created by the excrement and bodies of the animals that she acquired.

Mary had multiple arrests for animal neglect during the course of her life—most notably in 1874 when Robert Chantrell's son from his first marriage challenged her assignment as probate over his father's estate, when during the testimony, a witness estimated that they had seen over a thousand dead cats removed from the property. In 1875, Mary obstructed an attempted search of her home to locate and remove neglected cats, threatening the searching officials with violence. She became homeless sometime after this, and in 1898, was found sleeping in a doorway in London, where she was arrested for vagrancy. When brought into court, Mary brought along a portfolio of her drawings as well as two cats that she had hidden under her coat. In this interaction, Mrs. Chantrell was described by the *South Wales Echo* as "an elderly woman of refinement and education" (p. 3); nevertheless, she was admitted twice over the subsequent year to a London asylum under similar circumstances, where she subsequently died in 1899.

IMPACT OF ANIMAL HOARDING

As demonstrated by the story of Mary Chantrell, animal hoarding has serious negative consequences for both the animals and the people involved. As previously noted, the animals involved in these cases are subject to extreme neglect, and suffer from crowding, unsanitary conditions, starvation, illness, injury, and death. The extent and the nature of the neglect that is seen in animal hoarding cases almost inevitably leads to euthanasia for the more seriously ill and dying animals. This is also the case where large numbers of animals are living with chronic or deteriorating health conditions, for those who cannot be effectively sheltered, or who are not adoptable.

Humans who hoard animals also suffer in substantial and concrete ways from their hoarding. First, there are potential legal consequences for those who come to the attention of law enforcement agencies or animal humane societies for animal hoarding. Second, the unsanitary living conditions, and accumulation of urine, feces, and other sequelae of large numbers of animals living in a closed environment typically leads to extreme squalor and dangerous, unsanitary living conditions. The health risks associated with such poor living conditions are substantial, and include flea and tick infestations; infections due to exposure to both animal waste and to the animals themselves (e.g., toxoplasmosis from cat feces, psittacosis from bird droppings); lung problems due to aerosolized pollutants and ammonia from urine; and injuries from falls due to rotting floorboards, spilled water or food, or pervasive animal waste. Approximately 60% of people who suffer from animal hoarding have floors that are covered with animal feces and urine, and a similar percent of animal-hoarding homes contain multiple dead animals. As is also seen with more typical object hoarding, unsafe homes due to animal hoarding can also have consequences for family members and others in the household. According to HARC, an estimated 10%–15% of animal hoarding cases also involve the presence of vulnerable and dependent adults or children. These individuals are at significant risk

Figures 6.1a and 6.1b: Drawings of Mrs. Chantrell's Home and Her Many Cats, Including Those Found Deceased *Source: From the* Illustrated Police News, *June 1, 1867 (right) and August 1, 1872 (below).*

of illness and even death from the hoarding-related health problems described above.

Since the Chantrell's time there have been many media reports of animal hoarding. Most, but not all, involved domestic animals, primarily cats and dogs, but also birds, exotic animals, and occasionally horses or farm animals. These reports are typically sensationalized, usually reporting on extreme cases, and are often presented as cases of animal cruelty or other criminal acts. However, as exemplified by Mrs. Chantrell, individuals suffering from animal hoarding do not see themselves as being cruel to animals; on the contrary, they see themselves as animal lovers, and, ironically, often as rescuers of animals that would otherwise be neglected or harmed. While little is still known about the causes of this complex and serious ailment, it should be treated as a mental health condition or psychiatric illness rather than as criminal behavior. Because of the clear lack of insight displayed by many, if not all, individuals who hoard animals, harm reduction approaches, which aim to minimize the negative impact of the problematic behaviors, should be considered when developing treatment plans or other interventions. Harm reduction is discussed in Chapter 11.

Chapter 7

Neurobiology of Hoarding Disorder

While it may be tempting to try to explain the occurrence of hoarding as the result of abandonment, loss, personality traits, human weakness, or abnormal attachment to objects, what we know of the origins of hoarding disorder is quite different. Like other neuropsychiatric illnesses, HD is heterogeneous in nature, and multiple factors contribute to its development. For most individuals, the specific causes of hoarding disorder are unknown. What we do know is that both biology and environment play important roles, and that multiple factors contribute to its development. In particular, as is true for other psychiatric illnesses, the susceptibility to developing hoarding disorder appears to have a strong genetic component.

GENETICS

Almost all human characteristics have an underlying genetic basis. This includes the traits that we commonly think of as being genetic in origin, such as height and eye color, as well as vulnerability to disease. Most people know that the risk for developing diseases or conditions such as diabetes, high blood pressure, and cancer can be inherited. This is also true for psychiatric disorders.

The majority of neuropsychiatric disorders, including HD, are biologically based. More specifically, an individual's risk for developing a particular psychiatric disorder, or their susceptibility to that disorder, is strongly influenced by their genetic makeup. However, this does not mean that a person's genetics will determine their fate, or that, if they have a strong family history of hoarding disorder, that they will inevitably develop HD themselves. The disorder itself is not inherited—only the risk for developing that disorder. It is critical to remember that risk factors can be modified.

HOW CAN YOU TELL IF A DISORDER LIKE HD IS GENETIC IN NATURE?

The most common way to determine whether a particular characteristic, trait, or disorder is genetic is to examine the pattern of expression of that trait in families. If a disease or trait has a genetic cause, or is inherited, it will occur more frequently in family members of affected individuals than it does in the general population. For example, if a disorder occurs in 2% of the population, and 20% of the family members of people with that disorder also have it, the risk to family members is 10 times higher than the general population risk. Thus, it is likely that the disorder in question is inherited.

Another way to determine whether a trait is genetic is to determine the heritability of the trait. Heritability can be thought of as the proportion of a trait that is due to genetic factors rather than to environmental or other factors. The degree of heritability, which ranges from 0 to 1 or from 0% to 100%, can be determined by comparing the rates of that trait in twins. Identical twins share 100% of their genetic material in common, while non-identical twins only share 50% of their genetic material in common, on average. If a trait is 100% heritable, or 100% genetic in origin, if one twin has that trait, then 100% of the time their identical twin will also have that trait, and 50% of the time their non-identical (or fraternal) twin will also have that trait.

Although essentially all of the psychiatric disorders are genetic in origin, none of them are 100% genetically determined. That is, genetics contribute to the risk of developing a psychiatric problem, but other influences, such as environmental factors, can either increase or decrease the risk that a person will actually develop that problem. It is also important to know that in the majority of people, hundreds of genes acting in concert with one another are responsible for increasing the risk of psychiatric illness. There is no single gene or genetic mutation that is responsible for all cases of any known psychiatric disorder. In a small number of families, one specific genetic mutation may be found to be responsible for causing a given illness in all of the affected members, but this is rare and is the exception rather than the rule.

GENETIC UNDERPINNINGS OF HOARDING

Because hoarding disorder affects fewer than 5% of the general population and is a relatively newly recognized diagnosis, genetic studies of HD are still in the early stages. There are only a few studies examining the heritability and patterns of inheritance of hoarding, and almost all of them have examined hoarding symptoms rather than the more strictly defined hoarding disorder. Nevertheless, the studies that do exist provide strong evidence that hoarding is in fact inherited.

HOARDING RUNS IN FAMILIES

Family or pedigree studies show that if one person has hoarding disorder, the odds are high that other people in the family will also experience problems with hoarding. First-degree relatives, that is, parents, siblings, and children of individuals who hoard have between a 20%–60% higher risk of developing hoarding themselves than they would if no one in their family had hoarding disorder. The heritability of hoarding as estimated by this type of study is between 35% and 71% (M. E.

Hirschtritt, Mathews, C.A., 2014). These rates appear to be higher in families where OCD is also a problem than in families where hoarding only is seen.

HERITABILITY OF HOARDING

The few twin studies that exist have refined the heritability estimates derived from the family studies, and taken together, suggest that the heritability of hoarding is around 50% (Iervolino et al., 2009; Iervolino, Rijsdijk, Cherkas, Fullana, & Mataix-Cols, 2011; Mathews, Delucchi, Cath, Willemsen, & Boomsma, 2014; Monzani, Rijsdijk, Harris, & Mataix-Cols, 2014). Twin studies also indicate that hoarding shares genetic factors with both OCD and with disorders that are related to OCD, including body dysmorphic disorder, and to a lesser extent, excoriation disorder (skin-picking disorder) and trichotillomania (hair-pulling disorder) (Monzani et al., 2014).

Although genetic studies clearly indicate that hoarding is in part determined by genetic factors, they also show that genetics are not fate. As is the case for other psychiatric illnesses, a person's genetic makeup merely determines whether they have higher or lower susceptibility to hoarding disorder, it does not guarantee that the person will develop hoarding problems. Other factors, as yet unknown, but likely environmental in nature, clearly contribute, either to increase the risk or, just as importantly, to decrease it.

There is no one gene or genetic mutation responsible for the development of hoarding disorder. Instead, hundreds of genes, each exerting a very small effect, act in concert to increase the susceptibility to developing HD in a given person. Different individuals, even within the same family, may have more of these genetic mutations while others have fewer. The relative proportion of HD risk genes that a given individual carries is called the *genetic load*. Those with a high genetic load are more likely to develop hoarding problems, even in the absence of environmental risk factors. Conversely, those with a low genetic load are less likely to develop hoarding disorder, even in the presence of environmental or other risk factors. Those who have an intermediate genetic load for hoarding may develop symptoms only in the context of other risk factors, which could be either genetic or non-genetic in nature.

NEUROCOGNITION AND HOARDING DISORDER

It is commonly known that cognitive function (e.g., learning, memory, and attention) peaks in early adulthood and changes (usually, but not always, declining) as one ages (Salthouse, 2009). Even individuals who never develop dementia do show changes in memory, learning, attention, speed of information processing, and abstract reasoning as they get older. Although most normal age-related cognitive changes begin to be apparent in the later decades of life, some changes in some aspects of cognitive functioning begin as early as the 20s or 30s.

There is some evidence to suggest that individuals with hoarding disorder may suffer from more than the normal age-related cognitive changes. People with HD commonly complain of problems with memory, attention, decision making, and organization. Although cognitive functioning is functionally normal in most people with HD, neuropsychological studies do suggest that hoarding disorder is associated with subtle changes in attention, memory, decision making, sorting, and categorization (Grisham & Baldwin, 2015; Woody, Kellman-McFarlane, & Welsted, 2014). There is also evidence to suggest that in at least some proportion of people with HD, these changes are more significant than would be expected due to normal aging, and may rise to the level of cognitive impairment, potentially affecting their daily functioning (Ayers, Dozier, Wetherell, Twamley, & Schiehser, 2016; Mackin et al., 2016; D. F. Tolin, Villavicencio, Umbach, & Kurtz, 2011). The main cognitive domains, and the data with respect to the presence or absence of impairment in people with hoarding disorder, are discussed next. It is important to remember, however, that cognitive impairment does not necessarily indicate dementia or incipient dementia. Despite the fact that rates of dementia are higher among people who have problems with hoarding, particularly in those who developed hoarding only later in life, these rates are still very low. The majority of people with hoarding disorder, especially those younger than 80, do not suffer from dementia.

MEMORY

Individuals with hoarding disorder often report memory problems, and in fact, they will sometimes say that they keep otherwise unneeded items as memory aids. However, most people with hoarding disorder do *not* have significant memory problems. Approximately 15% to 25% of individuals with HD do have observable decrements in memory compared to what would be expected for their age when they are formally tested (Mackin et al., 2011; Mackin et al., 2016). However, even among these individuals, for the most part the observed deficits are actually mild, such that they can be observed on testing but are not clinically apparent. In other words, for most people, memory deficits may be observed on formal testing, but do not affect their daily functioning.

What people with hoarding *do* have, however, is low confidence in their memories (Hartl et al., 2004). What this means is that, even when there are no objective memory impairments, individuals who hoard do not trust that their memories are accurate or that they will be able to remember things accurately. People with hoarding disorder not only report lower confidence in their memories, they also tend to feel that the outcomes of forgetting something will be more catastrophic. Perhaps because of these fears, those who hoard report a stronger desire to keep their objects in sight, perhaps as a way to mitigate their fears of catastrophe if they do forget something.

DECISION MAKING

Difficulty with decision making is also reported quite frequently by people who suffer from hoarding disorder (R. O. Frost & Gross, 1993;

G. Steketee & Frost, 2003). Decision making is a complex function and is influenced by many factors. Emotional state, perceived and subjective value of the choices involved in the decision, and attentional state all affect someone's ability to make even simple decisions.

Unlike memory, where objective measurement is quite straightforward, there are many ways to assess someone's ability to make decisions. This variability of measurement and differences in the definition of what constitutes problems with decision making have complicated the assessment of this cognitive domain in hoarding.

There are many types of decision making, two of which are particularly relevant for HD—perceptual decision making, and value-based decision making (Summerfield & Tsetsos, 2012). Perceptual decision making involves using accumulated evidence from the senses (such as sight, sound, touch), to choose between two or more alternatives on the basis of observed characteristics. Deciding whether a truck is bigger than a car by looking at it from all angles, and perhaps measuring it, is an example of perceptual decision making. Value-based decision making, as the name implies, is much more subjective, and involves making a choice between one or more options or items based on the perceived value, worth, or potential benefit of each of the options (Summerfield & Tsetsos, 2012). Deciding between ice cream or a cookie for dessert is an example of value-based decision making—the choice depends on how much the individual likes each of the choices, the cost of each of them, perhaps what they had for dessert the day prior.

All of the studies that have explicitly examined decision making in hoarding have used measures of value-based decision making. None have directly examined perceptual decision making. Although the existing studies vary quite a bit in their methods and in what they set out to assess, some patterns are beginning to emerge.

First, as was the case for memory, people with hoarding disorder consistently *report* that they are indecisive, or that they have problems with decision making (R. O. Frost & Gross, 1993; R. O. Frost & Shows, 1993; Grisham, Norberg, Williams, Certoma, & Kadib, 2010; G. Steketee & Frost, 2003). It is perhaps self-evident that individuals who hoard report difficulties in deciding what to keep and what to discard. In addition, these people also subjectively report difficulties in everyday decision making, unrelated to discarding.

Second, people with hoarding disorder objectively do have more difficulty in deciding whether or not to discard a given item than do people without HD, *but only when the items belong to them.* Individuals with hoarding disorder do not differ from healthy control individuals in their ability to discard items that belong to someone else (D. F. Tolin et al., 2012).

Third, individuals with HD do not differ from other individuals on objective laboratory tests of decision making. Studies that use standard value-based decision-making tasks such as the Iowa Gambling Task or the Risk and Ambiguity Task indicate that people with hoarding disorder perform as well as people who do not have hoarding disorder (Mackin et al., 2016; Pushkarskaya et al., 2017).

Finally, and most importantly, newer studies confirm that, when the task is not related to discarding personal items, performance on decision-making tasks are the same for people who have hoarding and for those who do not. What appears to be different, however, is the type of decision-making *style* employed by individuals with hoarding disorder. This can be seen most effectively in studies that examine the outcomes of decision making under conditions of uncertainty or risk. For example, when people are offered the choice between a 100% chance of receiving a small reward, and a 50% chance of receiving a large reward, in a task involving multiple trials, most people will use adaptive strategies. That is, they will explore different strategies, and will eventually settle on an approach that is responsive to what has happened before, for example, taking fewer risks after they lose a trial and taking more risks after they win.

People with HD, in contrast, do not tend to alter their strategies after wins or losses. Rather than incorporating information from previous successes or failures to update their approach for the future, they employ a stable, typically risk-neutral, strategy for all trials in a given task, regardless of feedback or outcome (Aranovich, Cavagnaro, Pitt,

Myung, & Mathews, 2017; Pushkarskaya, Tolin, Henick, Levy, & Pittenger, 2018).

Although the reasons that people with hoarding tend to use risk-neutral, feedback-insensitive strategies for making decisions are unknown, it has been hypothesized that this approach may be a result of the difficulty in tolerating uncertainty that many people who hoard experience (Pushkarskaya et al., 2018). This lack of sensitivity to environmental changes such as a previous win or loss on a risk-taking game may also be due to cognitive inflexibility, which is discussed later in this chapter. Somewhat unexpectedly, the end result is that people with hoarding disorder tend to win (or lose) about the same amount as their nonhoarding peers do on gambling or other decision-making tasks. However, they take longer to achieve this result. That is, people with HD are ultimately as successful as their age-matched peers in their decision-making strategies, but these strategies are less efficient and require more trials, more time, and ultimately, more effort.

ATTENTION AND WORKING MEMORY

Attention can be defined as the ability to selectively process information; and working memory, which is a closely related function, is the ability to retain information for a short time span for immediate use. Both are critical components of cognitive functioning, and when impaired, can adversely impact learning, long-term memory, decision making, error recognition, and task completion.

Many people with HD report that they have difficulties with attention, and as discussed in Chapter 5, rates of the inattentive subtype of ADHD are approximately 3 times higher in people with hoarding disorder than in the general population, at least in some studies (Fullana et al., 2013). Even when a formal diagnosis of ADHD cannot be made because the other diagnostic criteria (such as age of onset before age 13 or impairment in multiple domains of functioning) are not present, people with hoarding disorder consistently score much higher on ADHD symptom questionnaires than do their age-matched peers, in particular, on the questions pertaining to inattention (Grisham et al., 2007; D. F. Tolin & Villavicencio, 2011).

Formal assessments of attention and working memory in hoarding disorder have had mixed results. There are no studies that consistently demonstrate impairment in measures of attention among people with HD compared to their age-matched peers. Some studies have suggested that individuals with HD may have longer reaction times (an indirect measure of inattention) when asked to perform a deliberately boring repetitive task that nevertheless requires focused attention (the continuous performance task), but others have not (Grisham et al., 2007; Mackin et al., 2011; Mackin et al., 2016; D. F. Tolin, Villavicencio, et al., 2011; J. J. Zakrzewski, Gillett, D.A., Vigil, O.R, et al., 2020). Studies using more complex tasks such as the digit span task, which requires remembering a series of numbers first forwards and then backwards, and requires both attention and working memory, have for the most part shown no differences between people with hoarding disorder and those without (Grisham et al., 2007; Mackin et al., 2016; Testa, Pantelis, & Fontenelle, 2011; J. J. Zakrzewski, Gillett, D.A., Vigil, O.R, et al., 2020). The most conservative interpretation of the available neuropsychological data is that although some people with HD may take longer to react or respond to a stimulus than others do, there is no clear evidence to suggest that attention itself is impaired in most people.

LEARNING

There is no indication that people with hoarding disorder have specific learning disorders or difficulties more commonly than do other people, at least from a clinical perspective. Similarly, people with HD have normal intelligence and intellectual functioning. For this reason, learning has not been extensively studied in a formal neuropsychological sense among people with hoarding disorder. To date, there are only a few studies that have assessed learning in HD. These studies, although still relatively small, confirm the clinical impressions that individuals with

HD generally do not have problems with learning (Mackin et al., 2011; Mackin et al., 2016).

CATEGORIZATION

Categorization, in neuropsychological terms, is the ability to sort items according to similar features or specific sets of rules. It is an important cognitive function because it determines how information is sorted and ordered, which subsequently has an effect on learning, memory, and organization.

Impaired categorization is often hypothesized as a key factor that underlies the behavioral manifestations of hoarding disorder. The underlying idea is that people with HD may have difficulty organizing information and finding commonalities between objects. As a result, they are likely to create more categories from a given number of objects than others might. This tendency to be under-inclusive, that is, to have more categories with fewer items in them, could then lead to difficulty in knowing what to discard because each category is seen as being equally as valuable as every other (Woody et al., 2014).

For example, it is much easier to discard a pair of shoes if a person has twenty pairs of shoes than if they have only one or two pairs, as the potential impact of the loss of any given pair is less in the former case than in the latter. Thus, if someone with hoarding disorder doesn't think of their shoes as fitting into a single overall group, but rather sees them as being in multiple separate categories (such as high heels, sneakers, and loafers), the relative value of each item appears to be greater, as each item is more unique. Taking this idea a step further, if there is only one item in each category (red high heels, blue high heels, red loafers, brown loafers, blue sneakers, red sneakers), it is difficult to discard anything, as every item represents a unique category, and its loss means the loss of an entire category of items.

Neuropsychological studies of categorization in HD fall into two types: Those that examine items of personal relevance to the partic-ipant, and those that use neutral objects that do not have an inherent use, such as differently shaped, sized, and colored blocks. In the first type of study, participants are asked to identify things or types of things (books, mail, clothing) of personal relevance to them, and are then given either the items themselves or cards with the names of those items. They are then asked to sort these items into groups or categories.

In the second type of study, participants are given neutral objects such as blocks, or cards with shapes or squares on them. They are asked to sort the items in as many different ways as they can (e.g., according to shape, color, size, number) or to identify, through trial and error, the underlying rule for sorting the objects, which is not stated directly but must be deduced.

Interestingly, people with hoarding disorder do not seem to sort their belongings into more categories than do healthy controls, although they do take longer to sort and they express feeling more anxiety related to the sorting (Grisham et al., 2010; Wincze, Steketee, & Frost, 2007). Similarly, on standard neuropsychological assessments of categorization using blocks or cards, people with HD do not show significant differences in their overall scores (number of correct sorts or number of correct categorization rules identified) compared to their age-matched peers when all responses across multiple trials are summed. People with HD do generally make more sorts or trials, though, and they also make more errors (or incorrect sorts). As with the studies using personal items, people with hoarding disorder also take longer to complete these types of sorting tasks than do healthy controls (Mackin et al., 2011; Mackin et al., 2016).

Perhaps of most relevance, the time taken on these sorting tasks actually increases with HD-specific treatment, and performance on the tasks improves (although performance does not improve by much). This is in contrast to performance on a similar neuropsychological task, the block design task. This task requires mental effort and information processing, but does not require categorization or sorting. Following HD-specific treatment, performance improves on the block design task, but time to completion does not significantly change (J. J. Zakrzewski, Gillett, D.A., Vigil, O.R, et al., 2020).

Taken together, the results of these studies suggest that differences in categorization and sorting may in fact be core components of hoarding disorder, although the manifestation of these differences may be in efficiency rather than in accuracy. In behavioral therapy for hoarding disorder, which is discussed in Chapter 9, participants are asked to actively sort their belongings and to choose which they are willing to discard in order to improve their ability to discard unneeded items. It is possible that repeatedly practicing sorting and discarding as is done in behavioral therapy causes individuals with HD to slow down and think more carefully about their belongings and their usefulness. An unexpected consequence of this type of deliberation may be that it generalizes to other types of decisions that require sorting or categorizing. That is, after treatment, people with HD may also take longer to complete (and also improve in) non-discarding tasks that require categorization, such as the neuropsychological sorting tasks.

VISUAL PROCESSING

There is some evidence to suggest that most, if not all of the abnormalities seen in HD are mediated through the visual system (Hough et al., 2016; Mackin et al., 2016). This is seen most clearly on two neuropsychological tasks that assess attention. The first is the digit span task, which requires listening to and then repeating a series of numbers out loud. Performance on this task, which is verbally mediated, is not usually impaired in hoarding. In contrast, performance on the continuous performance task, which requires pushing a button every time a particular image shows on a screen (and thus is visually mediated), more consistently identifies impairments in people with hoarding relative to healthy age-matched controls.

Neuroimaging studies using functional magnetic resonance imaging (fMRI) and studies of brain function using electroencephalography (EEG) provide support for the idea that visual processing is inefficient among individuals with hoarding disorder (Hough et al., 2016). It is important to note that *vision* is not affected—that is, people with hoarding disorder do not necessarily have worse (or better) eyesight than anyone else. Similarly, there is no evidence that their visual processing is inaccurate. Instead, the brains of people with hoarding disorder appear to process what they see *accurately but inefficiently*, requiring activation of more of the visual cortex, the visual processing center of the brain, than is needed for the same tasks in people without hoarding disorder. These findings are in line with the neuropsychological studies of decision-making and categorization, which also suggest that neurocognitive inefficiency, rather than cognitive impairment or disability, is at the heart of the perceived cognitive problems reported by so many people with hoarding disorder.

ERROR MONITORING

One of the most widely held hypotheses regarding the underlying causes of hoarding disorder is the idea that people with HD cannot tolerate uncertainty, and in particular, cannot tolerate the idea that they may make a mistake or an error. This fear of making an error, the theory goes, leads to the keeping rather than the discarding of items, in case the items may be needed again in the future. In other words, people with HD choose to keep things that they don't actually need to prevent making a potential mistake by discarding them.

There is a growing body of evidence to support the hypothesis that the brain's error processing system, and in particular, the brain's automatic reaction to errors (also called error monitoring), is indeed atypical in HD. Interestingly, people with HD do not actually commit more errors than their age-matched peers do on standard neuropsychological tasks. Instead, it is how the brain processes or reacts to those errors that differs between those with hoarding disorder and those without.

Error monitoring, which is sometimes also called performance monitoring, is a crucial cognitive function. As the name implies, error or performance monitoring provides important feedback to the brain when an error or mistake is made on a given task. The recognition of a mismatch between the actual response and the intended response (the error) by the brain then leads to increased attention, to an adjustment of the strategy, and, presumably, to improved performance in the future. Interestingly, the function of error monitoring is preconscious; that is, it is activated whenever an error is made, regardless of whether the person consciously recognizes that they have made a mistake or not.

The brain's error monitoring system can be studied using electroencephalography, or EEG. EEG is used to measure the electrical activity (or brainwave) generated by different regions of the brain under certain conditions, or in response to specific stimuli. In the error monitoring studies, participants are asked to do a repetitive simple task, such as pushing a button when a *K* rather than a *Z* appears unexpectedly sandwiched between a series of four flanking *Z*'s. The intention is to essentially generate mostly correct responses, accompanied by a few errors, in order to compare the brain's response on correct trials to its response on error trials. The EEG waveform that measures error monitoring by the brain is called the *error related negativity* (ERN) ("negativity" because the brainwave goes down rather than up from the baseline in traditional depictions of the waveforms).

People with obsessive compulsive disorder, as would be expected, consistently have enhanced ERNs. That is, their ERN waveforms show a larger negative deflection in response to an error than do the waveforms of healthy controls. This indicates a magnified response to errors, consistent with the hypothesis that people with OCD are more vigilant than are others, particularly with regard to errors.

If hoarding disorder is fundamentally related to fear of making an error, as has been hypothesized, it then stands to reason that the ERN would also be amplified among individuals with HD. Surprisingly, the opposite is true. People with hoarding disorder have ERNs that are *smaller* in amplitude than those of healthy controls, and are much smaller than those of people with OCD (Mathews, Perez, et al., 2016; / Baldwin, Whitford, & Grisham, 2019). Instead of being increased, their preconscious response to errors is blunted.

People with HD also do not respond emotionally or physiologically to errors in the same way as others do. Although they *report* feeling more upset than controls do after making an error on simple laboratory tasks, their objective responses to errors tell a different story. Both their facial reactions and their physiological reactions to errors are blunted or dampened in people with hoarding disorder compared to controls and to people with OCD (J. J. Zakrzewski et al., 2018).

As mentioned previously, people with hoarding disorder do not make any more errors than do individuals with OCD or than do healthy controls on these simple laboratory tasks. They can also consciously recognize and correct their errors in the moment when asked to do so, just as others who do not have hoarding disorder can. However, when asked to estimate how many errors they made after the task is completed, they are inaccurate in their estimations, both overestimating their error rates, and underestimating their error rates. This is in contrast to healthy controls, who are quite accurate in their estimations, and also in contrast to those with OCD, who consistently overestimate the number of errors that they made (J. J. Zakrzewski et al., 2018).

So what does this all mean? Unfortunately, as with much of the research on hoarding disorder, the larger picture isn't entirely clear yet. However, the blunted EEG and physiological responses, as well as the decreased facial reactions to errors, all suggest that people with HD may not be able to actually trust their brains or their bodies to accurately process the fact that they have made an error, *even as they automatically act to correct that error.* This disconnect between the automatic error correction and the brain's preconscious error monitoring system could then lead to a conscious response—an abnormal fear of making a mistake. Learning from one's errors depends on effective monitoring and appropriate feedback. Regardless of whether one makes more mistakes than others, or even regardless of whether one corrects one's mistakes, if the brain doesn't process it appropriately, no one can effectively learn from their mistakes.

COGNITIVE FLEXIBILITY

Cognitive flexibility is the capacity to switch attention and focus between two or more mental sets or concepts, or to think about two or more concepts simultaneously. It can also be described as the ability to adapt to new situations or new information or the capacity to pay attention to relevant information or stimuli and to ignore or inhibit irrelevant information or stimuli. High levels of cognitive flexibility allow individuals to change focus and selectively allocate attention based on the changing environment and changing demands of a given situation (Carbonella & Timpano, 2016).

Cognitive flexibility is also the executive function that allows an individual to switch from a behavior or way of thinking that is habitual and to take on a new behavior or way of thinking. A parent who initially blames a child for a broken vase because the child has broken multiple objects in the home previously, but changes her mind when she sees the paw prints on the tablecloth where the vase stood, is exhibiting cognitive flexibility. A child who switches tactics in the middle of a game when he recognizes that he is losing is also exhibiting cognitive flexibility.

Cognitive flexibility is a crucial executive function that impacts planning, organization, memory, and learning. Impaired cognitive flexibility is seen in a variety of psychiatric illnesses, including autism, schizophrenia, eating disorders, and OCD. There is also increasing evidence to suggest that cognitive flexibility is impaired in people with hoarding disorder (Carbonella & Timpano, 2016).

People with hoarding consistently take longer to respond and are less accurate on behavioral tasks that require rapidly switching their responses in reaction to external stimuli than without hoarding. For example, when participating in a task that required one response after hearing a single auditory tone and a different response after hearing two auditory tones, participants with high levels of hoarding behaviors had more difficulty in changing their answers appropriately than did those with low levels of hoarding behaviors (Carbonella & Timpano,

2016). People with hoarding also spend more time paying attention to an initial signal, and have difficulty effectively switching their attention to a subsequent, more relevant signal on neuropsychological tasks, even when they objectively know that the first signal is a distractor that they shouldn't pay attention to (Carbonella & Timpano, 2016).

This cognitive inflexibility also impacts learning and decision-making strategies among people with hoarding disorder. As discussed more extensively in the previous section on decision-making, several studies have shown that people with HD are not sensitive to the outcomes of their decisions and do not change their strategies based on previous experience (Aranovich et al., 2017; Pushkarskaya et al., 2017; Pushkarskaya et al., 2018).

In other words, people with HD do not change their way of doing things in response to environmental feedback. Instead, they adopt one consistent approach, which does not change across the length of the task, regardless of changes in the outcome. For example, in neuropsychological tasks that use gambling as a way of studying decision making, healthy individuals will explore a variety of approaches, and ultimately will settle on a style of responding that balances risk and reward. In contrast, people with HD will choose an initial strategy of responding, and will not change their strategies, even if the initial approach is not successful and results in a series of losses (Aranovich et al., 2017; Pushkarskaya et al., 2018).

Quite interestingly, the data also show that this cognitive inflexibility does not necessarily result in poorer performance, at least on the surface. People who have problems with hoarding tend to win as much money (or as many points) on these gambling tasks as do people who do not have problems with hoarding (Aranovich et al., 2017; Carbonella & Timpano, 2016; Pushkarskaya et al., 2017; Pushkarskaya et al., 2018). A little deeper investigation suggests that people with HD do pay a cost for their inability to adapt, however. Although they ultimately arrive at the same outcomes, individuals with HD tend to take a longer time, and to require more trials or responses to arrive at the same result than do those without HD. This increased effort, or as one research group terms it, "slow, step-by-step deliberation," is not only time-consuming but is also inefficient, and may put an excessive strain on the cognitive capabilities of people with hoarding disorder (Pushkarskaya et al., 2018, p. 507). This continuous state of cognitive overload might then be perceived by the person experiencing it as problems with attention, memory, and decision making, potentially explaining the discrepancies between what individuals with HD report that they experience and what is observed in formal neuropsychological assessments.

EXCESSIVE EMOTIONAL ATTACHMENT TO OBJECTS

Affected individuals and their families and friends report that a common feature of hoarding disorder is an abnormal or excessive attachment to objects. People with hoarding disorder save their belongings and acquire unneeded additional items for a variety of reasons, but many of these relate to sentimentality, comfort, and safety (R. O. Frost & Hartl, 1996). People with hoarding tendencies report being "hypersentimental," that is, attaching more personal meaning to items than other people do, and also attaching meaning to items that others would not feel similarly about.

Some people with HD report feeling that their possessions are an extension of themselves, and thus that it would be a violation of sorts to discard them. They may also feel safer or more comfortable when surrounded by their possessions than they do in other contexts, and be reluctant to discard them because they do not want to experience a feeling of loss when the item is gone. The subjective reports of an emotional component in HD are supported by studies of brain activation patterns among people who hoard, which is discussed in detail in the next section.

NEURAL CIRCUITRY OF HD

Although the neural circuitry of HD has not yet been completely worked out, the few studies that do exist are beginning to converge. As a preface to discussing what is known of the potential differences in brain structure and function between people who have hoarding disorder and those who do not, the brain regions that have been most consistently implicated in HD and their functions are described below.

The brain is divided into three main components, the cerebrum, the cerebellum, and the brainstem. The brainstem is the most primitive part of the brain, and controls respiration and cardiac function. It also plays an important role in regulating the sleep cycle and the central nervous system, thus regulating consciousness.

The cerebellum's main role is to regulate motor movements. Although the cerebellum is not responsible for the initiation of movement, it does fine-tune movement, and is responsible for coordination, precision of movement, equilibrium, balance, and posture. Although its role is not as well understood, emerging evidence also implicates the cerebellum in attentional, language, and emotional processing (Wolf, Rapoport, & Schweizer, 2009).

The cerebrum contains the cerebral cortex, which is divided into the left and the right hemispheres, and several subcortical structures, including the olfactory bulb, the hypothalamus, and the basal ganglia. The lobes of the cerebral cortex include the frontal lobe, which is the most anterior, or front-facing lobe, the parietal lobe, which is behind the frontal lobe and on the most dorsal, or top, part of the brain, the temporal lobe, which lies under the parietal lobe and behind the frontal lobe, and the occipital lobe, which is the most posterior lobe, lying behind the parietal and temporal lobes.

Unlike studies of OCD, in which both cortical and noncortical brain structures (such as the basal ganglia) appear to be equally important, most neuroimaging of studies of HD have focused on the role of the cerebral cortex. Although some subcortical and noncortical brain structures may play a role in the development and expression of HD, it appears that hoarding and associated symptoms likely arise primarily from cortical dysfunction. The areas of the cortex that have been the most consistently implicated in hoarding disorder, and their functions, are described next.

PREFRONTAL CORTEX

The prefrontal cortex, or PFC, is the most anterior (or front) part of the cerebral cortex, as well as the most exterior. It lies just over (on top of) the anterior cingulate cortex, and is divided into dorsal (upper) and ventral (lower), lateral (outside) and medial (inside) components. The PFC plays an important role in the synthesis of inputs from other parts of the brain, and as such is critical for planning, organization, and decision making. It is also involved in the formation of personality and in the development of social behavior (E. K. Miller, Freedman, & Wallis, 2002).

ANTERIOR CINGULATE CORTEX

The anterior cingulate cortex, or ACC, lies just under the frontal gyrus or frontal cortex. The anterior cingulate cortex plays a role in error detection, decision making, impulse control, and motivation. The ACC is divided into two components, the dorsal, or upper, ACC and the ventral, or lower, ACC. The dorsal ACC is the cognitive component of the ACC, while the ventral ACC is the emotional component. The ACC connects to the prefrontal and parietal cortex, as well as to the amygdala, nucleus accumbens, hypothalamus, and hippocampus (which is the memory center of the brain). The ACC also regulates blood pressure and heart rate.

ORBITOFRONTAL CORTEX

The orbitofrontal cortex, or OFC, is a part of the frontal lobes of the cerebral cortex that is located immediately above the orbits of the eyes. It connects to the amygdala, to the lateral prefrontal cortex, and to the parahippocampus. The OFC recieves signals from many parts of the brain, including the insula, amygdala, and hypothalamus. It is involved in many aspects of decision making and responding. In particular, the OFC is implicated in the role that emotion and reward play in decision making, as well as in valuation in choice, response inhibition, and in regulation of social behavior. The OFC is consistently implicated in OCD, where it is generally reported as being hyperactive, as well as in other psychiatric and addictive disorders.

INSULA

The insular cortex, or insula, is a part of the cerebral cortex that lies in the lateral sulcus, which is the crevice separating the frontal, parietal, and temporal lobes. The insula has connections to many other areas of the brain, including the amygdala and the somatosensory cortex, the thalamus, the temporal and occipital lobes, the opercular and orbitofrontal cortex. The role of the insula is broad, and includes regulation of the body's homeostasis, consciousness, and emotion, including empathy, perception, motor control, self-awareness, and cognitive functioning.

The insula also plays an important role in salience, which is a component of attention that allows for someone to recognize that a particular event or aspect of the environment is relevant or important, and to differentiate it from all of the other things in the background. The insula is known to be activated in addictions, and deterioration of the insula is seen in a variety of degenerative disorders, including frontotemporal dementia and Alzheimer's disease.

AMYGDALA

There are two amygdalae, one in each of the two cortical hemispheres. They are often colloquially referred to collectively in the singular as the amygdala. The amygdala is located in the temporal lobe of the cerebral cortex, and plays a critical role in emotional responses, particularly fear, anxiety, and aggression. It is a part of the limbic system, a series of cortical brain structures (including the cingulate cortex and the orbitofrontal cortex) that regulate emotion and motivation. The amygdala is also involved in memory, emotional learning, reward, and decision making.

BRAIN LESIONS AND HOARDING

One of the biggest challenges in neuroscience and the study of the causes of neuropsychiatric disorders is that scientists do not have direct access to the tissue or structure of interest. While oncologists can take a biopsy from a liver, a lung, or a breast to determine whether cancer cells are present, and internists can examine the function of the kidneys and pancreas and prostate using blood tests, the same methods are not available to psychiatrists.

There are no blood tests that directly (or even indirectly) measure brain function; and biopsies, while technically possible, are reserved for the most severe and life-threatening brain diseases. Radiographic techniques for imaging the brain, including computed tomography (CT) scans, magnetic resonance imaging (MRI), positron emission tomography (PET) scans, and magnetoencephalography (MEG), are becoming more and more useful as research tools in psychiatry, but are not yet useful for routine clinical practice. These methods are excellent for identifying structural damage or deterioration to specific brain regions, as happens in neurological disorders such as traumatic brain injury, stroke, multiple sclerosis, and dementia. However, they are less good at identifying changes in brain function. Most psychiatric illnesses do not have known abnormalities in brain structure, at least at the level that can be identified by current neuroimaging technologies. Thus, the approaches and techniques that are used to study brain function as it relates to psychiatric illness in humans, including neuroimaging, have relied heavily on serendipity, and on observant clinicians from nonpsychiatric fields for hints as to the brain structures that might be most relevant for specific psychiatric illnesses.

For example, some of the most useful clues as to which brain regions are involved in hoarding disorder have come from studies of individuals who have sustained brain lesions or trauma. Close clinical observation of these individuals and how their behavior does and does not change following the trauma can provide important information about the underlying function of the affected brain structure. Individual case histories, when collected and jointly examined, allow scientists and clinicians to identify patterns of behavior associated with brain lesions or other types of dysfunction in particular brain areas. Such identified patterns can then be used to design studies that test specific hypotheses, thus confirming or refuting the observed associations.

In the case of hoarding disorder, the focus of observation has primarily been on individuals who develop abnormal collecting behavior following brain injury or illness. As discussed throughout this book, difficulty discarding, not active collecting, is the fundamental core symptom of hoarding disorder. However, collecting behaviors, particularly when they arise acutely following an injury, are more likely to be identified and remarked upon than would difficulty discarding. Difficulty discarding is a passive behavior, while collecting is active, and therefore, more obvious to observers.

The Story of Phineas Gage

One of the earliest and well-known case histories of this type is that of Phineas Gage. Phineas Gage was a railroad worker who lived in the mid-1800s. While working on a railroad project in Vermont in 1848, Mr. Gage was injured in an explosion, when a three and a half foot long, 13-pound tamping rod was driven upward through his jaw, behind his left eye, into the left side of his brain, and out the top of his skull.

Remarkably, after being thrown backward by the explosion and experiencing a few convulsions, Mr. Gage was able to sit up, stand, and even speak. The tamping rod, covered in blood and brain tissue, was recovered about 80 ft away from the site of the accident, having been blown there by the strength of the explosion. After getting up, Mr. Gage rode into town on an oxcart, where he presented to Dr. John Harlow, who noted "he bore his sufferings with firmness and directed my attention to the hole in his cheek, saying 'the iron entered there and passed through my head.'" (Harlow, 1868, p. 277). Thus began a long career as a medical study subject, a career that continues to this day, over 150 years after his death.

After a treatment that involved several surgeries to remove bone fragments, blood clots, and infected brain material, as well as a long convalescence, Phineas Gage returned to what was, in retrospect, a remarkably functional life, given the extent of his injuries. His memory and intelligence were not affected by the injury, and, superficially, at least, he was able to think clearly and to process information.

However, despite his seemingly normal cognitive capacities, Mr. Gage was unable to return to his work on the railroad. This is because, as is noted in Harlow's account, and in other case studies, his personality was dramatically changed. Whereas prior to the accident, he was calm, well-regulated, and balanced, after the accident, Mr. Gage's behavior was unpredictable, he was obstinate, impulsive and erratic, and showed little concern or empathy for the people around him. He started projects in a fit of fancy, and abandoned them just as quickly, never finishing any. He also engaged in what was at the time termed coarse, profane, gross, and vulgar behavior, "to such a degree that his society was intolerable to decent people." (Harlow, 1851).

Phineas Gage became a kind of medical side show, and he would appear as Exhibit A when his case was presented to medical societies across the northeast United States. However, despite ongoing interest from the medical community, appearing at such events did not earn him a living, nor did similar attempts to act as a kind of medical museum exhibit for the public. Mr. Gage continued to try to work throughout his life, moving first to Chile and then to San Francisco in search of employment. However, he was unable to sustain employment for very long, in part because of his profound personality change, and in part due to his progressively deteriorating neurological condition. In 1860, at the age of 37, he began to experience seizures, which rapidly increased in frequency and severity. He died of status epilepticus, a form of continuous and unremitting seizure activity, on May 21, 1860.

So why is the story of Phineas Gage relevant to hoarding? The answer to this question lies in the clinical observations of his doctor, John Martyn Harlow. In addition to the changes in personality and demeanor that were reported by Harlow and subsequently confirmed by many others, Mr. Gage appears to developed "great fondness for pets and souvenirs, especially for children, horses and dogs—only exceeded by his attachment for his tamping iron, which was his constant companion during the remainder of his life."(Harlow, 1868, p. 277).

This description of Phineas Gage's behavior following his injury is remarkably vague and bears only a passing resemblance to what is now thought of as pathological collecting. Nevertheless, this description is enough to become the core of an emerging pattern, especially when combined with information collected by later clinicians from other medical cases reporting on similar types of brain injury.

In particular, Phineas Gage sustained damage to the mesial (or middle) portion of the frontal cortex, and subsequently developed a type of collecting behavior that he had not demonstrated prior to his injury. Subsequent clinical investigations have identified a number of additional individuals with damage to this region of the brain. Careful assessment of these individuals, both clinically and neuroanatomically, have produced compelling evidence to suggest that the prefrontal cortex is intimately involved in the development of abnormal collecting behaviors (Anderson et al., 2005).

For example, a study published in 2005 combined detailed neuroimaging data for 86 people who had sustained injury to the cerebrum in adulthood, with careful clinical assessments of the behaviors of these individuals. This study identified 13 people who exhibited severe, problematic collecting behaviors following their injuries. None of these individuals had any evidence of hoarding or collecting behaviors prior to the injury.

While each of the 13 participants who had hoarding disorder also had other areas of brain damage, the only point of convergence among all 13 was damage to the mesial prefrontal cortex, and in particular, the anterior cingulate cortex and the frontal pole, the most anterior part of the prefrontal cortex. Importantly, none of these 13 individuals had damage in subcortical regions that have been suggested to be the source of hoarding behaviors in animals (Anderson et al., 2005).

Similarly, studies of pathological collecting and frontotemporal dementia provide evidence, albeit indirect, for a role of the prefrontal cortex in pathological collecting and hoarding. People with frontotemporal dementia, or FTD, and specifically those with the particular form of FTD called *behavioral variant FTD*, experience progressive declines in self-awareness, insight, and self-care. A substantial portion of individuals with behavioral variant FTD also develop Diogenes syndrome, which is characterized by a combination of extreme self-neglect and hoarding or collecting behaviors. Close examination of five such patients, along with neuroimaging pinpointing the areas of brain deterioration, confirms the role of the fronto-limbic system of the brain (Finney & Mendez, 2017).

Subsequent studies examining structural and functional differences between people who hoard and those who do not have provided additional support for the role of the frontal lobe, and in particular, components of the prefrontal cortex, in the development of hoarding behaviors. For example, a study examining brain volumes using structural MRI found a significantly increased gray matter volume in the prefrontal cortex among those with hoarding disorder, but not in those with OCD compared to healthy controls (Yamada et al., 2018).

In contrast to OCD, where a clear functional network of interrelated brain regions that contribute to the development and maintenance of symptoms, the neural circuitry of HD has not yet been elucidated. However, functional MRI studies, which examine patterns of brain activity, have identified a variety of possible brain regions and networks that may be implicated in HD.

In general, these studies find that individuals with HD show *more* brain activity in regions that are involved in affect and emotion when asked to make decisions about discarding their own items compared to that found in healthy controls (D. F. Tolin et al., 2012). However, they also show *less* brain activity than do healthy control participants in these same regions when asked to perform tasks that are not related to personal decision making (Hough et al., 2016; Stevens, 2019).

Brain regions that have been the most consistently implicated in HD include the anterior cingulate cortex (ACC) and the insula, which together make up the cortical components of the cingulo-opercular network (Hough et al., 2016; Tolin, Kiehl, et al., 2009; Tolin, Stevens, et al., 2012; Tolin, Witt, & Stevens, 2014). As discussed, the ACC and the insula play an important role in error monitoring or error detection, decision making, and motivation, all of which have been hypothesized to be altered in people with HD.

Other brain regions that have been implicated, albeit less consistently, as being of relevance for HD include the dorsolateral prefrontal cortex or the DLPFC, the orbitofrontal cortex or OFC, and the amygdala (An et al., 2009; Hough et al., 2016; Mataix-Cols et al., 2004; D. F. Tolin, Kiehl, Worhunsky, Book, & Maltby, 2009). Both the DLPFC and the OFC are involved in planning, organization, and stimulus responding, while the amygdala is involved in memory, emotional learning, and reward. All three brain structures, the DLPFC, the OFC, and the amygdala, are involved in decision making, and in particular, in emotional aspects of decision making.

Finally, one study has suggested that, in addition to the regions described above, people with hoarding disorder also demonstrate over-activation of the primary visual cortex when engaging in tasks that require cognitive flexibility (Hough et al., 2016).

PUTTING IT ALL TOGETHER

As can be seen in the previous sections, understanding whether there are actually consistent cognitive or neuropsychological deficits among people with hoarding disorder, and if so, exactly what they consist of, and from where in the brain they originate, is a complex and difficult task. However, although our understanding of hoarding disorder is still in its infancy scientifically speaking, a picture is beginning to emerge.

Figure 7.1 ties together the most reliable neuropsychological findings for HD in a hypothesized model.

In the proposed model depicted in Figure 7.1, the core deficits in hoarding disorder are not in learning, memory, attention, or decision making, as was originally hypothesized. Instead, this model suggests that people with HD exhibit inefficient visual processing and categorization, a mismatch between subjective and objective physiological response to errors, and reduced cognitive flexibility. These abnormalities in turn lead to the inability to (a) efficiently process and organize information, (b) adapt to changing circumstances or new information, and (c) accurately assess whether an error has been committed.

These difficulties in turn lead to an increased overall cognitive load, as well as to perceived problems with attention and low confidence in memory, which subsequently lead to a fear of making an error and difficulty with decision making. These problems, when added to an excessive emotional attachment to objects, even those that are unneeded or objectively valueless, subsequently leads to difficulty discarding.

Data from the neuroimaging studies, which are now beginning to converge, provide additional support for this theoretical model. These studies have demonstrated that people with hoarding disorder have

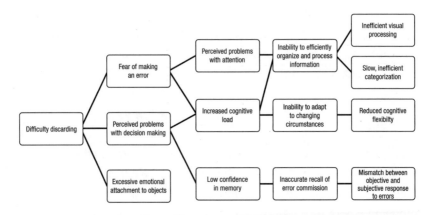

Figure 7.1: Hypothesized Model of Neuropsychological Deficits in Hoarding Disorder and Their Role in Difficulty Discarding

generalized hyperactivation of visual cortex, possibly indicating inefficient visual processing. They also demonstrate a bimodal or biphasic response in the cingulo-opercular network among people with HD, with over-activation of the ACC and insula, which are involved in error monitoring, decision making, and cognitive flexibility, when making personal decisions, but under-activation of these brain structures during other tasks. Finally, studies suggest—although somewhat less robustly—that abnormalities in the DLPFC and the OFC, which are involved in planning and organization, as well as in the emotional aspects of decision making, may also exist in people who are diagnosed with hoarding disorder.

OVER-INCLUSIVE SPEECH IN HOARDING DISORDER

One observation that is frequently voiced by both clinicians and researchers who work with people suffering from hoarding disorder regards their distinctive style of speech. Anecdotally, experienced clinicians say that they can often identify people suffering from hoarding disorder just by talking to them, even without any mention of hoarding symptoms, clutter, or excessive acquisition. These experts say that individuals with HD are often not only very talkative, much more so than their friends and family members, but they also exhibit what is termed over-inclusive speech patterns (R. O. Frost, Steketee, G., 2010).

Over-inclusive speech is, broadly speaking, the tendency to provide more details than are necessary within a given conversation or interaction. In addition to being verbose, people with HD tend to be either circumstantial or tangential in their speech, or both (Weintraub, Brown, & Timpano, 2018). In other words, when asked straightforward questions, people with HD will often get sidetracked in their answers.

Sometimes, after getting sidetracked and talking about a topic that is peripherally related to the original question or discussion people with HD will return to the original point or question (circumstantial speech). Other times, in the course of their verbal detours, they will completely lose track of what was asked (tangential speech). In both circumstantial and tangential speech, irrelevant and unnecessary details that are not directly related to the topic of discussion are provided.

People with hoarding disorder who exhibit over-inclusive speech, when asked, will often say that they are not sure what information is important for the listener to know. Therefore, in order to be as helpful as possible, they try to include everything that they can think of that might potentially be relevant. In other words, in the effort to keep from providing too little information, they will actually provide too much, leaving the listener overwhelmed and confused. Unless the interviewer is exceptionally skilled at directing the discussion, the tendency towards over-inclusiveness can actually impede efficient and effective conversation, history-taking, or therapeutic treatments.

Researchers have noted that these speech patterns bear a resemblance to the behavioral manifestations of hoarding disorder, in that they reflect an inability to efficiently sort or categorize information for dissemination, in much the same way that difficulty discarding represents an inability to distinguish valuable from unneeded objects (Weintraub et al., 2018). It is perhaps not a coincidence that in a sample of people with high levels of hoarding behaviors, unusual speech patterns were strongly associated with self-reported cognitive complaints, including forgetfulness, failures of memory, distractibility, and difficulties with sequencing (Weintraub et al., 2018). These observations suggest that over-inclusive speech may in fact be another symptom of the cognitive inflexibility and inefficiency in information processing that is increasingly thought to underlie hoarding disorder.

THE ROLE OF INSIGHT FROM A NEUROBIOLOGICAL PERSPECTIVE

As discussed in Chapter 1, people with hoarding disorder frequently have impaired insight with regard to their symptoms and the impact that their symptoms have on themselves and on others. Insight is a heterogeneous and complex concept, and as with many such constructs, it is not known precisely from which area of the brain insight, or lack thereof, arises.

Once again, studies of individuals with brain lesions or neurodegenerative disorder that affect specific brain regions or structures can provide some clues. Studies of metacognition, a form of insight that relates to the ability to put one's own patterns of thinking and belief structures into a larger context, can also be of help. These studies suggest that metacognition or insight arise from the prefrontal cortex, and in particular, the fronto-limbic system (Finney & Mendez, 2017; Yamada et al., 2018).

As discussed, the fronto-limbic system contains several of the brain regions that have been implicated in hoarding disorder, including the anterior cingulate cortex, the orbitofrontal cortex, and the amygdala. Similarly, the insula, another cortical region that is consistently implicated in hoarding disorder, is clearly associated with anosognosia (see Chapter 1), a type of lack of insight that is common among people with dementia or with brain injuries that affect the parietal lobe, where the insula resides.

Unfortunately, no neuroimaging studies have yet examined the relationship between level of insight and degree of activation in either the fronto-limbic structures or the insula among individuals with hoarding disorder. Similarly, there are currently no studies examining the relationships between the neuropsychological deficits seen in HD and insight. This is in part because insight is difficult to measure in healthy controls, who by definition do not have psychiatric symptoms in which insight can be easily assessed, and in part because people with HD who have poor insight into their hoarding symptoms do not tend to participate in research.

SUMMARY

The neurobiology of hoarding disorder is clearly complex, and as more is learned about the neural underpinnings of this fascinating disorder, it is also becoming clear that the deficits are relatively subtle in nature. Standard neuropsychological assessments and neuroimaging approaches provide hints regarding what may be going awry in the brain of someone who is suffering from hoarding disorder, but they are not yet sophisticated enough to pinpoint the underlying causes. Work still needs to be done to fully understand the underpinnings, both biological and psychological, of this common but mystifying disorder.

Chapter 8

Pharmacological Treatment of Hoarding Disorder

The practice of psychiatry, like much of medicine, is sometimes more of an art than a science. This is especially true for the pharmacological treatment of hoarding disorder. As described in the preceding chapters, our understanding of the epidemiology and biology of HD, and the full extent of its various clinical presentations, is still nascent, although interest in this field has grown and the science is rapidly expanding. Whereas the psychological treatment of HD is relatively well characterized (see Chapter 9), the pharmacological treatment of HD is still in its infancy.

When developing treatments for newly recognized disorders, particularly medication-based treatments, the first, and often the most effective, approach is to test the efficacy and safety of treatments that are already available and known to work in similar or related disorders. The reason for this is simple: One must start somewhere. As was the case for many of the studies aimed at understanding the causes and neurobiology of hoarding disorder described in Chapter 7, the starting point for identifying potentially effective treatment approaches for HD is to look to those medications that have previously been shown to work in OCD or other related disorders.

Although the trial-and-error approach based on the successful treatment of other conditions can seem unscientific on the surface, this method has been useful in identifying effective treatments for many disorders. For example, the chemotherapeutic agent bleomycin, which is used to treat Hodgkin's lymphoma, can also be used to treat testicular cancer, cervical cancer, cancers of the head and neck, and many other conditions, despite the fact that the underlying causes of these cancers are not the same (Prescribers' Digital Reference, 2020). Similarly, many psychiatric medications that were originally developed to treat one condition (for example, depression) have been successfully used to treat a myriad of psychiatric disorders and symptoms (such as anxiety, eating disorders, and OCD).

STEPS TO IDENTIFYING MEDICATIONS FOR HOARDING DISORDER

There are several common approaches or types of study that aim to determine whether a specific medication is useful for a given disorder. These studies are more or less progressive in terms of both sample size and in terms of scientific rigor. As the study designs increase in the degree of scientific rigor, the amount and quality of information obtained from them improves. As outlined in Figure 8.1, the typical studies in such a progression range from case reports and case series, which are post-hoc examinations of data that were originally collected for clinical purposes to prospectively designed randomized clinical trials (RCTs). The following sections discuss these two ends of the progression, as well as two additional intermediate study designs, retrospective reanalyses of existing RCTs for another, related disorder, and prospective open-label studies.

Case reports and case series are often the first step in determining whether a specific treatment or type of treatment is likely to be of use in improving symptoms or curing a particular condition. Case reports recount the experience of one or two patients with a particular treat-

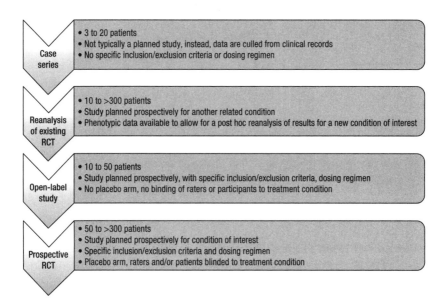

Figure 8.1: Common Progression of Studies in the Investigation of the Utility of a Specific Medication in Treating Psychiatric or Other Illnesses. As noted in the text, not all study types are conducted for a given treatment, nor are they always completed sequentially, if they are conducted.

ment, while case series report on outcomes in a few to a few dozen patients. Case reports typically examine the effects of medications approved by the Food and Drug Administration (FDA) for use in one disorder that have been repurposed for use in a different condition for which it has not been studied or approved. This type of use of a medication in a condition for which it has not been FDA approved is called *off-label* use.

Because case reports and case series involve retrospective examination of data that were collected in the course of clinical treatment, rather than being prospectively designed research studies, they are opportunistic, real-world studies. They are also by definition unblinded, or open-label. That is, the both the clinician and the patient know what the proposed treatment is.

This type of study has many limitations, the two most important being the small sample sizes and the unblinded nature of the data collection and analysis. As anyone who treats patients knows, no two people are alike. Symptom presentations and symptom severity vary tremendously, even within patients who have the same underlying disorder. Many other factors are variable between patients also, including the number and type of co-occurring conditions, previous treatment history, age, sex, and so forth. The experience of one or two individuals with hoarding disorder and Treatment X may therefore have no bearing on whether Treatment X is useful in treating patients with hoarding disorder in general.

Similarly, because both the patient and the provider know what treatment is being given, and both (presumably) hope that it will be effective, there is threat of potential (unconscious) bias toward positive outcomes in reporting the results of case reports or case series. This bias toward the positive is thought to be caused by the so-called *placebo effect*. The placebo effect describes the phenomenon wherein the very act of being provided with a medication can lead to symptom improvement, even if there is no active ingredient in that medication (in other words, a placebo) or if the medication doesn't work for the condition of interest.

Case reports or case series, while limited in their utility for a number of reasons, do have some value. For clinicians and patients for whom all else has failed, they can provide initial hints into the tolerability, acceptability, and perhaps the likely usefulness of a treatment of interest. When no good treatments are available, or a patient has not been able to tolerate or has not responded to the standard treatments, clinicians often turn to case reports to identify alternative approaches. As such, these studies can provide hope, and a way of identifying off-label or nontraditional approaches to treatment refractory patients or for newly-recognized disorders.

RANDOMIZED CLINICAL TRIALS

At the other end of the progression of treatment studies are prospective, double-blind randomized clinical trials (RCT) with a placebo control group, the gold standard methodology for identifying effective medications for a given condition or disease. In this type of study, some proportion of the participants (typically 50%) are randomly assigned to receive a placebo, or inactive form of the medication, while the rest are assigned to receive the active treatment. Those participants who receive the placebo are in the control group. In a double-blind study, neither the patient nor the person assessing the outcomes (the rater) knows whether the active treatment or the placebo is being administered; they are both *blinded* to the treatment condition.

RCTs can be very powerful, particularly when well-designed, but they are not typically the first line of inquiry for a given treatment of interest. RCTs are expensive to conduct, because, in order to provide meaningful results, they also require large numbers of subjects. In the case of placebo-controlled trials, where some subjects will be randomly assigned to receive a placebo, the identification and recruitment of sufficient numbers of participants who are willing to take the chance that they will not receive an active form of the medication is also required.

For many illnesses and medical conditions, and even for some problems that require surgical intervention, some proportion of individuals who receive a clinical intervention will improve, even when there is no demonstrated clinically meaningful treatment involved. This rate of response to an inactive treatment or clinical intervention is called the *placebo response rate*. For most psychiatric disorders, the placebo response rate is between 20%–30%. In order to determine whether a given medication or treatment is useful, the study must have sufficient numbers of participants to overcome the effects of the placebo response rate and allow for the detection of the degree of improvement that is due to the active medication, if any. This is because the placebo response is expected to occur for both groups of patients, including those who are in the control group and are thus taking the placebo, and those who are in the active treatment group. The response that is due to the medication, over and above the effects of the placebo, is called the active or absolute response.

Prospective double-blind placebo controlled RCTs, when well done, can provide definitive evidence not only of whether or not a given treatment is effective, but also can help to quantify how much improvement can be expected. In particular, the average degree of symptom improvement or response rate that is due to the active effects of the treatment, over and above any placebo response, is the outcome of interest. Most pharmacological treatments for psychiatric disorders result in a 30%–60% response rate. When the response rate for the placebo group is considered, (usually between 20%–30%) this translates into a 20%–40% actual (or absolute) response for the active treatment.

The strength of the placebo response to a given treatment is affected by a number of variables. This includes the disorder itself (for example, generally OCD has a lower placebo response rate than does major depression), number of active treatment groups (also called treatment arms), length of the study, number of study sites, and the presence of a placebo lead-in prior to the actual trial (Li et al., 2019). In a placebo lead-in, all participants, regardless of the treatment arm to which they are assigned, are given a week or two of placebo prior to entering into the actual RCT. Participants are not told that they are being given a placebo during this time, and their symptoms are measured at the end of the lead-in period. The purpose of this component of the study is to identify anyone who shows substantial improvement in symptoms without actually receiving an active treatment. Those subjects who do show improvement in the lead-in phase are disqualified from participating in the RCT. The idea behind a placebo lead-in is to reduce the number of people in both arms of the study (both active treatment and placebo groups) who are likely to have a placebo response, thus, making it easier to determine whether the medication has true benefit.

Even though they represent the gold standard in terms of research designs, because RCTs can be logistically complex and expensive to conduct, they are often the last in the progression of studies outlined in Figure 8.1, rather than the first. Given the large number of factors that potentially affect the treatment response, interpretation of the outcome of any given clinical trial in a way that provides useful clinical guidance is complex. Thus, multiple well-designed, rigorously controlled studies are often necessary to really determine the utility of any particular treatment in psychiatry. If a particular medication has never been studied for the condition of interest, and thus there are no preliminary indications as to its likely effectiveness in treating that condition, it is difficult to convince either funders or potential participants to take a risk on an RCT. Preliminary data that suggest some benefit, even if the data are imperfect, are often needed first. Such preliminary data can come from a variety of sources. These include case reports or case series, prospective open-label clinical trials, and, in special cases when there is symptom overlap, reanalyses of RCTs conducted previously for another, potentially related disorder.

REANALYSES OF EXISTING RANDOMIZED CLINICAL TRIALS

A relatively uncommon study design, albeit one that can be very useful in generating preliminary data, is the reanalysis of existing data from previously conducted RCTs. Also called retrospective analysis, this approach takes existing data from a randomized clinical trial of one disorder and reanalyzes the outcomes using a new, secondary phenotype (in other words, a new disorder, symptom, or trait) as the condition of interest. For example, the investigators of a randomized clinical trial studying the efficacy of a new antidepressant for major depression may also collect information about other psychiatric symptoms or illnesses, such as anxiety disorders. After the study is completed, the investigators can then take the original data and reanalyze the outcomes with respect to anxiety disorders rather than with respect to major depressive disorder.

Although not definitive, this type of analysis of preexisting data can provide some hints regarding whether a medication can be repurposed from treatment of one condition to treatment of another. If the participants in the study who have depression and a co-occurring anxiety disorder respond better to the medication under study than do individuals who have depression but do not have anxiety, that medication would be of potential interest as a treatment for primary anxiety disorders.

There are some caveats to this type of post-hoc analysis, however. By definition the randomization of participants in the original study is focused on the primary disorder of interest (in this example, major depression) and not the subsequent disorder (anxiety). Random assignment to a particular treatment group—active medication or placebo—is done to distribute any underlying baseline characteristics of the participants that may impact treatment response across all treatment arms. For example, if younger people are more likely to respond to the treatment under study than older people, and younger people are more concentrated in the active treatment group, the results may suggest a greater response to treatment than actually exists, due to a bias in the distribution of participants between groups.

In the example above, participants are not randomized by anxiety diagnoses, but rather by depression. Thus, the participants who have both anxiety and depression may not be similar to those who have only depression in terms of key characteristics (sex, age, treatment history, and so forth). For this reason, any reanalysis to examine the effects of the treatment on anxiety will lose the benefits of the original randomization. Care must be taken in the analysis step to control for the potential effects of baseline characteristics of the participants that may confound the results.

Despite the potential complications, retrospective analyses retain many of the advantages that were built into the original randomized clinical trial. Any procedures that were designed to prevent bias or overinterpretation of outcomes, such as blinding, as well as procedures aimed at identifying optimal dosing or other relevant aspects of treatment, are retained. Thus, assuming that the appropriate clinical or phenotypic data are available for examination, retrospective analyses of well-conducted, rigorous randomized clinical trials can provide important and useful information.

PROSPECTIVE OPEN-LABEL STUDIES

Open label studies or clinical trials often follow case series and retrospective reanalyses in the path toward determining whether a particular medication or treatment is beneficial. As the name implies, in an open-label study, both the scientists or clinicians administering the treatment and the patients receiving the treatment know what medications they are receiving and what the hoped-for outcome is. These studies are designed in advance, with the dosing of the medication and the number of participants needed predetermined before the trial starts.

The problem with open-label studies is that they introduce a tremendous potential for unconscious bias toward a positive result. As with case series, and indeed, in any clinical trial, both the researchers and the participants in an open-label trial usually hope that the treatment will work. As many studies have conclusively demonstrated, for everything from pain control to neurosurgery for Parkinson's disorder, this hope can actually influence the perceived outcome through the placebo effect (Albin, 2002; Damien, Colloca, Bellei-Rodriguez, & Marchand, 2018).

SO WHY CONDUCT OPEN-LABEL STUDIES?

The answer to why open-label studies are still being conducted is simple—logistics. In a randomized clinical trial, one third to one half of the participants will not receive the treatment of interest. Instead, they will receive a placebo (or in some study designs, a treatment that is already in use). For many people who are suffering, this chance is not worth taking—their symptoms are problematic, often they have not responded to prior attempts at treatment, and they want relief. It is thus sometimes easier to recruit participants into an open-label study than it is into an RCT with a placebo group.

Open-label trials also require fewer participants than do RCTs. The outcome of interest is simply symptom improvement from pretreatment to posttreatment across all subjects. Compare this to an RCT, where the outcome is also symptom improvement pre- to posttreatment, but it is measured as the differences between the participants in the active treatment group and those in the comparison (placebo) group. The placebo response must be subtracted from the overall response in order to identify the component that is due to the active treatment. The number of participants required to identify a meaningful difference between these two groups is thus much higher than the number needed to simply identify a meaningful improvement within one group.

However, this brings us back to the fundamental problem with open-label studies—the problem of the placebo response. Some number of participants, typically around 20% to 40%, will experience an improvement in their symptoms simply by being in the study (Li, Nasir, Olten, & Bloch, 2019). Although it might not matter to either the clinician or the patient that the observed symptom improvement is not really due to the treatment being tested, the placebo response does not tend to last much past the end of the study. This is why it is important to distinguish a placebo response from a true response to an active medication, and also why prospective double-blind RCTs include a placebo control group and often a placebo lead-in. Nevertheless, open-label studies can be useful for providing preliminary indications as to whether a specific treatment may be beneficial for use in a new disorder. For many interventions, well-controlled, randomized, double-blind clinical trials are only conducted after an initial benefit is identified through open-label studies.

PHARMACOTHERAPY FOR HOARDING DISORDER

Unfortunately, the existing literature on pharmacological treatments for hoarding disorder is quite limited. Current treatment recommendations for medication management of HD stem from a mix of case series, open-label trials, and reanalyses of placebo-controlled, RCTs for OCD. There have been no prospective, randomized double-blinded medication trials for hoarding disorder, or for hoarding symptoms in the context of OCD.

The studies that do exist focus mostly on the selective serotonin reuptake inhibitors, or SSRIs. There are also a few studies examining other classes of medications, including serotonin-norepinephrine reuptake inhibitors (SNRIs), psychostimulants, and neuroleptics. These studies are summarized in Figure 8.2 and discussed in detail in the following sections. First will be a brief description of the relevant neurotransmitters, the chemicals that communicate between neurons in the brain and the rest of the nervous system, and of the classes of medications that act on those neurotransmitters.

SEROTONIN

Serotonin, which is also known as 5-hydroxytryptamine, is a monoamine neurotransmitter that is present throughout the nervous system, including the central nervous system (brain and spinal cord), peripheral nervous system (nerves and nerve endings), and enteric nervous system (which governs the gastrointestinal tract). Serotonin has a variety of functions in the body, including in gastric motility, vasoconstriction and vasodilation, sleep, appetite, sexual behavior, and temperature (Beattie & Smith, 2008).

Serotonin is best known for its role in the regulation of mood and anxiety. With a few exceptions, nearly all of the pharmacological agents that are currently used to treat mood and anxiety disorders have an impact on the serotonergic system. In fact, antidepressants, and specifically serotonin reuptake inhibitors, are the second most commonly prescribed class of medications in the United States, second only to medications that lower lipid levels (Stone, 2018).

NOREPINEPHRINE

Norepinephrine is a catecholamine that is sometimes referred to as noradrenalin. Norepinephrine is synthesized from dopamine, and can be subsequently catalyzed into epinephrine, both in the central nervous system and in the peripheral nervous system.

Norepinephrine is best known for its role in the fight-or-flight response. In the body, norepinephrine increases heart rate and blood pressure, triggers the release of glucose, and increases blood flow to muscle. In the brain, norepinephrine increases arousal, alertness, attention, and vigilance. As might be expected for a chemical that increases the brain and body's readiness to fight or flee, norepinephrine release also increases anxiety and can cause restlessness. Many of the medications that are used to treat depression and anxiety, particularly the types of anxiety with prominent physiological symptoms, target the norepinephrine system.

DOPAMINE

Dopamine, or 3,4-dihydroxyphenethylamine, is another neurotransmitter in the catecholamine family (National Center for Biotechnology Information, 2019). Dopamine is synthesized in many parts of the body, including the central nervous system, the adrenal glands, the kidney, and even in immune cells.

Dopamine plays a major role in motor control, motivation, and reward. Alterations in dopamine levels or in dopamine activity have been implicated in many conditions that are characterized by disordered movement, motivation, and reward. These include Parkinson's disease, attention deficit hyperactivity disorder (ADHD), schizophrenia, depression, and addiction.

There are many other compounds that act as neurotransmitters in the central nervous system, too many to discuss here. These additional compounds also likely play important roles in brain functioning (and malfunctioning). However, serotonin, norepinephrine, and dopamine are of particular relevance for the treatment of psychiatric disorders, including hoarding disorder. Most of the medications currently in use for depression, anxiety, psychotic disorders, OCD, ADHD, and other psychiatric disorders that co-occur with hoarding disorder act on one or more of these neurotransmitter systems. The classes of potential relevance to hoarding disorder are discussed next.

SEROTONIN REUPTAKE INHIBITORS

Of all the antidepressants and antianxiety agents currently on the market, the selective serotonin reuptake inhibitors (SSRIs) are the most commonly prescribed, both in the United States and elsewhere. As the name implies, the SSRIs block the reabsorption (reuptake) of serotonin after its release from the neuron into the synaptic cleft (the space between the transmitting and receiving neuron), thus functionally increasing the amount of serotonin that is available in the system (Staff, 2019). As with most psychotropic medications, the mechanism of action of the SSRIs in treating depression and anxiety is not well understood. It is clear, however, that their therapeutic effect is not due merely to the increase in the amount of available serotonin in the system, but rather to downstream effects that occur after several weeks to months of treatment.

Because SSRIs are safe and have relatively few side effects, in particular compared to other psychotropic medications, they have been studied in and shown to be effective for many psychiatric disorders, including major depressive disorder, OCD, anxiety disorders, eating disorders, and autism spectrum disorders. SSRIs have also been examined for the treatment of hoarding symptoms.

SEROTONIN-NOREPINEPHRINE REUPTAKE INHIBITORS

Serotonin-norepinephrine reuptake inhibitors (SNRIs) are a comparatively new class of antidepressant medications. SNRIs block the reuptake or reabsorption of both serotonin and norepinephrine from the synaptic cleft and were developed to build and expand on the success of the SSRIs in treating mood and anxiety symptoms.

Because the SNRIs block the reuptake of both norepinephrine and serotonin, they are thought to have utility in treating a wider range of symptoms than the SSRIs. For example, SNRIs may be more useful than SSRIs in the treatment of individuals who have prominent sleep disturbances, or in those who have physiological arousal (such as increased heart rate or shortness of breath) as a part of their anxiety disorder. Although this class of medications are used to treat depression and anxiety, they have actually been of more utility in another area of medicine: These drugs are now also commonly used to treat chronic pain.

Approved indications for the use of SNRIs includes neuropathic pain, fibromyalgia, and chronic musculoskeletal pain, in addition to depression, PTSD, generalized anxiety disorder, and social anxiety disorder. One SNRI, atomoxetine, is approved primarily for use in ADHD. As discussed below, both of these non-mood/anxiety indications may be of benefit in the pharmacological treatment of hoarding disorder.

NEUROLEPTICS

Neuroleptics, which are also known as antipsychotics because they were first used to treat the positive symptoms of schizophrenia and other psychotic disorders, are useful for treating a variety of psychiatric disorders. These medications primarily act on the dopamine system. There are two classes of neuroleptics currently available, first-generation neuroleptics, and second-generation neuroleptics. First-generation neuroleptics cause a blockade of dopamine receptors in the brain (and elsewhere) and are most commonly used to treat schizophrenia and other psychotic disorders.

The newer, or second-generation neuroleptics, have a wider range of uses in psychiatry. Like their earlier counterparts, second-generation neuroleptics primarily act to block dopamine receptors, but they also act on serotonin receptors. This activity in the serotonin system has two potential benefits. First, the serotonergic properties of second-generation neuroleptics are thought to reduce the rate of side effects such as muscle stiffness, restlessness, and abnormal movements that are off-target (unintended) effects of all neuroleptics. Second, the serotonergic effects of these medications may also have direct benefits on symptoms such as insomnia, anxiety, and mood regulation.

In addition to being useful in treating psychosis, the second-generation neuroleptics are thus also of benefit as primary or adjunctive agents in the treatment of mood disorders, including depression and bipolar disorder. They have also been shown to be useful in improving outcomes for OCD when used in conjunction with an SSRI (M. E. Hirschtritt, Bloch, & Mathews, 2017).

PSYCHOSTIMULANTS

Psychostimulants are a class of drug that increases activity of (or stimulates) the central nervous system. Psychostimulants range from legal and available without a prescription (caffeine), to legal and available without a prescription but controlled (pseudoephedrine), to prescribed and highly regulated (methylphenidate), to illegal (methamphetamine).

As a class, psychostimulants act on multiple neurotransmitters and receptors, including the dopaminergic, noradrenergic, serotonergic, adrenergic, and adenosine systems. However, the stimulants commonly used to treat psychiatric symptoms most prominently stimulate the release of, or block reuptake of, dopamine and norepinephrine.

Psychostimulants increase alertness and arousal, improve focus, attention, and endurance, and enhance motivation and productivity. However, they also have a high abuse potential, partly because tolerance to their positive effects can develop, and users can feel a subjective crash in mood and arousal as their effects wear off. For this reason, most stimulants used in clinical practice are classified as Schedule II drugs by the Drug Enforcement Administration, and thus require a special license to prescribe.

In psychiatry, psychostimulants are most commonly prescribed to treat ADHD and are effective in treating hyperactivity, impulsivity, and inattention in children and adults. They do not directly treat the executive dysfunction that is commonly seen among individuals with ADHD, but improvement in the other symptoms can lead to increased organization and planning skills as a secondary benefit. Other uses of psychostimulants include treatment for narcolepsy, binge eating disorder, and in some cases, depression. Because of their benefits in treating ADHD, they are also of potential interest for the treatment of hoarding disorder.

THE USE OF SSRIS TO TREAT HOARDING

Most of the data on treatment of hoarding using SSRIs comes from reanalysis of RCTs examining the efficacy of this class of medications for obsessive compulsive disorder. Fluvoxamine, citalopram, and sertraline have all been examined in retrospective analyses of randomized clinical trials for OCD (Bloch et al., 2014). Collectively, these studies indicate that, as a group, individuals with OCD who also have prominent hoarding symptoms have somewhat poorer treatment responses to the SSRIs when compared to those with OCD who do not have hoarding. Reanalyses of the data by type of OCD symptom also indicate that, as a symptom, hoarding does not respond as well to the SSRIs as do other types of OCD symptoms such as contamination or checking. However, these studies do suggest that there may be some benefit to using SSRIs for the treatment of hoarding. Although hoarding does not seem to be as responsive to SSRIs as other types of OCD symptoms, between 40% and 60% of individuals with hoarding symptoms will have at least a partial response to SSRI treatment (defined as at least a 25% improvement in symptoms).

One prospective, open-label trial on the effect of one of the SSRIs, paroxetine, on hoarding symptoms in individuals with OCD has also been conducted (Saxena et al., 2007). This study compared treatment outcomes of 32 individuals with OCD and co-occurring hoarding to 47 individuals with OCD who did not have hoarding. The results of this study suggested that hoarding symptoms, when measured by two questions on the Yale Brown Obsessive Compulsive Scale (YBOCS), responded as well to paroxetine treatment as did other types of OCD symptoms.

However, when changes in hoarding symptoms were measured pre- to posttreatment with the UCLA Hoarding Symptom Severity Scale (UHSS), an instrument that was more specifically designed to assess hoarding (see Chapter 3), the results were somewhat different.

Among individuals without prominent hoarding symptoms, UHSS scores, which can range from 0 to 40, went from a mean of 4.7 pretreatment to a mean of 2.5 posttreatment. This decrease technically translates into a symptom improvement of 46%. However, a 2.2 point improvement is not clinically meaningful, particularly in this range of scores, which is well below the standard cutoff for clinically significant hoarding symptoms (≥ 20). In contrast, among those study participants who had high levels of hoarding symptoms, UHSS scores decreased by an average of 6 points, from a mean of 26 pretreatment to a mean score of 19.7 posttreatment. This translates into a 24% improvement in hoarding symptom severity.

Thus, although the results of this study do indicate that paroxetine was associated with some improvement in hoarding symptoms, this improvement was only moderate at best. Importantly, the average posttreatment hoarding severity score for those with primary hoarding was near the suggested UHSS cutoff score of 20, suggesting that most of these participants continued to have significant and problematic hoarding symptoms after treatment with paroxetine.

Perhaps more importantly, paroxetine was not well tolerated by many of the participants in either arm of the trial (OCD with hoarding and OCD without hoarding). The proportion of those who either dropped out of the study or were not able to achieve optimal doses of paroxetine due to side effects or other adverse effects was relatively high. Only 16 of the 79 participants (20%) were able to tolerate the target dose of 60 mg per day, while 18 (23%) either dropped out before completing the treatment or were only able to tolerate doses below 40 mg per day.

The results of the studies on the use of SSRIs for hoarding, when taken together, indicate that response of hoarding symptoms to SSRIs, while quantifiable, is suboptimal. This is not to say, however, that SSRIs are completely ineffective in treating hoarding symptoms. Clinicians can tell their patients that, in general, 40% to 60% of individuals will have some response to treatment with an SSRI, and that, on average, hoarding symptoms will improve by about 25%. For a disorder that is exceedingly functionally impairing and usually becomes progressively more severe over time in the absence of treatment, a 25% improvement in symptoms can translate into a measurably improved quality of life.

There is also another potential use for SSRIs in the treatment of HD. As discussed in Chapter 4, 50% of people with hoarding will also have major depressive disorder, while 30%–50% will have an anxiety disorder. These co-occurring conditions, which are a major source of distress and impairment, *are* likely to improve, and in many cases, remit, with SSRI treatment. Improvement in depression and anxiety symptoms can improve quality of life for individuals with HD and may also thus improve patients' ability to participate in psychotherapeutic interventions for hoarding. These interventions are discussed in Chapter 9.

SNRI TREATMENT FOR HOARDING

There have been only two studies of SNRIs for hoarding, one study of venlafaxine, and one of atomoxetine. Unlike the studies of the SSRIs, both of these studies were conducted in participants with primary hoarding disorder and used assessments that were specifically designed to measure hoarding symptoms, making their results more directly relevant for clinicians who treat HD.

The first, a 12-week-long study of extended-release venlafaxine, was conducted in 24 individuals with primary hoarding disorder (Saxena & Sumner, 2014). Venlafaxine was chosen in for this clinical trial because it is well tolerated among middle-aged and older adults, particularly at the higher doses that may be required for effective treatment of HD. This medication also has reasonably good efficacy for depression among individuals who have not responded to SSRIs.

Participants in this study were much more representative of individuals with hoarding disorder than were the participants in the SSRI studies discussed previously. They ranged in age from early 30s to late 60s and had moderate to severe hoarding symptoms. Nearly a third had co-occurring depression, while 10% to 20% had co-occurring ADHD or anxiety symptoms. Only one participant had co-occurring OCD.

As expected, venlafaxine was generally well tolerated in this study.

The possible dose range used in this study was between 37.5 mg to 300 mg per day, and the mean dose that was achieved at the end of the study was approximately 200 mg per day, representing a moderate dose. At the end of the 12 weeks, hoarding symptoms had improved by about 30% to 35% across the sample. Seventy percent of the 24 participants had at least a 30% improvement in hoarding symptoms and were rated as much improved following treatment.

Importantly, co-occurring mood and anxiety symptoms also improved with venlafaxine treatment. In fact, venlafaxine had more pronounced effects on depression and anxiety in this sample than it did on hoarding. Depression symptoms improved by an average of 48%, while anxiety symptoms improved by 43% on average. Similarly, obsessive compulsive symptoms in this sample improved by an average of 39%.

Interestingly, most of the pretreatment characteristics that were collected did not predict hoarding symptom treatment response. Severity of hoarding, mood, anxiety, or obsessive compulsive symptoms prior to initiation of venlafaxine did not predict improvement in hoarding symptoms, nor did the dose of venlafaxine used. In fact, the only predictor of treatment response was age, with older individuals showing a poorer treatment response to venlafaxine than younger individuals.

The second study examined the effect of 12 weeks of treatment with atomoxetine on hoarding symptoms and on attention among 12 individuals with HD (Grassi et al., 2016). Atomoxetine is a potent norepinephrine reuptake inhibitor. It has also been shown to have serotonin reuptake properties in animal studies, but its effect on serotonin reuptake at clinical doses in humans is still in question. It is approved for use as a treatment for ADHD in children, adolescents, and adults. It has also been used to treat emotional lability, cognition, mood dysregulation, and executive function in a variety of disorders, including schizophrenia and Parkinson's disease (Moukhtarian, Cooper, Vassos, Moran, & Asherson, 2017; Solmi et al., 2019; Warner, Ottman, & Brown, 2018).

The potential use of atomoxetine in hoarding disorder is based on the observed increased rates of ADHD among individuals with HD (see Chapter 5) and because of the consistent reports of executive dysfunction among individuals with HD (see Chapter 7). The idea is that, rather than targeting hoarding symptoms, functional improvement in HD may also be achieved by targeting problems with attention and concentration, or by improving executive functioning.

The 12 participants in the atomoxetine study were similar to those in the venlafaxine study—they were middle-aged and older adults with moderate to severe hoarding symptoms and a range of comorbid psychiatric conditions (Grassi et al., 2016). Unlike the venlafaxine study, however, most of the participants in this study were also taking a range of other psychotropic medications, including quetiapine, risperidone, alprazolam, citalopram, mirtazapine, or lorazepam.

After 12 weeks of treatment, participants were taking a mean of 63 mg of atomoxetine daily (total possible range of 40 mg to 80 mg), and this medication was generally well tolerated. Hoarding symptoms improved by approximately 40% across the entire group. Half of the sample met the predefined response criteria (35% or greater reduction in hoarding symptom severity, and a rating of much improved or better). Among the 6 participants who were classified as treatment responders, hoarding symptom severity improved by an average of 57%.

Symptoms of inattention and impulsivity, both symptoms of ADHD, also improved with atomoxetine treatment. Inattention symptoms improved by 18% and impulsive symptoms improved by about 19% from baseline to posttreatment. In contrast to the venlafaxine study, however, there were no significant changes in anxiety or depression scores pre- to posttreatment, although it should be noted that these symptom scores were low at baseline for the majority of participants (Grassi et al., 2016).

The authors of the atomoxetine study suggest that their results are consistent with the results of the venlafaxine study, and suggest that in both, noradrenergic effects play a prominent role in treatment response. They note that at higher doses (e.g., above 200 mg per day) the noradrenergic effects of venlafaxine are primary, while at lower doses, the serotonergic effects are more dominant.

The results of these studies suggest that SNRIs, and norepinephrine reuptake inhibitors (NRIs) such as atomoxetine, may be more effective in the treatment of hoarding than are the SSRIs. As discussed, confidence in the results of these studies is limited by the pitfalls inherent in any open-label trial, that is, the likelihood that the reported outcomes are overestimates of the true treatment response. Nonetheless, in the absence of double-blind randomized controlled clinical trials, these studies provide some direction for clinicians with regard to pharmacological management of this complex disorder.

NEUROLEPTIC TREATMENT OF HOARDING

Only one study has examined the use of a neuroleptic agent in the treatment of hoarding symptoms (Bogan, Koran, Chuong, Vapnik, & Bystritsky, 2005). This study was a reanalysis of an open-label clinical trial of quetiapine as an adjunct to SSRI treatment in treatment refractory OCD. Eight of the 30 patients had hoarding as their primary symptom.

Participants received quetiapine augmentation for 8 weeks, with doses ranging from 25–200 mg daily. The mean dose across the sample was 170 mg. Treatment response was defined as at least a 25% percent improvement in OCD symptom severity from baseline to post-treatment. Unfortunately, only 1 of the 8 participants with hoarding in this study responded to quetiapine with a 25% or better improvement. As with the paroxetine study, participants in this study reported a high rate of adverse side effects, most prominently sedation, fatigue, and forgetfulness. Increased appetite, dry mouth, and restlessness were also reported in more than 10% of the sample. These results suggest that, for most people with HD, quetiapine is not likely to be a useful first line treatment. However, given the utility of neuroleptics in the treatment of psychosis, this class of medications may be useful for treatment of people with HD who have poor insight into their symptoms or are delusional.

USE OF STIMULANTS TO TREAT HOARDING

As with the atomoxetine study, the idea behind the use of stimulants in people with hoarding disorder arises from two observations. The first is that individuals with HD frequently report problems with attention, decision making, and procrastination. The second is that, as discussed in Chapter 5, rates of ADHD, particularly the inattentive subtype of ADHD, may be increased in people with hoarding disorder.

The use of stimulants to treat hoarding and related symptoms has been reported in only a few individuals, including one case study using amphetamine salts in a single individual, and one open-label prospective case series of extended release methylphenidate in four individuals.

In the case study, a patient with hoarding disorder, ADHD, and schizotypal personality disorder reported unsuccessful treatment with a variety of pharmacological and non-pharmacological approaches over the course of a decade for extreme hoarding, including electroconvulsive therapy. After presenting to the authors of the case study for treatment, he was started on fluvoxamine and risperidone, which led to some improvement on this combination. Methylphenidate was subsequently added, but was not tolerated. The authors report that when amphetamine salt was added to his medication regimen, the patient's motivation and organization improved, his tendency to procrastinate lessened, and over time, his hoarding symptoms also improved to the point where he was able to accept help in clearing paths in his home (Kaplan & Hollander, 2004).

In the open-label trial, four patients with hoarding disorder were given between 36–54 mg of extended-release methylphenidate, a commonly used treatment for ADHD, for 4 weeks (Rodriguez et al., 2013). The participants in this study ranged in age from 36 to 48 years old, and all four had either comorbid major depressive disorder or dysthymia, while three of the four had a co-occurring anxiety disorder. Two were on stable doses of either an SSRI or an SNRI, or both. All participants had previously tried and failed at least one SSRI.

Although none of these four patients met criteria for ADHD, all reported moderate to high levels of problems with attention prior to treatment. Following 4 weeks of treatment with methylphenidate, three of the four participants reported substantial improvements (greater than 50%) on a self-report measure of attention. All four participants showed small but measurable improvements in objective measures of attention using a computerized task called the continuous performance task (CPT). However, only two reported improvement in hoarding symptoms. One participant had a 32% reduction in hoarding symptom severity after 4 weeks of methylphenidate treatment, while the other had a 25% reduction in hoarding symptom severity. The other two participants reported no change in their hoarding symptoms.

Interestingly, the two participants who reported improvement in hoarding symptoms also reported the greatest improvements in attention symptoms pre- to posttreatment (67% and 63% reduction in inattentive symptoms, respectively). However, there was no association between degree of improvement on the objective measures of attention using the CPT and self-reported improvement for either inattention or hoarding symptoms.

Perhaps most importantly, methylphenidate was not well tolerated by the participants. All reported substantial side effects, including insomnia, palpitations, and decreased appetite. Despite the self-reported improvements in attention and, for some individuals, in hoarding symptoms, none of the participants elected to continue treatment with methylphenidate at the conclusion of the trial.

WHAT SHOULD CLINICIANS TELL THEIR PATIENTS ABOUT PHARMACOTHERAPY FOR HOARDING?

Unfortunately, there is no easy answer to this question. Although some medications and medication classes show promise for the treatment of hoarding disorder, no rigorous randomized clinical trials have yet been conducted for any medication. This is where the art of medicine comes

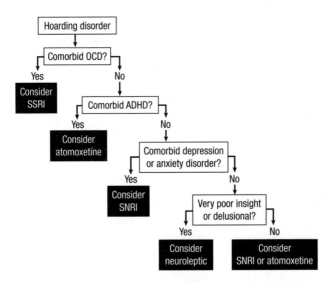

Figure 8.2: Proposed Treatment Algorithm for the Treatment of Hoarding Disorder. Note that SSRI treatment for hoarding with co-occurring OCD should target OCD-appropriate doses, which are 2 to 3 times higher than standard doses used to treat depression. For individuals with HD who exhibit delusional symptoms, in addition to instituting neuroleptic treatment, consider dementia as a possible additional or alternative diagnosis (see Chapter 4 for details).

into play—taking what little is known of the science and interpreting it for an individual patient. Figure 8.2 outlines one potential algorithm for pharmacological treatment of hoarding disorder. Because there are no clear answers with regard to which medications are likely to be best at reducing hoarding symptoms in and of themselves, other components of hoarding disorder as a clinical syndrome can also be useful in aiding decision making.

For example, despite the data indicating that hoarding is less responsive to SSRIs than are other types of obsessive compulsive symptoms, SSRIs as a class are the standard of care for medication management of OCD, and they show clear benefits for obsessive compulsive symptoms, including hoarding, although hoarding symptoms may be somewhat less responsive than other types of OCD symptoms (M. E. Hirschtritt et al., 2017). No other class of medications is currently recommended as a first-line treatment for OCD. Thus, for patients with hoarding disorder and co-occurring OCD, SSRIs, at doses that have been shown to be effective in treating OCD, are a reasonable first choice.

For individuals with co-occurring anxiety or depressive disorders, either SSRIs or SNRIs are a good starting point. SSRIs are effective and FDA approved for both depression and anxiety, and as such, can be used to treat these conditions in people with HD. As described above, in an open-label trial, the SNRI venlafaxine showed good efficacy in primary hoarding disorder, and it is also FDA approved for the treatment of both major depressive disorder and generalized anxiety disorder. Although the other SNRIs have not been studied, it is also reasonable to consider these medications in the treatment of hoarding.

Although conclusions regarding the use of agents other than SSRIs and SNRIs draw more heavily on the art of medicine than the science, the existing data regarding the other classes of psychiatric medications, both for HD and for other psychiatric symptoms, can be of some help. For example, for patients who have hoarding disorder and co-occurring ADHD, atomoxetine is a reasonable starting point. Not only is atomoxetine approved by the FDA for the treatment of ADHD, but one open-label study has shown that atomoxetine may also have promise in the treatment of hoarding symptoms.

Similarly, neuroleptics may be useful in some patients with HD, in particular, among those with delusions or very poor insight. The data for the utility of neuroleptics in HD are sparse, and the one retrospective study examining quetiapine in individuals with OCD and hoarding symptoms showed only small improvements. Nevertheless, neuroleptics have clear efficacy in the treatment of psychotic symptoms, as well as in mood disorders, and thus may be of some benefit for the subgroup of patients whose lack of insight can mimic psychosis at times.

Finally, in the absence of other co-occurring psychiatric disorders, both venlafaxine and atomoxetine have shown promise in the treatment of HD and should be considered as potential first line agents.

The data suggest that both venlafaxine and atomoxetine can improve hoarding symptoms, at least in open-label studies. At standard FDA recommended doses, these two medications show similar efficacies, with 70% to 75% of patients showing meaningful (albeit moderate) reductions in symptom severity.

It is also clear, however, that pharmacotherapy is not an optimal treatment for hoarding disorder. No medication or class of medications has been studied in depth, and even in open-label trials, none has shown more than moderate improvement in hoarding symptoms. Medication management is a reasonable choice in the absence of other options. But there are other treatments for hoarding disorder that have been rigorously studied and do show clear efficacy in improving symptoms. These treatments, which are psychotherapeutic interventions based on cognitive behavioral therapy models, are discussed in Chapter 9.

Chapter 9

Psychotherapy for Hoarding Disorder

Hoarding disorder, like most conditions that develop in adulthood, is a chronic rather than an acute illness. Like diabetes and hypertension, depression and posttraumatic stress disorder, management rather than cure is the goal of treatment for hoarding, at least from a practical perspective. Although some patients respond exceedingly well to a given treatment, and their symptoms completely resolve or remit, this pattern is the exception rather than the rule. The majority of people with moderate or severe hoarding disorder will continue to have some level of difficulty discarding, or problems with excessive acquiring, or both, on an ongoing basis.

However, this does not mean that treatment is futile. As with diabetes and depression, appropriate treatment can significantly improve the quality of life for many individuals with HD, even if complete remission of symptoms is not achieved. Reducing clutter can improve the safety and functionality of living spaces. Minimizing or decreasing acquisition of superfluous items can improve an individual's financial status and continuing to work on discarding unneeded or worn-out items can help to maintain the gains that are made in treatment.

Psychotherapy is the mainstay of treatment for hoarding disorder—but not just any form of psychotherapy. Traditional psychodynamic psychotherapy, which is also colloquially called "talk therapy" and focuses on identifying the triggers and antecedents to a particular maladaptive behavior in order to produce change, has not been shown to be effective for HD. While useful for improving many aspects of functioning, examining one's childhood, life story, and patterns of behavior that have developed over one's life does not seem to improve hoarding symptoms or reduce a person's difficulty in discarding unneeded objects.

Instead, a specific form of evidence-based psychotherapy, or variations on this form, are used to treat hoarding disorder. These treatments all derive from a combination of psychotherapeutic approaches to treating obsessive compulsive disorder, anxiety disorders, and addictions. In its most fundamental form, treatment of hoarding disorder combines elements of cognitive behavioral therapy (CBT), which is used to treat OCD and anxiety disorders, with elements of motivational interviewing (MI), which is used to treat addiction.

There are two primary differences between CBT and motivational interviewing techniques and psychodynamic psychotherapy. The emphasis for CBT and motivational interviewing is on the individual's present and the future rather than on their past. That is, these forms of treatment focus on what is happening at the current time in a person's life, and on where that person wants to be or how they want to be living in the future.

This is in contrast to psychodynamic therapies that focus on an individual's childhood and early life, with the idea that their past experiences are responsible (at least in part) for their current state. In other words, psychodynamic psychotherapy focuses on the *why*, as in "why did this happen to me?" and CBT focuses on the *what* and *how*, as in "what do I need to do to get better?" and "how do I make it better?"

The interaction styles between therapist and client also differ in these types of therapies. Psychodynamic psychotherapy is traditionally exploratory, and the therapist acts as a guide, a listener, and an interpreter. The client is encouraged to explore freely, to talk about not only their experiences and emotions but also their dreams, fantasies, and fears. The idea is that patients will, over time, learn to identify recurring patterns in their lives and to gain insight about the causes of these patterns, both healthy and maladaptive.

CBT and motivational interviewing, on the other hand, are more structured and more directive in nature. Instead of encouraging the client to freely explore any topic that might interest them, the focus is on methodically assessing when and how specific problems, and in particular, unwanted behaviors arise, and then in systematically working to change them. Although CBT and MI are a collaboration between the therapist and the client, the therapist takes an active role in assigning tasks for the client to complete, either in the office or at home.

WHAT EXACTLY IS CBT?

Cognitive behavioral therapy (CBT) is an overarching term that captures a variety of specific types of therapy that all share some common elements. CBT is a time-limited, structured form of treatment that was developed in the 1950s and 1960s by Albert Ellis, who developed a psychotherapeutic approach that he called rational emotive behavior therapy, and Aaron Beck, who developed a treatment that he called cognitive therapy.

CBT-based approaches combine the work of Ellis and Beck and are based on the following concepts: (1) How people think (cognition), how they act (behavior), and how they feel (emotion) all interact with one another. (2) The problem being addressed (in this case, hoarding) is caused by faulty or unhelpful ways of thinking or unhelpful patterns of learned behavior, at least in part. (3) These ways of thinking and unhelpful patterns of behavior can be changed (American Psychological Association, 2020).

Cognitive behavioral therapy typically has three primary components: psychoeducation, cognitive restructuring, and behavioral intervention. As discussed above, inherent in this type of approach is the idea that why the problem arose is not as important in effectively treating it as identifying exactly what the problem is, how it manifests, and developing strategies to change it.

For hoarding disorder, the *psychoeducation* component usually lasts for one or two sessions and consists of teaching the client (and family members, if they are engaged in treatment) about what hoarding disorder is, what is known of its causes, and what to expect from treatment. Following the initial education sessions, one or two sessions are then devoted to helping the client identify and begin to develop more awareness of when and how their symptoms manifest in a variety of contexts, and to recognize the fears and triggers that may be associated with their behaviors.

The *cognitive restructuring* component then follows. The goal of cognitive restructuring is to identify mental distortions, maladaptive cognitions, and erroneous ways of thinking related to hoarding behaviors, and to change them to better reflect reality. Cognitive restructuring can be completed as a separate, self-contained unit. More typically, the cognitive and behavioral parts of CBT for hoarding disorder are intermingled as the therapist and the patient work to identify and challenge recurring beliefs and fears and to test them over many sessions.

Inherent in the cognitive restructuring component of treatment is helping the client to identify and build on sources of motivation, both internal and external. This process is critical to helping the client continue to engage in treatment, identify the underlying emotional attachment to particular items and the patterns of thought surrounding this attachment, set goals, and plan how to effectively and realistically reach these goals.

For hoarding disorder, a therapist will use cognitive restructuring techniques to help the patients challenge the thoughts and beliefs that underlie the desire to keep or to acquire a specific item. Patients are asked to think through their fears of discarding in a structured way, often using an "if/then" type of statement, in order to subsequently challenge those fears by actually testing them.

For example, a commonly voiced fear among people with hoarding disorder can be expressed as follows: "*If* I throw this newspaper away, *then* I will worry about possibly needing the information in it in the future. I will get so anxious about the newspaper and whether or not I might need it that I won't be able to focus on anything else."

The first step in the therapeutic process for a patient who voices is to write it down. The therapist would then ask the patient to identify and write down as many possible alternative outcomes (the *then* part of the articulated statement) as they can. If they cannot identify any alternatives, as is common, particularly early in the course of treatment, the therapist may suggest some. An example alternative if/then statement for the fear described above is the following: "*If* I throw this newspaper away, *then* I will feel anxious for a little while." The therapist, and later in the course of treatment, the patient, may add a *but* statement that follows the *then* clause. In this example, the complete alternative statement would be written as follows: "*If* I throw this newspaper away, *then* I will feel anxious for a little while, *but* when something else comes up that I have to pay attention to, I will forget about the newspaper."

The client is then asked to test the fear and the possible alternatives that they and the therapist have identified by actually throwing the newspaper away or recycling it. They are then asked to go about their normal business over the next day or two, and then to sit down, think back about the experience, and write down their actual response to discarding the newspaper if they were successful in doing so. This is the *behavioral* component of CBT, and it is also called an *exposure*. Back in therapy the following session, the client and the therapist think together about the discarding experiment, or exposure, and identify whether and how the actual outcome differed from the original feared outcome.

If, as expected, the client finds that discarding the newspaper was easier than they thought it would be, and that their anxiety did indeed only last for a short period of time, the therapist and client would next work together to devise another exposure that builds on the first. They may practice discarding one newspaper a day, every day for an entire week, to see how that feels.

If, on the other hand, the client finds that the exposure went exactly as they had feared, and they were indeed paralyzed by anxiety, the therapist would take a step back, and work with the client to identify and test a somewhat less strongly held fear. Instead of actually discarding the newspaper, for example, the client may choose to sort the newspapers in a particular area of their home and put them all together into one place in preparation for eventual recycling. Or they may decide to bring the newspaper to the therapist's office for safekeeping, with the idea that, the first step would be to remove it from the home, and the second step would then be for the therapist to discard it the following week, with the permission of the client, of course.

This approach is called *graded exposure*, and, as the name implies, it involves exposing oneself to a feared situation in a graded fashion. Graded exposures for hoarding can involve sorting specific items into a small number of categories (for example into piles labeled "need," "don't need," and "not sure"), imagining discarding a specific item, practicing discarding it (such as bringing it to the therapist's office), and actually discarding the item.

A critical component of the success of graded exposures is repetition. That is, discarding one item among a group of unneeded items is not enough to develop and maintain behavioral change. Instead, as with any habit or maladaptive behavior, the new or desired behavior must be practiced daily or near daily, built upon, and reinforced, to successfully replace the old, undesired behavior.

The idea behind graded exposures is that, over time, the fear related to discarding will diminish until it eventually disappears. Although the initial exposures may be difficult, and, in some cases, the anxiety may actually spike during the actual act of discarding, with repetition, the brain learns that it can tolerate letting go of the item, and that the feared outcome does not actually come to pass.

A similar approach can be used for excessive acquisition in hoarding disorder. In the case of excessive acquiring, individuals are encouraged to practice non-acquiring as their exposures. That is, when a client sees an item that they think may be of use, such as a flyer in a doctor's office, initially they may be asked to avoid picking it up. If this is successful, they may then be asked, the next time they are in a similar situation, to pick the flyer up and to read it, but then to put it back rather than taking it with them.

For acquirers, part of the behavior change may also be to learn to avoid places (such as thrift stores) or events (such as flea markets) that trigger the desire to purchase unnecessary items. Over time, as the ability to resist temptation strengthens, the individual may practice window shopping, that is, looking, but not buying anything, in the places that they used to frequent.

There are many ways to devise exposures in the behavioral component of CBT. Part of the success of treatment lies in the therapist's ability to work with a specific client to identify a series of exposures that have meaning and are achievable for that individual, as one size does not fit all. Insight, motivation, resilience, and severity of symptoms all play a role in an individual's ability to effectively participate in CBT. Of these, the most important predictor of improvement appears to be motivation. Thus, if a client or patient is ambivalent about treatment, or their lack of insight into the impact of their hoarding causes them to have low motivation for change, motivational interviewing techniques can be helpful.

WHAT IS MOTIVATIONAL INTERVIEWING?

Motivational interviewing is a type of psychotherapeutic approach that, like CBT, is both directive and collaborative (Rollnick, 1995). The fundamental goal of motivational interviewing differs from that of CBT, however. As described, the goal of CBT is to directly affect behavioral change through ongoing practice in changing maladaptive patterns of thought and behavior. In contrast, the goal of motivational interviewing is to help a client identify, examine, and resolve their ambivalence around making a desired change.

Motivational interviewing, or MI, was developed by Drs. Stephen Rollnick and William Miller in the early 1980s. It has been used for many types of maladaptive behaviors and psychiatric illnesses, but it is best known in the treatment of addictions. Like CBT, motivational interviewing is an umbrella term that describes the principles underlying several types of psychotherapy, including motivational enhancement therapy and behavior change counseling, among others.

There are seven key principles that underlie all forms of MI: (1) Motivation to change is elicited by the client, not by the therapist. (2) It is the client's job to identify and name the ambivalence surrounding their symptoms, and to resolve it. (3) Although MI is directive, persuasion, coercion, or confrontation by the therapist are not effective approaches. (4) The therapist's style should be quiet and open, to facilitate eliciting information from the client. (5) The therapist is directive only in the service of helping the client to identify and resolve the ambivalence for themselves, rather than in telling the client what to do or how to do it. (6) Readiness to change is not an innate trait that the client either does or does not have. Instead, readiness to change fluctuates over time and with environment. It is the product of interpersonal interactions. (7) The therapeutic relationship is a true partnership. While the therapist may have specific skills, they do not act as an expert in this form of treatment. Instead, the client has autonomy, and thus bears the responsibility for making choices and for accepting the consequences of those choices.

The four processes of motivational interviewing are to *engage, focus, evoke,* and *plan* (W. R. Miller, Rollnick, S., 2013). *Engaging* involves two steps, getting to know the client and their struggles, and expressing empathy. This component of MI is typically open ended, and the primary role of the therapist is to listen, to allow the client to open up and explore their reasons for coming to treatment, as well as their hopes, their expectations, and their fears about treatment. As the therapist listens and helps the client explore their motivations for treatment, they also express empathy for the client and their struggles, without judgement and without directive suggestions.

Focusing involves helping the client identify an area or a problem that they want to work on, and in particular, one where they are struggling to make the needed changes. This component of MI involves helping the client to identify their motivation to change, or in other words, both *if* and *why* the patient might want to make a change in their life or behavior. The focusing phase is analogous to the "what" component of CBT, and essentially asks the question, "what are the problems that you wish to work on?" It is important in this step to allow the client to identify the goal, without the therapist pushing a preconceived goal on them. In this step, the therapist will also help the client to identify and foster discrepancies between their current behaviors and the behaviors (or state) that they wish to achieve.

After identifying a series of potential goals or desired changes within the context of the larger goal or outcome, the therapist can take one of three stances in treatment—they can either direct the client toward a particular area to work on, they can let the client decide the goal independently and follow their lead, or they can guide the client toward a goal by helping them to prioritize areas of highest importance.

In the *evoking* step, the therapist works with the client to help them identify the reasons for change. In this component of MI, which is also known as the "Why?" step, the client is asked to put into words the specific reasons that they want to change their behavior. The function of this step is twofold. First, asking the client to articulate their reasons for the desired change often reinforces those reasons, and helps the client recognize that there are more reasons than they realized to make the wanted change. Second, it helps the client (and the therapist) identify the strongest underlying motivations and develop potential strategies and solutions to effectively address those motivations.

It is important to remember that this component of the treatment is client-led rather than therapist-led. That is, the client is responsible for recognizing and articulating their underlying reasons for wanting change and for working on solutions and action steps aimed at achieving the desired change. The therapist's role is to ask questions that help guide the client toward solutions, rather than to provide advice or "answers." The exception to this is if a client cannot identify potential solutions—or gets stuck—then the therapist can, with permission, provide some ideas to help get the process started or to move it along.

In the planning step, the therapist helps the client to design a strategy for changing their behavior and encourages and supports their commitment to making the change. This step is analogous to the "how" aspect of CBT and is very practical in nature. Although the therapist can assist, it is the role of the client to come up with a step-by-step action plan. The action plan should have a series of targeted smaller goals that adhere to the SMART principle, that is they are *S*pecific, *M*easurable, *A*chievable, *R*elevant, and *T*imely (or *T*ime Bound).

For people with hoarding disorder, addressing ambivalence is a critical component of treatment. Although individuals who enter treatment for HD are usually quite motivated to improve their living space and their quality of life, they almost always express significant ambivalence about the steps that are required to achieve this, in particular, ambivalence about discarding. In addition to fear of needing an item after it has been discarded, people with HD are also motivated to keep things because of attachment. While they may worry that they will forget a particular event or person, or will need a particular item in the future if they discard it, they may also feel a sentimental attachment to the item. Asking someone with a strong emotional attachment to a particular item to discard it without helping the person to identify, understand, and challenge their ambivalence around that item is unlikely to be a successful form of treatment.

The vignette presented next illustrates the importance of finding appropriate motivational factors to help people with HD effectively engage in treatment. This vignette, and the vignette presented in Chapter 10, describe the real-life experiences of people living with hoarding disorder and their attempts to find help. To protect the privacy of these individuals, the stories are composites of multiple people with similar experiences rather than the case history of any single person. For similar reasons, some potentially identifying details have been changed.

Motivation and the Department of Motor Vehicles

Marvin is a 74-year-old veteran with a long and distinguished military record. As a young man, he served in the Korean War, where he was an army mechanic. At the end of the war, Marvin reenlisted in the army, as he enjoyed the structure provided by the military. He continued to work as an auto mechanic, moving his family from time to time, as he was deployed to various army bases around the United States. When he retired from the military in his late 40s, Marvin found a job working in car repair at a dealership, where he stayed until retiring at age 66.

Marvin has lived alone since his wife of 35 years died of heart disease. He has adult children who live in another state but visit him often. He is fully connected to the Veteran's Administration Medical Center (VAMC), where he gets his health care, and he is active in many veterans' associations in his city, from which he derives social support and a sense of purpose. Marvin is fiercely independent and resists efforts by his children to get him to move nearer to them, in part because he is unwilling to leave the organizations to which he belongs.

Marvin describes himself as a "lifelong saver," perhaps because he grew up poor. He was taught as a child that to throw something away was to waste it, and he learned to repurpose and reuse as much as possible. During the Korean War, obtaining parts for the Jeeps and other vehicles that he serviced was often difficult, and Marvin learned to both save and to scrounge parts whenever he could.

After the war, Marvin found that his saving ways were no longer needed, and in fact, at times they became problematic, such as when he wanted to put an old part in a vehicle instead of ordering a new one. Marvin learned to use only new materials in his job, but as he said, "the habit was too hard to change, and besides, it is what I was taught to do." He found himself bringing the old, discarded parts home from work.

Over the course of 30 years, Marvin filled multiple storage sheds in his backyard with discarded car parts. He took pride in helping his neighbors with their auto repairs and was especially pleased when he was able to find a part in his stash that was useful to someone else. Over time, Marvin began picking up and keeping other items, particularly tools, screws, nails, and fasteners of all types. He began to fill up coffee cans in his home with these items, which he would collect on his daily walks in the neighborhood.

Marvin continued with this pattern for many years. As far as his family or neighbors knew, his collecting habit did not cause any him difficulties, other than the fact that his house eventually began to look like a workshop, with tools and fasteners covering all available surfaces. However, during the course of a routine yearly physical at the VAMC, Marvin's internist noticed some scrapes that looked like road burn on the fingertips of his left hand and inquired about them. Marvin sheepishly admitted that they were indeed road burn, and that he acquired them during the course of what he called his "collecting trips."

When the internist inquired further, she found that Marvin had begun driving slowly around his neighborhood with both car doors open. He said that he was looking for screws and nails on or alongside the road. Marvin was initially worried that he or one of his neighbors would drive over these items, causing them to suffer tire damage. When he found a screw or a nail or any other piece of hardware or equipment, he reached out of the door while the car was still moving and scooped it up, adding it to his collection once he reached home.

The internist was appropriately worried about this behavior, which she told Marvin was unsafe. She referred him to a psychiatrist at the VAMC who specialized in hoarding disorder. Marvin was initially unwilling to see a psychiatrist, as he had never heard of hoarding disorder, and further, didn't think that his collecting was problematic. He did agree that his collecting trips might be unsafe, but he worried that the nails on the side of the road might be even more unsafe and was unwilling to stop the activity.

The internist let the issue drop for the time being, but she made a note to follow up with Marvin about this unusual behavior at his next check-up, as she saw him every 3 months for his chronic medical conditions. At his follow-up visit, Marvin admitted that he was still driving on his collecting trips. In addition to picking up screws and nails and similar items, he had begun to pick up roadkill, or dead animals that had been hit by traffic, on his drives. He used the same technique, which was to drive with his doors open and to lean out of the moving vehicle to scoop up the animal carcass whenever he saw one.

The internist was more alarmed by this behavior, as she now worried that Marvin, in addition to the potential safety risk due to unsafe driving, was putting himself at risk of injury or the acquisition of zoonotic infections from dead or wounded animals. She gave Marvin the choice of seeing the psychiatrist that she had mentioned previously or being sent to the emergency room for an evaluation. Marvin, who trusted his internist, although he disagreed with her assessment of the risk potential, chose to see the psychiatrist.

After committing to a course of action, Marvin was the type to see it through. He came willingly to his psychiatric appointments and participated in the sessions. He practiced discarding his collection of nails and screws, reluctantly at first, but with more enthusiasm once he learned that charity organizations that repaired homes for the elderly were happy to accept them.

However, Marvin was unable to give up his collecting trips. He recognized the logical facts—that the nails and screws were fairly infrequent, and that he might in fact pose more of a danger to other drivers than the loose hardware did. He admitted that picking up dead animals from the road was probably not necessary, as there was a government agency responsible for such things.

Marvin and his psychiatrist spent a number of sessions exploring his reasons for collecting along the roadside, as well as trying to identify reasons that he might want (or be willing to) change his behavior. As is often the case in HD, the logical reasons for stopping were not sufficient to instigate change in Marvin. The idea that he might be putting himself or others at risk, although important to him, did not seem to be sufficient motivation for change.

Finally, one day there was an unexpected breakthrough. Marvin was late to his appointment, which was highly unusual. He apologized, and explained that while he typically avoided highway driving in favor of back roads, he was running late for the appointment, and thus took the interstate. While en route to the VAMC, Marvin saw a hammer lying on the median. He said, somewhat sheepishly, that he just couldn't let it stay there, even though it was not in the road and thus was not endangering any drivers. He thought that the charity where he donated his collection of hardware would greatly appreciate the gift of a hammer.

Marvin got off the interstate at the next exit, doubled back, and then got back on the highway a few exits before the place where he had seen the hammer. He drove deliberately slow in the left lane in order to find the exact spot, and when he arrived, he pulled over suddenly, got out with the engine still running, picked up the hammer, got back into the car, and pulled back into traffic.

Following this narration, the psychiatrist exclaimed, "You were lucky you weren't killed! Or seen by the police. They may have taken your driver's license away for reckless driving." No more was said about this incident, and the session went on, although Marvin was unusually quiet. He was more quiet than usual for the next few visits as well, although he continued to work on sorting and discarding as usual.

However, some time later, Marvin came to a therapy session and told the psychiatrist "I've stopped my collecting trips." When he was questioned about this pronouncement in more detail, Marvin admitted that the psychiatrist's comment from the earlier session had stuck with him. He explained that while he was not really worried about the risk of dying, the idea that his behavior might lead him to lose his driver's license really bothered him. He noted that his children were always threatening to call the Department of Motor Vehicles and have them take away his license because of his age.

Marvin did not take these threats seriously, as he believed that as long as he could pass the driver's test, his license was safe no matter what his age. But the psychiatrist had inadvertently provided him with a new fear, and in the context of that, the motivation to change. While he had initially started treatment for hoarding at the request of his internist, over time, he began to value the sessions for themselves, and enjoyed finding ways to usefully repurpose the clutter that had pervaded his home. However, Marvin found it harder to give up collecting, as he called it. Although he logically recognized that he should at least stop driving with his doors open in order to scoop things up from the roadside, he could not find the will to do it, even with the help of therapy. The combination of ongoing treatment with a successful outcome in other aspects of his life, combined with the very real fear of losing his independence, provided the motivation that Marvin needed for change.

HOW WELL DOES PSYCHOTHERAPY FOR HOARDING DISORDER WORK?

Perhaps because the scientists who began the study of hoarding disorder in the early 1990s were psychologists and social workers, psychotherapeutic approaches to treat HD are significantly more advanced than are pharmacologic approaches. Perhaps for this reason, the evidence also suggests that the use of psychotherapy in the treatment of HD is more effective than the use of medications. In addition, refinements to the basic therapeutic techniques aimed at improving access to care or enhancing treatment outcomes are continually being developed. Studies have examined the utility of both individual and group treatment for HD; other research has been conducted to explore modifications and enhancements to the standard CBT plus MI approach described above.

INDIVIDUAL CBT-BASED PSYCHOTHERAPY

Studies researching the outcomes of individual psychotherapy for hoarding disorder suggest that this approach results in between 20%–38% improvement in symptoms, with a 28% reduction in hoarding symptom severity, on average (Mathews et al., 2018; Mathews, Uhm, et al., 2016; Thompson, Fernandez de la Cruz, Mataix-Cols, & Onwumere,

2017). These studies differed in several ways, including the number of CBT sessions conducted (range of 20 to 40 visits), whether home visits were or were not included, and in one case, which is discussed in more detail later in this chapter, whether additional modules aimed at addressing cognitive problems was included. The improvement rate results for HD-specific individual therapy are remarkably consistent across studies, despite differences in study design, characteristics of the participants (such as older adults, adults with intellectual disability), or baseline hoarding symptom severity.

However, as is the case with most treatments, not all participants in the studies of individual psychotherapy showed significant improvement. In general, only about one third of people participating in individual psychotherapy across most studies achieved clinically meaningful improvement in their hoarding symptoms, and very few achieved functional remission. Most continued to experience significant problems with hoarding at the end of treatment.

GROUP CBT-BASED PSYCHOTHERAPY

Group treatment for hoarding disorder typically follows a similar structure to that seen in individual psychotherapy. The major exception is that in group therapy, between 8 and 12 individuals meet weekly with a therapist instead of participating in one-on-one sessions. Because this means less time for attention focusing on any individual group member, a key aspect of group treatment is effective facilitation, that is, helping to ensure that everyone has a chance to participate in an equitable fashion.

Studies examining the utility of group treatment for HD indicate that the results are similar to those for individual treatment, although there is more variability in outcomes between individual studies. Hoarding symptom severity was reduced by between 13% and 30%, with most studies reporting between 22% and 28% improvement (Mathews et al., 2018; Mathews, Uhm, et al., 2016; Moulding, Nedeljkovic, Kyrios, Osborne, & Mogan, 2017).

The structure of the group treatments varied somewhat more than those of the individual treatments, perhaps explaining some of the variability in outcomes. The number of sessions were typically fewer than the studies examining individual treatment, and ranged from 16 to 20. Some studies included home visits, while others did not, and one study included not only four home visits, but also four visits by a non-clinician coach who helped participants with their discarding assignments (J. Muroff, Steketee, Bratiotis, & Ross, 2012).

A meta-analysis that included data from all of the available studies of both group and individual psychotherapy suggested that a higher number of treatment sessions and more home visits, but not treatment modality (e.g., individual vs. group), were associated with greater reduction in symptoms (D. F. Tolin, Frost, R.O., Steketee, & Muroff, 2015). In addition, the data from the meta-analysis suggested that studies with high proportions of women or those with younger participants tended to show higher rates of improvement, although subsequent studies have not confirmed these findings (Mathews et al., 2018).

The good news arising from these studies is that, while not everyone benefits equally, CBT-based psychotherapy is clearly beneficial, at least for some individuals with hoarding disorder. Its effectiveness appears to be robust to variability in the structure of the treatment. That is, while more treatment sessions and the presence of home visits somewhat improved outcomes, the degree of improvement seen by these additions was relatively small. In addition, two naturalistic studies in which treatment was provided for clinical rather than for research reasons suggest that targeted psychotherapy for HD can be effective even without highly trained research-oriented therapists providing the treatment (Mathews, Uhm, et al., 2016; Moulding et al., 2017).

In fact, because of the strong evidence that CBT-based, clinician-led psychotherapy for HD is effective in a variety of settings, a therapists' guide, a group facilitator's guide, and a workbook for patients that corresponds to these guides, has been published by the Treatments That Work series and are available for general use (J. Muroff, Underwood, P., Steketee, G., 2014; G. Steketee, Frost, R.O., 2014; G Steketee, Frost, R.O., 2014).

MODIFIED CBT APPROACHES TO TREATMENT FOR HOARDING

Over the years, several adjustments to the core CBT+MI-based treatment for HD have been developed. In addition to home visits or non-clinician coaches, other changes to the standard approaches have included the use of lay individuals who have lived experience of hoarding disorder, rather than clinicians, as group facilitators; the addition of a cognitive rehabilitation component; and the incorporation of a type of therapy called compassion focused therapy, or CFT. Table 9.1 lists the different types of psychotherapy that have some evidence base behind their use, and details the characteristics and typical response rates for each.

PEER-FACILITATED TREATMENT

Because there are a limited number of clinicians with expertise in treating hoarding disorder, finding effective approaches that do not rely on clinician experts has been a high priority. Although self-help approaches, which are detailed in Chapter 10, are one option for individuals who do not have access to appropriate clinical care, peer-facilitated treatment and support groups have emerged as a promising alternative to clinician-led groups or individual psychotherapy.

In peer-facilitated treatment, or PFT, individuals who have lived experience of hoarding disorder, ideally those who have undergone (or are still undergoing) treatment, act as group facilitators. Training in group facilitation and in the basic concepts of CBT-based treatment for HD are provided in the form of a two-day workshop. Peer-facilitated treatment uses the same workbook for participants that is used in clinician-led group treatment for HD, and a facilitator's guide has been developed and is freely available from the authors Lee Shuer and Randy Frost on their mutual support website (https://www.mutual-support .com/the_buried_in_treasures_workshop). Mr. Shuer and his team also offer the facilitators' workshop for interested individuals.

Studies indicate that PFT is as effective as clinician-led group treatment for hoarding disorder (Mathews et al., 2018; Mathews, Uhm, et al., 2016; D. F. Tolin et al., 2015). In a large RCT of group psychotherapy that compared group CBT to PFT in over 300 individuals with HD (Mathews et al., 2018), participants who were randomly assigned to peer-facilitated treatment showed as much improvement by the end of the study as those who were randomly assigned to clinician-led therapy (Mathews et al., 2018). The average percent reduction in hoarding symptom severity was essentially equal between the two groups (25.6% for PFT and 27.7% for CBT). Perhaps more importantly, more than half of the participants in both groups experienced clinically meaningful improvement, and more than a third had their symptoms decrease to below the clinical cutoff for hoarding disorder, in other words, to functional remission (Mathews et al., 2018).

In contrast to the previous findings, neither gender nor age was associated with response to treatment in this study. Instead, the only characteristic of the individual participants that predicted a better treatment outcome across both groups was higher hoarding severity at the beginning of treatment. While this may seem paradoxical initially, and is in contrast to a previous, much smaller study that found the reverse (J. Muroff, Steketee, Frost, R.O., & Tolin, 2014), it is not actually all that surprising. Individuals with more severe symptoms at baseline actually have more room to improve than do those with milder symptoms, and thus received additional benefit from the treatment.

Other predictors of symptom improvement identified by this study represent characteristics of the treatment rather than of the individual, and these differed somewhat by treatment type. Although the underlying structure and content of both the CBT and the PFT groups were similar, the groups differed in the manner in which they were conducted. The clinicians facilitating the CBT groups asked participants to sign a treatment contract at the beginning of the first session. This contract asked each participant to agree to attend a minimum number of sessions, arrive to the sessions on time, and complete the weekly assigned homework (Uhm et al., 2016).

The PFT groups, in contrast, collaboratively arrived at and agreed to adhere to a "comfort agreement," which outlined the general expectations for each participant. The facilitators, who were not professional therapists but rather members of the community who also suffered from hoarding disorder, aided in the development of this document but did not dictate its content.

Similarly, the facilitators of the PFT groups encouraged the participants to identify and make use of a "clutter buddy." A clutter buddy is someone, typically a friend or family member, who agrees to help hold the participant accountable and encourage them when they struggle to complete their homework for the group. In contrast, the therapists in the CBT group assigned clutter buddies such that group members were partnered with each other in pairs or trios as mutual clutter buddies. Participants were allowed to refuse to participate in the clutter buddy component of treatment, but it was an "opt out" rather than the "opt in" employed by the PFT facilitators.

As expected, for both the CBT and the PFT groups, higher rates of homework completion were associated with better outcomes at the end of the 15 or 16 weeks of treatment. For the PFT groups, which had a less restrictive attendance policy and did not require clutter buddies, attending more group sessions and having a clutter buddy were also associated with better outcomes. These variables were not associated with treatment improvement in the CBT group. Although these findings require confirmation in additional studies, they do suggest that more active participation in treatment, as defined by rates of group attendance, completion of homework, and active use of a clutter buddy, are important predictors of treatment response. Therefore, individuals who are planning to conduct group treatments for HD, whether they are mental health professionals or peers with lived experience of hoarding, should consider incorporating the more structured methods used in the CBT arm of this study to assist participants with motivation and compliance with treatment in order to optimize treatment gains.

HOW LONG ARE TREATMENT GAINS MAINTAINED?

Only two studies have evaluated the durability of treatment response to psychotherapy for HD. One of these studies examined the outcomes at one year posttreatment for 31 people who completed 26 weeks of clinician-led individual CBT for hoarding disorder (J. Muroff et al., 2014). The other examined the outcomes at between 3 months and 2 years (mean of 14 months) after the end of treatment in over 200 of the participants in the RCT comparing 15 weeks of group PFT to 16 weeks of group clinician-led CBT (Mathews et al., 2018).

Both of these studies found that, overall, the gains made in psychotherapy were maintained for at least a year, on average. For both the CBT and the PFT treatment groups, there were no significant differences between hoarding severity scores as measured by the Saving-Inventory, Revised (SI-R) immediately posttreatment and at longitudinal follow up a year later (Mathews et al., 2018; J. Muroff et al., 2014). For example, mean SI-R scores in the RCT went from approximately 65 at pretreatment to about 47 posttreatment. An average of 14 months later, the average SI-R score for participants in this study was approximately 48. In the smaller CBT study, the average pretreatment SI-R scores were also around 65, with posttreatment scores dropping to an average of 46. At follow-up between 3 and 12 months later, the SI-R score for this participant group remained low, with an average score of 45.

WHAT PREDICTS SUCCESS IN TREATMENT?

Although both of these studies indicated that treatment response was maintained for many individuals as far as two years after treatment, the predictors of treatment response at 1 year following treatment differed between studies. The smaller study that examined clinician-led CBT found that only gender was associated with long-term treatment outcome—being male was associated with a poorer treatment response both immediately following treatment and 1 year later (J. Muroff et al.,

2014). Unfortunately, however, there were only six men participating in this study, making it hard to generalize the findings.

The second study, which had a larger sample size, found that gender was not associated with treatment outcome. Instead, receiving ongoing help with decluttering after taking part in treatment was associated with long-term maintenance of gains for both the CBT and the PFT treatment arms. Ongoing help was defined in many ways in this study, and included attending ongoing drop-in support groups, allowing family members or friends to assist with decluttering, working with a professional organizer, or continuing in formal HD-specific psychotherapy. Results also showed that for the PFT group, but not for the CBT group, having a clutter buddy, attending more group sessions, and completing more of the assigned homework was associated with greater improvement.

The differences between the predictors of treatment outcome for the CBT and PFT groups are most likely due to the differences in how the groups were conducted. As discussed, the facilitators of the CBT groups were clinicians and they used the tools that many therapists employ to help clients effectively engage in treatment, including setting clear expectations through the use of treatment contracts. The PFT facilitators utilized a collaborative style that engaged participants in a discussion of what the rules for participation should be rather than predefining them for the group.

Given the fairly strong differences in style, and the fact that the participants were randomly assigned to one of the two types of treatment instead of being allowed to choose, it is all the more remarkable that the two types of treatment were equally successful. Interestingly, both types of treatment were deemed acceptable to the participants—the majority did not express a strong preference for one style over the other, either before they began treatment or after they completed treatment. Taken together, the results of these studies suggest that PFT is a viable option for treatment of HD, and that, even with a relatively short treatment time (15 or 16 group sessions spread over 20 weeks), group psychotherapy for HD can be effective.

ADDING COGNITIVE REHABILITATION TO CBT

Because individuals with HD often report difficulties with categorization, organization, attention, and memory, one group of clinical experts in HD has explored adding techniques aimed at addressing these problems to CBT-based treatments for hoarding disorder. This group has tested a form of cognitive rehabilitation plus CBT for hoarding disorder in older adults with HD, with good results.

This intervention is termed *CREST,* which stands for *C*ognitive *R*ehabilitation and *E*xposure/*S*orting *T*herapy. The idea behind CREST is that neurocognitive dysfunction, although relatively subtle on formal testing, may limit someone's ability to effectively participate in hoarding-specific treatment. CREST consists of 24 to 26 individual treatment sessions and eliminates the cognitive restructuring piece of CBT entirely. However, other components, including the behavioral sessions that focus on practice sorting and discarding, the training that helps to reduce acquiring, and the psychoeducation session(s) are retained. Instead of cognitive restructuring, which is usually the "C" in CBT, the first six sessions of CREST are dedicated to compensatory cognitive training (Ayers et al., 2014).

Compensatory cognitive training is a structured manualized cognitive rehabilitation approach to help improve cognitive flexibility, categorization, problem solving, and prospective memory that was initially developed for individuals with psychotic disorders (Twamley, Vella, Burton, Heaton, & Jeste, 2012). Compensatory cognitive training is very practical in nature, and makes use of tools such as daily calendars, to-do-lists, prioritization lists, goal-setting, reminder tools, brainstorming, and the designation of specific places for important items (Ayers, Dozier, Twamley, et al., 2018).

CREST has been tested in an open trial of 11 older adults with HD and in a randomized controlled trial comparing CREST to case management in 58 older adults with HD (Ayers, Dozier, Twamley, et al., 2018; Ayers, Saxena, et al., 2014). The open-label study consisted of 24 sessions. In between 3 and 6 of those sessions, clinicians went to participants' homes to assist the participants with practicing the assigned discarding exposures.

Participants in the open trial were between 60 and 80 years old and had moderate hoarding symptoms at baseline. All 11 completed the treatment, with no attrition, suggesting that it was a well-tolerated intervention. Hoarding-severity symptoms improved by about 37% on average following treatment. Eight of the 11 participants had at least a 35% improvement in symptoms, and were considered to be responders, while 3 were considered to be partial responders, with 23%–25% treatment response. Notably, the three partial responders had the highest pretreatment hoarding symptom severity scores in the group, and two of the three also had co-occurring OCD (Ayers, Saxena, et al., 2014).

The structure of the therapy in the randomized clinical trial of CREST was similar to that of the open-label trial, but also included two additional sessions dedicated to relapse prevention and maintenance of gains. Home visits were also an integral part of this study. The last two discarding sessions (Sessions 23 and 24) were also longer—while most sessions were an hour long, these sessions, which took place in the participants' home, lasted between 2 and 4 hours, and were focused on advanced and prolonged exposure to sorting and discarding (Ayers, Dozier, Twamley, et al., 2018).

Treatment response in this study was defined as achieving subclinical levels of hoarding symptoms, defined as a score of 40 or less on the SI-R, a score of 4 or less on the CIR, or a score of much or very much improved on a 5 point scale that assesses degree of clinical improvement independent of disorder). Participants were older adults, with a mean age of 67, and 70% were women. Pretreatment SI-R scores were somewhat lower than in the previously described studies, with a mean of 58, consistent with moderate impairment. Attrition was somewhat higher in the RCT than in the open-label study, with approximately 20% of participants in the CREST treatment arm and 30% of participants in the case management control arm dropping out before the end of treatment.

Interestingly, participants in both treatment arms showed improvement pre-to posttreatment. The results for the CREST group are described first; the results for the case management group are described next. Participants in the CREST arm demonstrated a 38% improvement, on average, with a mean SI-R score of 46 at 3 months (mid treatment) and a mean SI-R score of 35 at 6 months (posttreatment). Sixty-four percent of participants in the CREST treatment were classified as responders at the end of treatment, with SI-R scores of less than 40. Average SI-R scores continued to be subclinical at 9- and 12-month follow ups (3 to 6 months after the end of treatment), with mean SI-R scores of 36 and 41, respectively.

Because CREST was specifically designed to address potential underlying neurocognitive impairments among individuals with HD, the research team also evaluated the effect of cognitive compensatory training on neuropsychological functioning. Most measures of cognitive functioning did not change following 26 sessions of either CREST or case management. However, three areas of executive functioning did improve with CREST. These were cognitive flexibility, inhibition, and task switching (Ayers, Davidson, Dozier, & Twamley, 2019). As discussed in Chapter 7, there is emerging evidence that impaired cognitive flexibility may be a core feature of HD. Thus, any treatment, such as CREST, which improves cognitive flexibility while also specifically addressing a patient's difficulties with discarding and acquisition, is likely to be of particular benefit for individuals with HD. Unfortunately, it appears that targeting cognitive flexibility alone (that is, without the exposure to and practice of sorting and discarding) is not effective in the treatment of hoarding disorder (DiMauro, 2014).

CASE MANAGEMENT FOR HOARDING

Case management, the form of treatment administered to the comparison group in the CREST RCT, is the most widely available intervention for hoarding disorder. In the community, case management is typically performed by nurses or social workers who specialize in working with older adults. In the CREST study, case management for participants in the control arm was conducted by nurses with geriatric expertise. These individuals provided 26 sessions of case management, which included evaluating safety and health, helping to provide linkages to appropriate medical care or other identified needs, providing support and advocacy and helping to mitigate safety problems. Case managers were specifically instructed not to help with decluttering or to provide other forms of intervention for hoarding, including CBT or cognitive rehabilitation. Case managers were allowed to move items from one location to another to mitigate an immediate danger to the participant's safety, but were not allowed to remove the items from the home (Ayers, Dozier, Twamley, et al., 2018).

Although designed to be a control (placebo) arm for the RCT, and thus not expected to demonstrate substantial levels of improvement, participants in the case management arm also showed significant reduction in hoarding symptoms, although not at the same magnitude as those in the CREST arm. Those who received case management showed an average 25% reduction in symptoms at the end of the 26 sessions. As with the CREST group, these gains were maintained for the 6 months following treatment. Perhaps most importantly, 42% of participants in the case management group improved sufficiently such that their hoarding symptoms were considered to be subthreshold at the end of treatment (SI-R scores less than 40).

ADDING COMPASSION FOCUSED THERAPY TO CBT

As discussed, cognitive compensatory training seeks to improve outcomes for HD by embedding treatment for potential neurocognitive deficits within the standard CBT structure. Another approach to improving on the original CBT-based treatments for HD is to focus not on cognition, but on the underlying problems with emotion regulation and emotional attachment that seem to co-occur with HD.

Compassion focused therapy (CFT) was developed in the mid 2000s by Dr. Paul Gilbert (Gilbert, 2010). The premise behind CFT is that human beings evolved in a social context, and that, for this reason, they are physiologically wired to respond to emotional stimuli, and in particular, positive caring stimuli. For some patients seeking psychotherapy, purely cognitive or behavioral approaches may not be effective because the emotional content that is triggered by cognitive restructuring techniques may be negative in nature rather than positive. In particular, shame, anger, and despair are emotional responses that may be inadvertently generated in response to CBT approaches. These emotions are specifically addressed by the techniques incorporated in CFT.

Compassion focused therapy uses a variety of techniques to address the feelings that may arise during therapy and impair progress in treatment. These practices include imagery, mindfulness, rhythmic breathing exercises, as well as emotion regulation training, and work to encourage self-compassion and to de-shame the problem at hand. This approach has been used to treat a variety of psychiatric disorders including posttraumatic stress disorder, depression, and eating disorders, and it has been shown to improve distress tolerance, disorder-specific negative cognitions, and physiological measures of emotion regulation (Chou et al., 2019).

The rationale for using CFT in the treatment of hoarding disorder arose from two observations. The first was that the existing cognitive behaviorally based approaches resulted in clinically significant improvement for only a subset of individuals; they were not effective or were only minimally effective for a substantial number of people. The second observation was that, although the overt symptoms may have improved with treatment, many of the underlying HD-related dysfunctions posited by Frost and Hartl (avoidance and difficulty making decisions, information processing deficits, emotional attachment to possessions, and hoarding-related beliefs regarding responsibility for and need to control objects) did not improve with treatment (Chou et al., 2019).

Only one study of CFT in hoarding disorder has been published to date (Chou et al., 2019). Rather than examining CFT as a first-line treatment, this study compared a modified CBT-based treatment that included components of both CFT and additional exposure and prac- tice with sorting and discarding to a second round of CBT. Participants in this study were recruited from those who had already completed a course of 15–16 weeks of group CBT for HD in the RCT discussed ear- lier that compared group CBT to group PFT.

To qualify for entry into the study on compassion focused therapy for HD, participants were required to be non- or partial-responders to the previous round of treatment, meaning that they had an SI-R hoarding symptom severity score of greater than 41 at the time of study enroll- ment. Baseline hoarding symptoms and other characteristics did not differ between the two groups at entry into treatment. Both acceptabil- ity of treatment and treatment outcomes were examined.

This study found that CFT was both well-liked by participants and effective in reducing hoarding symptoms. All of those in the CFT group rated the treatment as good or excellent, while 79% of those in the CBT group rated the treatment as good or excellent. Completion rates indicated that, at least as a second round of treatment, CFT was preferred over CBT. While 72% of the 20 participants in the CFT group completed treatment, only 37% of the 20 participants in the CBT group completed treatment.

In addition to being highly acceptable to the participants, CFT for hoarding disorder also resulted in significant improvement in a variety of hoarding symptom domains. More than 75% of the CFT participants were treatment responders, such that their hoarding symptom severity dropped to subthreshold levels (defined as SI-R scores <42) following treatment. Overall hoarding severity improved by 33%, and significant improvement was seen in all three of the specific symptom domains, including difficulty discarding, clutter, and excessive acquisition.

Participants who completed a second round of HD-specific CBT also showed improvement, but to a much lower degree. Only 23% of the participants who completed the CBT group were treatment respond- ers. Overall hoarding severity dropped by 15% in this treatment arm, and of the specific hoarding-related symptom domains, only excessive acquisition improved significantly. Difficulty discarding and clutter improved only to a small degree, or did not improve at all.

SO HOW MIGHT COMPASSION FOCUSED THERAPY WORK TO IMPROVE CBT-BASED TREATMENT FOR HD?

Although the answer to this is not entirely clear, and it is important to note that no randomized clinical trials of CFT have yet been conducted, exploratory analyses of the pilot study might provide some clues. While participating in a second round of CBT resulted in improved decision making and decreased self-shame, participating in CFT appeared to have an impact on a much broader array of hoarding-specific dysfunctions.

As with the participants in the second round of CBT, those in the CFT arm also experienced improved decision making and decreased self-shame. However, participants in the CFT group also showed decreased avoidance, decreased self-criticism, decreased shame when making an error, and improved distress tolerance (Chou et al., 2019). Notable improvements in these domains were not seen among participants in the CBT arm. Self-criticism and shame are commonly found feelings among individuals with HD (Chou, Tsoh, et al., 2018). Although preliminary, and requiring replication in an RCT, this study suggests that directly targeting these and other symptoms of poor distress tolerance may provide additional benefits over and above the traditional elements of cognitive restructuring and exposure to and practice with sorting and discarding.

CRITICAL TIME INTERVENTION FOR SEVERE HOARDING DISORDER

Another form of case management that has been examined in the treatment of hoarding disorder is critical time intervention, or CTI. CTI is a case management model that provides support and resources to individuals in a collaborative and flexible manner at a critical time of their lives. This evidence-based approach has been successfully used for other vulnerable populations, including individuals who are at risk of eviction or homelessness due to psychiatric or other problems.

TABLE 9.1: TYPES AND CHARACTERISTICS OF PSYCHOTHERAPEUTIC TREATMENT FOR HOARDING DISORDER

Treatment type	Core elements	Format
CBT	Psychoeducation; cognitive restructuring; motivational interviewing; practice sorting, discarding, and reducing acquisition	Group or individual
PFT	Psychoeducation; cognitive restructuring; practice sorting, discarding, and reducing acquisition	Group
CREST	Psychoeducation; practice sorting, discarding, and reducing acquisition; cognitive rehabilitation	Individual
Case management	Support, advocacy, safety monitoring, linkage with medical providers	Individual
CTI case management	Support, linkage with medical providers, referrals to facilitated support group	Individual
CFT+CBT	Practice sorting, discarding, and reducing acquisition; mindfulness; compassion focused exercises; distress tolerance	Group

Dr. Carolyn Rodriguez and colleagues studied the impact of critical time intervention over the course of 9 months in 14 adults with hoarding disorder who were at acute risk for eviction (Millen et al., 2020). In this study, case managers spent the first 3 months establishing rapport, assessing the risk of eviction, arranging for psychiatric evaluations and coordinating treatment referrals to a peer-facilitated support group, and to medication management, if needed. This initial phase involved face-to-face meetings at least weekly. The subsequent 4 months were focused on increasing independence and reducing the level of engage-

Other relevant factors	Type of Facilitator	Number of sessions	Average symptom improvement (%)
1–4 home visits optional; Clutter buddies assigned from within group	Clinician, usually psychologist	16–26	~28%
Clutter buddies suggested but not assigned or required	Nonprofessional facilitators, typically with lived experience of hoarding disorder	15	27%
3–6 home visits	Clinician, usually psychologist	24–26	38%
Home visits as needed	Clinician, usually nurse or social worker	Weekly for 6 months	25%
Phased intensity of treatment	Clinician, usually nurse or social worker	9 months, variable intensity	25%
As second round of treatment following CBT	Clinician, usually psychologist	16	33%

ment by the case manager. Meetings or check-ins were conducted every other week, and avoidance of relapse was the primary goal. The final 2 months were aimed at optimizing existing support networks to maintain progress. Check-ins were conducted on a monthly basis during this phase. Outcomes were defined both as the reduction in hoarding symptom severity, but also as the utilization of available services.

Eighty percent of the participants (11 of the 14) completed the study, suggesting that it was acceptable to most. As expected for individuals at high risk of eviction from hoarding disorder, baseline hoarding severity symptoms were in the severe range. Of the 14 participants who began the study, 100% attended the peer-facilitated support group at least once, 64% utilized the legal counseling that was offered, 64% accepted help in decluttering their homes, half accepted a psychiatric evaluation, and 43% accepted help in coordinating a support network.

Over the course of the 9 months of intervention, hoarding symptom severity decreased by an average of 25%, which is similar to the reduction in symptoms seen for case management in previous studies (Ayers, Dozier, Twamley, et al., 2018). Most importantly, none of the participants was evicted during the time of the study. Taken together, the studies of case management suggest that modest improvements in symptom severity can be expected, possibly sufficient to prevent eviction in individuals at high risk of losing their home. However, these studies also indicate that this form of intervention is not as successful as more traditional psychotherapeutic interventions, and should only be used when other, more effective, forms of treatment are not available.

SUMMARY

As discussed at the beginning of this chapter, psychotherapy is currently the mainstay of treatment for hoarding disorder. Although there is still a great deal of room for improvement, the currently available forms of psychotherapeutic treatments for HD clearly lead to a reduction of hoarding symptoms for many individuals. The core, and likely most important feature, of psychotherapy for HD is the behavioral component, that is, exposure to and ongoing practice in sorting. However, the addition of specific modules focusing on emotion regulation, distress tolerance, or neurocognitive dysfunction may be beneficial, at least for some individuals.

Chapter 10

Self-Help Options

Although, as discussed in Chapter 9, CBT-based psychotherapy (plus cognitive rehabilitation if available) is the most effective form of treatment for hoarding disorder, not everyone has access to this treatment or is willing to see a mental health care provider or other clinician. There are self-help options that may be of use for individuals who choose not to participate in psychotherapy, or for those who do not have access to hoarding-specific treatment providers. These include options such as participating in internet-based support groups and online chat rooms, as well as joining in-person support groups, working with professional organizers, and using step-by-step workbooks that are similar to those often used by psychotherapists.

INTERNET-BASED SUPPORT GROUPS

With the rise of the internet and the abundance of information available on every topic imaginable, there are increasingly more resources available to help people with hoarding disorder. Merely entering the phrase "help for hoarding" into any internet search engine returns over eight million hits within seconds. Clicking onto any of these links leads to information from reputable professional and advocacy sources such as the American Psychiatric Association (APA), International OCD Foundation (IOCDF), the Anxiety and Depression Association of America (ADAA), and Mayo Clinic. Unfortunately, such a search will also link to less reputable sites.

Some of the sites identified by an internet search are run by professional clean-out or junk-removal companies, while others advertise residential treatment programs or private therapy practices. Still other websites are for online support groups, some of which are moderated by therapists or other clinicians and some by individuals with hoarding disorder or by family members of those with hoarding. Many of these organizations and groups are legitimate, and do in fact have expertise in effectively helping individuals with hoarding disorder, but some are not.

HOW DOES SOMEONE FIND EFFECTIVE HELP FOR HOARDING DISORDER ONLINE?

Fortunately, many of the professional websites that are dedicated to mental health topics have a section devoted to helping people locate resources. Advocacy organizations like the APA, the IOCDF, and the ADAA maintain lists of helpful resources, including those on the internet that they have vetted for accuracy. In some cases, these organizations also maintain lists of therapists and support groups, searchable by geographic location or specialty, who work with individuals and families who suffer from hoarding disorder.

12-STEP GROUPS

Another option, both in person and increasingly online, are 12-step groups for hoarding and cluttering. These groups, which are run by a parent organization called the Clutterers' Anonymous World Service Organization (https://clutterersanonymous.org/), are modeled after the original Alcoholics' Anonymous, or AA, 12-step program. These groups are called 12-step facilitation groups because they propound a stepped, facilitated approach to recovery.

The 12 steps of Clutterers' Anonymous are similar to those used in AA. They include (1) admitting powerlessness over clutter, (2) believing in a higher power that can provide help, (3) deciding to turn over control to that higher power, (4) conducting an inventory, both of one's flaws and assets, and more practically, of one's belongings, (5) admitting to the higher power and to other people the nature and extent of the cluttering problem, (6) being willing to let go of the clutter, (7) asking the higher power for help in removing the obstacles to decluttering, (8) listing the people that have been harmed by one's cluttering and related behaviors, (9) making amends to those people, (10) admitting to being wrong, (11) prayer and meditation, and (12) spiritual awakening.

As can be seen in the language of the 12 steps, both AA and Clutterers' Anonymous are based on spiritual principles, that is, that an individual is powerless over their problem, and as such, the problem or problems will not improve until the individual gives over control to a higher power (e.g., God, the Universe, or another, more personally defined higher power). Individuals who have successfully completed the program act as sponsors to newer members who are still actively struggling. The fundamental belief behind AA and other 12-step groups is that recovery requires a spiritual awakening, which is achieved by working through the 12 steps of the program with their sponsor's help.

AA has a long history, and over 25 years of data suggest that it is very effective in helping people with alcohol use disorders achieve and maintain sobriety (Kelly, 2017; Kelly, Stout, Magill, Tonigan, & Pagano, 2010). In some randomized clinical trials, AA and similar 12- step facilitated groups were more effective in helping people to remain abstinent from alcohol for a year or more than were cognitive behavioral therapy or motivational interviewing/motivational therapy (Kelly, 2017).

The mechanisms by which 12-step groups for alcohol and other addictions work are also relatively well understood. The key mechanisms of change are (a) helping people change their social networks in such a way as to enhance their ability to stay sober, (b) improving coping skills and self-efficacy, and (c) increasing and maintain motivation to stay sober across time. Interestingly, although inherently a spiritual approach, AA does not seem to effect change and increase abstinence through mechanisms related to spirituality, except perhaps for a subgroup of those with severe alcoholism (Kelly, 2017; Kelly et al., 2010). For AA to be successful, it is not necessary for someone to believe in God or a higher power. It is only necessary to actively participate in all components of the program.

In addition to AA, there are also 12-step groups for a variety of other forms of addiction or other related problems, including Narcotics' Anonymous, Adult Children of Alcoholics, Overeaters' Anonymous, and Gamblers' Anonymous. Some of these, such as Narcotics Anonymous, are well studied, and, like AA, have been shown to be of benefit to at least a subgroup of individuals. For others, there is little to no data available for their impact.

Unfortunately, Clutterers' Anonymous falls into the latter category. There have as yet been no published studies examining whether a 12-step approach is helpful for people with hoarding disorder. This is not to say that Clutterers' Anonymous is not helpful, it is just that it has not been formally studied. For some individuals, particularly those who are drawn to the 12-step approach, a facilitated group with built-in support may well be of benefit, especially if no more-organized formal treatment options are available.

SOCIAL MEDIA

Increasingly, conversations among people with similar interests, beliefs, or problems are taking place on social media and in online chatrooms. Hoarding and cluttering are no exception. Many of the major social media platforms and chatrooms, including Facebook, Reddit, Discord, Meetup.com, and Wireclub have hoarding-related groups. These groups are typically not facilitated but instead are informal discussions between individuals who are suffering from a common problem and seeking community, support, or guidance.

Informal chatrooms and support groups on social media should be distinguished from online support groups that are run by professional clean-out or junk-removal companies. The organizations sponsoring these groups, which have names like CleanOutYourJunk.com (not a real name), are often looking for clients.

While these sponsored support groups may in fact be helpful to some individuals, they may also be predatory, as the motivation behind them is typically commercial in nature. Therefore, a thorough investigation of the nature of the group and the individuals behind it, is important, as is the case with any resource found on the internet that is not recommended by a trusted, known, and reputable source.

Only one study has examined the effectiveness of internet support groups for hoarding disorder (J. Muroff, Steketee, Himle, & Frost, 2010). This study examined the impact of a private hoarding and cluttering support group that was hosted on the health groups section of Yahoo.com. The Yahoo support group was developed and moderated by people who themselves suffered from hoarding disorder in the late 1990s in an attempt to remedy the problem of limited access to therapists and other clinicians with expertise in treating hoarding disorder.

It is important to note that this support group differed from the majority of online support groups in a number of ways. First, participation was by invitation only following a formal application procedure. Only people with hoarding disorder were eligible for participation—family members, friends, professional organizers, clinicians, researchers, and other individuals who did not themselves suffer from hoarding were not allowed into the group.

Second, members were required to actively work on their hoarding, and to post their behavioral goals and their progress (or lack of progress) on a regular basis. Individuals who needed time away from the group could request a "breather," but otherwise, if a member fell into a prolonged period of inactivity, they were removed from participation.

Third, the format of the group was structured according to the cognitive behavioral principles described in Chapter 9 and included tools for cognitive restructuring, sorting, and practice discarding. The leaders and members supported one another in these efforts, and the leaders regularly sought input from clinicians with expertise in treating in hoarding disorder.

Individuals who agreed to participate in the study were either active in the support group, which was limited to about 100 individuals at any given time, or were on the waiting list for entry into the group. Each participant completed a series of questionnaires at the beginning of the study and every 3 months for up to 15 months. These questionnaires included several of the standardized hoarding assessments described in Chapter 3, including the Saving Inventory, Revised (SI-R), and the Clutter Image Rating Scale (CIR).

Hoarding severity was measured at each timepoint, and the percent improvement was calculated. For those participants who were in the active treatment arm, degree of participation in the group, which was calculated as the number of postings that the participant logged during the study period, was also examined.

Did the support group work? The answer to this question is "sort of." Surprisingly, both the people who participated in the facilitated online hoarding support group, and those who were on the waiting list had some reductions in their hoarding symptoms. For the people on the waitlist, hoarding symptom severity as measured by the SI-R was moderate to severe at baseline (mean score of 70), and decreased by an average of about 5 points, or by about 7%, over the course of 6 months. The CIR score, which is a visual assessment of the amount of clutter in the home, did not change significantly for those individuals who were on the waitlist.

Participants in the active treatment arm who had joined the online group just prior to entering the research study had similar outcomes. These individuals had hoarding severity scores that were similar to those in the waitlist (mean SI-R score of 65) at the baseline assessment, indicating moderately severe problems. Their SIR scores decreased by 6 points, or about 9%, after 6 months of participation. Unlike the people on the waitlist, CIR scores for recent entrants into the support group also decreased after 6 months, by about 18%.

Interestingly, people who had been in the group for a while before entering the research study showed the least improvement. As expected, these individuals had lower hoarding severity scores at the beginning of the study (mean SI-R scores of 55.5) than did either participants on the waitlist or those who had recently joined the group, perhaps indicating that they had already been somewhat successful in their efforts to declutter. However, at the end of the 6 months, their symptom severity scores had only decreased by an average of 2.6 points, or less than 5%, suggesting that additional time in the group had a relatively small impact.

Only a small number of participants completed assessments at all five time points over 15 months. The analyses of symptom change in this subgroup suggested that the longer-term outcomes for those participants who stuck with the group for a year or more were somewhat more promising. The average hoarding severity score for this small group of participants was lower at the first measurement than it was for the larger cohort (mean SI-R of 56.6, which is mild to moderate hoarding, compared to 65–70, which represents moderate to severe hoarding). At each subsequent timepoint following the baseline assessment, the change in hoarding severity was relatively small, in the range of only a few points. However, at the end of 15 months, these individuals had experienced, on average, a 9-point reduction in their SI-R scores, representing a nearly 16% decrease in symptoms.

While these results are not as impressive as the results of the treatment studies described in Chapter 9, they do suggest that, with time and dedication, individuals who do not have access to professional clinical treatment may still be able to help with their hoarding symptoms using online support groups.

PROFESSIONAL ORGANIZERS

Another form of help that does not fall under the rubric of formal treatment, but can nevertheless be useful, is working with a professional organizer. As the name implies, the role of professional organizers is to help their clients organize and more effectively manage specific aspects of their lives. Like doctors and therapists, who specialize in different types of illness or treatment approaches, professional organizers can also specialize. For example, some professional organizers specialize in working with clients who have attention deficit hyperactivity disorder, while others work with high level executives who must learn how to more effectively multitask to maintain efficiency at work.

Fortunately, some professional organizers focus on helping people who have hoarding disorder, or as it is called in their industry, "chronic disorganization." In fact, there is a professional organization for this subgroup of organizers called the Institute for Challenging Disorganization (ICD). Members of the ICD use approaches that are similar to those employed by therapists who specialize in treating hoarding disorder, and in fact, many professional organizers who belong to the ICD work closely with clinicians.

The ICD has independently developed a definition of chronic disorganization that is outlined in Table 10.1. The first two components of chronic disorganization align closely with Criteria A (persistent difficulty in discarding items) and C (accumulation of possessions that congest and clutter living spaces) from the *DSM-5* definition of hoarding disorder. Interestingly, the additional components of the ICD definition of chronic disorganization capture some of the ancillary symptoms that are not part of the formal diagnosis but are known to frequently co-occur with hoarding disorder.

TABLE 10.1: DEFINITION OF CHRONIC DISORGANIZATION ACCORDING TO THE INSTITUTE FOR CHALLENGING DISORGANIZATION (ICD)

- accumulation of large quantities of objects, documents, papers, or possessions beyond apparent necessity or pleasure
- difficulty parting with things and letting go
- a wide range of interests and many uncompleted projects
- need for visual clues to remind one to take action
- tendency to be easily distracted or lose concentration
- poor time-management skills

Source: Adapted from the Institute for Challenging Disorganization, 2010–2019

WORKBOOKS

Another form of individual self-help for hoarding disorder is the use of structured workbooks. Such workbooks are typically written by experts in the field and are designed to provide information; psychoeducation; and a practical, step-by-step guide to decluttering, reducing acquisition, and discarding.

There are two such workbooks currently available for purchase. These are *Buried in Treasures: Help for Compulsive Acquiring, Saving, and Hoarding* (D. F. Tolin, Steketee,G., Frost, R.O., 2007), written by Drs. David Tolin, Randy Frost, and Gail Steketee, and the second edition of *Treatment for Hoarding Disorder Workbook* (G Steketee, Frost, R.O., 2014), written by Drs. Gail Steketee and Randy Frost.

As can be seen, Gail Steketee and Randy Frost, the two scientists who first formulated the modern concept of hoarding disorder, are authors of both of these workbooks, and as might be expected, the content of the two workbooks is similar. The primary difference is that *Buried in Treasures* was designed to be used by the person with hoarding disorder in the absence of a guiding therapist, while the *Treatment for Hoarding Disorder* workbook was originally designed to be used with the guidance and oversight of a clinician (although it can also be used without a clinician's help). The publication of a facilitator's guide for the *Buried in Treasures* workbook has allowed for the development of effective group treatment that is driven not by clinicians but by people who themselves suffer from hoarding disorder and have undergone treatment. This form of treatment, peer-facilitated treatment, or PFT, was discussed in Chapter 9.

Both workbooks are based on the same principles that form the basis for psychotherapeutic approaches to treating hoarding disorder. These include (a) cognitive behavioral therapy or CBT; (b) approaches aimed at identifying, increasing, and maintaining sources of motivation; and (c) finding and using a support system. Although the language is less technical and more straightforward, the content of the *Buried in Treasures* workbook parallels that of the *Treatment for Hoarding Disorder* workbook.

After explaining what hoarding disorder is and what is known of its causes, these workbooks then contain a section aimed at helping readers determine whether they have hoarding problems, and if so, the impact that hoarding has on their lives, their daily functioning, and their safety. This is followed by chapters that detail practical steps to help the reader work on the two core elements of the program: sorting (and eventually discarding) current possessions; and limiting or eliminating the acquisition of additional unneeded objects, termed *non-acquiring*.

The cognitive elements of these workbooks involve challenging the thoughts and beliefs that underlie the participant's need to keep or acquire a specific item. The authors make liberal use of a common tool in cognitive therapy, the "if/then" statement, which was described in Chapter 9. This type of prompt asks participants to think through their fears of discarding in a structured way, in order to subsequently challenge those fears by actually testing them.

The behavioral elements of the workbooks involve systematically working on the skills of sorting, discarding, and non-acquiring in a graded fashion. The participant writes down their if/then statement in the space provided in the workbook and is then asked to test it and come back to the workbook to write down the outcome. For example, a commonly expressed fear among people with hoarding disorder might be written as follows: "*If* I throw this newspaper away, *then* I will worry about possibly needing the information in it in the future."

After writing the fear down, the participant is then asked to actually throw the newspaper away or recycle it. They then come back to the workbook in a few days and note their responses to discarding, both what they felt immediately after throwing the newspaper away, and what they feel as they are writing a day or two after the exposure. This response is termed the outcome of the test. The participant is then asked to think about the actual outcome and compare it to the fear embodied in the if/then statement. This process thus directs to come to a conclusion about their experience (that is *hopefully* different from the original fear).

In this example, after discarding the newspaper as part of the test, the participant may find that the outcome is different than they anticipated. Instead of worrying about the fate of the newspaper for days, they might find that they worried about needing the information in the newspaper for only a few minutes, or perhaps for an hour or two immediately afterward. The participant is then asked to draw a new conclusion, based on the outcome, about the impact of their discarding the newspaper. The conclusion might sound something like this: "I may be worried about letting something in my house go for a little bit, but ultimately, I do just fine without it. I guess I am more resilient than I thought I was."

THE IMPORTANCE OF A SUPPORT NETWORK

It is not yet known whether certain components of any of the approaches discussed in this book are more important than other components. However, data from peer-facilitated treatment groups, which are discussed in Chapter 9, indicate that receiving support, in particular, receiving targeted support from a nonjudgmental friend or family member or another individual who is going through a similar process of decluttering, often called a "clutter buddy," may be an important contributor to symptom reduction (Mathews et al., 2018).

Support from both a specific individual and from the larger community of sufferers is a common component of many of the treatments discussed here, including clinician-led therapy groups, peer-facilitated treatment groups, 12-step programs such as Clutterer's Anonymous, and the internet-based support groups discussed in this chapter. It is also inherent in the work that professional organizers do with their clients. Regardless of the type of approach that is chosen, finding a nonjudgmental clutter buddy can help to increase motivation and accountability, and is strongly encouraged. The vignette below describes the positive effect that a support system can have on an individual suffering from hoarding disorder.

Thrift Stores, Dumpsters, and College Students

Janice is a 66-year-old woman who came in for evaluation of possible hoarding disorder at the insistence of her two grown daughters, who were concerned that the state of her home was threatening their mother's safety. Janice lived in a university town, had a master's degree in social work, and had recently retired from a long and successful professional career. She presented for the clinical evaluation rather reluctantly, stating that although she knew that she had "a little too much stuff," she didn't really think it was that much of a problem. She knew that her daughters were worried about her, however, so she agreed to an assessment.

Janice explained that she had been a collector for as long as she could remember, but that it never got in the way of her functioning. She typically collected unusual items, and in particular liked things in pairs, such as salt and pepper shakers in unique shapes or styles. After her husband died unexpectedly 15 years previously, she began to visit thrift stores as a way of passing the time. Although she initially just "browsed," Janice rapidly found herself "feeling sorry" for the objects that she saw in the thrift stores, particularly the ones that remained unsold week after week.

Over time, Janice found herself buying more and more of these unwanted objects, especially those that came in pairs, but also many other types of things. Although she had excellent insight, and clearly knew objectively that the things she bought were not alive, and thus didn't have feelings, Janice sheepishly reported feeling that she couldn't stand the idea that they were unwanted and unused. Once she got her purchases home, however, she admitted that she put them away somewhere, and never really looked at them again.

When queried about the impact that her collecting had on her life, Janice initially said that it really wasn't a problem. When asked more specifically about potential ways that collecting and keeping these items might affect her, it became clear to the treatment provider and to Janice, that her behaviors were in fact causing problems. For example, most of the surfaces in her home were covered with objects. She could no longer use her kitchen or dining room tables, nor the chairs in her living room, because of the boxes and bags stacked on top of them. Her stove and kitchen countertops had piles of dishware—more than she could ever use—all purchased from thrift shops.

Although Janice's floors were clear of clutter, she had items piled on the old-fashioned heaters in her home and on the stovetop. She had difficulty finding a clear place to sit to eat dinner, and she often would perch on the edge of a chair to eat, rather than moving the items that occupied it. Finally, Janice admitted that she was spending more money to buy and "rescue" the thrift shop items than she could really afford, and in fact was having use her savings in order to pay her bills.

At the end of the initial appointment with the therapist, Janice said, "I guess, after all this discussion, I can see that I really do have a problem. My daughters were right. But what do I do about it?" After a thorough discussion of the options, Janice decided that she did not want to pursue either therapy or medications. She felt that with a bit of external support she could handle the problem herself. She was also not interested in working with a professional organizer, noting that she would feel ashamed of the state of her house, and that she was afraid that she could not afford the fees that such a professional would charge. However, she was willing to consider the idea of having someone come to her home to help her declutter. A plan was devised that involved having Janice work with a couple of college students that she hired on an hourly basis specifically for this purpose. Janice agreed to come to the clinic monthly for periodic check-ins, to keep her accountable to "an external authority figure," as she put it. She rented a dumpster, and she and the college students got to work.

Initially, Janice found that the decluttering was hard work. She insisted on personally handling, examining, and sorting every item in her house, even junk mail and garbage. However, over time, she was able to delegate increasingly more to the college students. Together, the team developed a structure that worked. Janice was able to identify categories of items that she felt comfortable trusting the students to handle—these included junk mail, old newspapers, and expired food items. They agreed that, for other categories, such as her thrift shop acquisitions, the students would collect all items of a similar type and put them in one place for Janice to inspect. She would then examine all of the items and decide which of a very limited number that she would keep. The rest would be donated to a women's homeless shelter for use or sale.

Six months after her initial visit, Janice came back to the clinic for her regular monthly check-in and declared success. She had filled up the dumpster and sent it for disposal the day before. The surfaces in her house were mostly clutter-free, and she could once again use them for their intended purposes. She had been able to successfully limit herself to owning only two of each type of item that she had been collecting—two sets of salt shakers, two sets of candle holders, and two sets of dinnerware. Best of all, her daughters were thrilled, and no longer felt reluctant to visit her or worried about her safety.

Janice said that, while she knew that she would always have an impulse to buy "unwanted" items, she had stopped going to thrift stores to browse. Although it was hard at first to give up this long-held habit, she found that the new routine of working with the students on a daily basis also led to a change in the structure of her entire day. After working to declutter for a few hours, the students would take the items to be donated with them when they left, and Janice would first head to the library, and then to the coffee shop. She started taking classes at the university extension, which not only filled her time more productively but also led to new social connections. Janice also felt such a strong connection to the college students that she had hired that she decided to continue working with them on an ongoing basis, to "keep her on track," as she said. The students, who Janice called her "clutter buddies," no longer spent 5 hours a day working with her. Instead, they came for about an hour or two a week, providing an objective set of eyes to identify items that might not be needed, to dispose of or donate these items, and to generally keep the clutter to a minimum.

This arrangement continued to work very well for both Janice and the college students over the following decade. The students, who developed close personal relationships with Janice, took responsibility for identifying their successors from the incoming classes of undergraduates and teaching them the ropes before they graduated from the university and left town. Janice, who had been a professional social worker before retiring, happily wrote letters of recommendation for the students in their pursuit of employment or graduate school and took great pleasure in following their careers. While she continued to struggle with clutter, her home remained livable and safe, and she took great pride in this fact.

Chapter 11

Impact on Family and Friends

As discussed in Chapter 2, hoarding disorder impacts not only the individual, it can also profoundly affect family members and friends, neighbors, and society as a whole. People who share a home with someone struggling with hoarding disorder are usually the most directly impacted, but many others who come into contact or care about these individuals will also be affected. Fortunately, family members and friends can also provide help and support for individuals with HD. This chapter first describes the signs that friends and relatives should look for if they suspect that their loved one suffers from hoarding problems and subsequently outlines some tools that can be used to mitigate the functional impairment caused by hoarding.

WHEN TO SUSPECT HOARDING DISORDER

Although some individuals will freely admit that they suffer from hoarding problems, many people with HD keep their families and friends at arm's length, and often no one knows about their struggles. It is not unusual for family members and friends to find out about their loved one's hoarding only after a significant illness requires that the individual receive in-home assistance. In some cases, when the person with hoarding prohibits anyone from entering their home, hoarding can remain unrecognized until after their death.

There is unfortunately no sure-fire way to know whether your loved one suffers from hoarding disorder short of actually inspecting their home. However, there are some warning signs that, if present, can provide an indication that an individual may have problems with hoarding. These warning signs are detailed next. If two or more of these signs are present, further exploration of other evidence of problematic hoarding may be warranted.

NO ONE IS ALLOWED IN THE HOME

One of the most important warning signs of potential hoarding problems is when an individual does not allow friends or family members, or in extreme cases, repair or maintenance professionals into the home. Individuals with HD are often ashamed of or embarrassed about their clutter, whether or not they consciously realize that they have a problem. When this is the case, they may limit access in order to prevent others' seeing the state of their home. They may suggest meeting at a coffee shop or other venue, or at someone else's home; or they may allow individuals to the entrance of their home but not beyond.

PLUMBING, HEATERS, OR APPLIANCES ARE FREQUENTLY NONFUNCTIONAL

In cases of severe hoarding, the individual's reluctance to allow others into the home extends to repair or maintenance personnel. If a friend or loved one has ongoing problems with broken or nonfunctioning appliances and does not seem to be able to get them repaired—or they are not motivated to get them repaired—hoarding disorder may be a potential cause. This is particularly a warning flag when it involves older individuals.

THE CAR OR WORKPLACE IS ALWAYS CLUTTERED

Symptoms of hoarding disorder are not limited to only one location or situation. People who have difficulty discarding items will not only manifest these problems in the home, they will typically also have these problems at work and in other places. Cars may be filled with papers, boxes, bags, old food containers, or other items, such that only the driver's seat is usable. Desks may be piled high with papers and books and other work-related items such that the workspace cannot be used properly or there is nowhere for a visitor to sit. In extreme cases, papers, books, old computers, and the like may be piled on the floor, leaving only a path to the desk or other workspace. As with the home, in extreme cases, someone suffering from HD may be reluctant to let others enter their offices, workspaces, or cars due to embarrassment or shame.

NO BARGAIN, NO MATTER HOW SMALL OR UNNEEDED, IS EVER REFUSED

Because over 80% of people with hoarding disorder also have problems with excessive acquisition, patterns of buying or collecting unneeded items may also indicate the presence of HD.

Individuals who suffer from HD with excessive acquisition may buy multiple sale items; collect flyers, brochures, and other free informational materials, regardless of their relevance; pick up items discarded on the street or frequent thrift shops. They may spend time on internet-based or cable shopping sites.

Sometimes an individual will purchase or pick up an item, not for themselves, but because they think someone else might benefit from it, or that they may gift it to someone at some point. In these cases, they often do not have a particular individual or event in mind, but rather a more generic feeling that the item will be useful at some undetermined future time.

EXCESSIVE FOCUS ON DETAIL

People with HD often report profound difficulty in organizing their lives, homes, or days, as well as problems in making everyday decisions. While neuropsychological studies of HD indicate that these executive functions are not objectively impaired for most people, these self-reported problems do indicate some type of underlying hoarding-related dysfunction. In some cases, subjective difficulty in organizing or decision making may actually be what is colloquially called a "forest-for-the-trees" problem, that is overwhelming focus on details (the "trees") at the expense of a more global perspective (the "forest").

People with hoarding disorder may be so focused on the details of a particular task that they cannot effectively see or achieve the ultimate end goal. They may believe that they need to obtain *all* potentially relevant information before even beginning a task. The prospect of actually obtaining all of that information, and sometimes the inability to know beforehand what information will actually be needed, can result in functional paralysis.

OVER-INCLUSIVE SPEECH

As discussed in Chapter 7, many people with hoarding disorder exhibit what can be thought of as a verbal form of difficulty discarding, or over-inclusive speech. While it is not a diagnostic criterion for HD and is not seen in every individual suffering from HD, many clinicians believe that over-inclusive speech is almost pathognomonic for hoarding disorder. Individuals who consistently have difficulty in "cutting to the chase," and giving only the relevant details in a conversation may have or be at risk for hoarding disorder.

Over-inclusive speech is essentially another form of the "forest-for-the-trees" symptom in that the person exhibiting it has difficulty seeing or presenting the big picture, and instead focuses on many small or tangential details in an effort to provide the listener with all potentially relevant information.

Of course, not everyone who doesn't like visitors in their home or likes to collect free things has hoarding disorder, just as not everyone with frequently broken appliances does. There are many other reasons for these behaviors or problems, most of them completely unrelated to psychiatric illness. Financial difficulties may underlie someone's bargain hunting or difficulty in repairing their home. Shyness or introversion may prevent people from letting folks into their homes. Therefore, it is important to remember that warning signs discussed in this chapter are just that. They are not intended to be diagnostic of HD, but only to provide clues, in the context of other indications, that problematic hoarding may be present.

THE IMPACT OF HD ON FAMILIES AND FRIENDS

Families and friends are often significantly adversely affected by hoarding disorder, both directly and indirectly. Those who live in the same household as someone who hoards can experience a variety of problems related both to the actual physical environment and to social functioning. Troubles related to the physical environment include difficulty in moving about the home safely, health hazards such as spoiled or rotting food, insect or rodent infestation, fire danger, blocked or inaccessible windows or entrances, and barriers to using furniture and other household goods for their intended purposes due to clutter.

Children may have no clear place to do their homework or may lose their schoolwork or other important items in the clutter. Spouses and roommates may find themselves retreating into one room that is designated as theirs to maintain a small clutter-free space. Families may go without heat or running water or suffer from financial difficulties because the individual with HD spends much of the household's disposable income on acquiring.

Interpersonal problems can include frequent arguments or ongoing conflict with the affected individual about their clutter and its impact, or unwillingness or inability of children, spouses, or roommates to allow friends or other guests into the home. This can result not only in familial conflict, but also in social isolation, both for the person with hoarding disorder, and for others in their household.

Conversely, family and friends who do not live in the hoarding household may be reluctant to enter the home or to bring young children or older people into the home, due to safety concerns or shame. They may express increasing anger or frustration to the person with HD, and in extreme cases, may cut off all contact with them. This not only leads to increasing social isolation for the person with HD but also deprives their family and friends of their company and presence. This is particularly a problem for older adults with HD, as they tend to have fewer people in their social circles due to death, illness, or relocation than do younger individuals.

In Chapter 2 we discussed the impacts of hoarding disorder on the affected individual. These include an increased rate of medical and psychiatric conditions as well as loss of work productivity, financial strain, and social isolation. Studies now suggest that the level of functional impairment is *equally* high among spouses and children of individuals with HD (Drury, Ajmi, Fernandez de la Cruz, Nordsletten, & Mataix-Cols, 2014). Family members of individuals with HD have high levels of frustration, social isolation, family discord, and marital conflict. They also report higher physical and emotional burdens than do family members who care for individuals with Alzheimer's disease, which is in itself indicative of the profound impact that hoarding has on family systems (Drury et al., 2014).

Children and spouses of those who hoard report social isolation and a tendency to withdraw from the outside world (Buscher, Dyson, & Cowdell, 2014). This is due to embarrassment about the condition of their home and reluctance to initiate social interactions because they feel that they cannot reciprocate any invitations that they may receive (Wilbram, Kellett, & Beail, 2008). These family members will also withdraw within the home, often to a safe, relatively clutter-free space, such as a bedroom or office. This tendency, although perhaps adaptive in the short run, can lead to increasing isolation and distance within the family structure.

Family and spousal conflict is also high in hoarding households. Arguments are common and are often instigated because of clutter, failure to discard, excessive buying or acquisition that leads to additional clutter, and financial strain. It is common for their children or siblings to reject an individual suffering from hoarding disorder, further contributing to family discord and social isolation (Buscher et al., 2014). Divorce rates among individuals with hoarding are high, and studies suggest that the rates are higher in this group than in the general population (Archer, 2019; Rees, 2018).

In addition to the problems already mentioned, adult children of individuals with HD report a reluctance to engage in normal social or personal relationships themselves, even once they have left the hoarding household (Rees, 2018). They continue to have ongoing conflicts with their parents and avoid interacting with them. As their parents age, children may worry about the safety and health of their parent and feel helpless to protect or care for them. Somewhat paradoxically, but also understandably, they also worry about and resent the fact that they are likely to be the ones left to clean up and dispose of the hoard after their parent dies (Rees, 2018).

ASSESSING THE FUNCTIONAL IMPACT OF HOARDING ON FAMILY MEMBERS

In part because hoarding affects more than the individual who suffers from hoarding disorder, Dr. David Mataix-Cols and colleagues have developed a scale to assess the functional and emotional impact of hoarding on family members. This scale, the Family Impact Scale for Hoarding (FISH), consists of 16 questions that are measured along a four-point scale ranging from "strongly disagree" to "strongly agree" (A.E. Nordsletten, 2014).

The FISH is divided into two components. The first measures family burden, assessing the degree to which the family member of the person with hoarding has difficulty using the rooms in the home, has had to move away or buy another home, or limits or does not visit the family member at all due to clutter. This component also assesses the degree to which the family member has had to modify their lives, including social life, leisure activities, work, or education due to their relative's hoarding, as well as the loss of productive workdays or income.

The second component assesses accommodation of the hoarding behaviors. These questions ask about avoidance of discarding either their own or their family member's belongings in order to avoid distress, avoidance of discussing discarding or clutter, and cleaning or discarding in secret to avoid causing distress to a family member. Additional questions assess the degree to which a relative will buy unneeded things at the request of the individual with HD, store their clutter, or shop for their relative in an attempt to limit their purchases.

As an assessment tool, the FISH is perhaps most appropriate for research purposes. However, the questions and content areas addressed by this instrument are important for clinicians to keep in mind, particularly given the data suggesting that the negative functional impact of hoarding can be as impairing for a family member as it is for the individual with HD. Family members of individuals with hoarding disorder may themselves benefit from clinical interventions such as referrals for mental health treatment, financial counseling, and social support networks.

WHAT TO DO IF A FAMILY MEMBER WON'T GET HELP

Although much of this book is focused on treating individuals who are seeking help for their problematic hoarding, there is also a substantial subgroup of individuals who do not, will not, or cannot seek help. Fortunately, there are still ways that family members and case managers can help these individuals, who often have severe hoarding symptoms, poor insight, or limited motivation.

If someone who suffers from hoarding disorder refuses to get help, the goal changes from treatment to harm reduction. The goal of the harm reduction approaches is exactly what the name implies, that is, improvement of symptoms to the point where safety and health are not threatened. Development of insight, remission of symptoms, and willingness to seek treatment, although desirable, are not the primary objective.

It is sometimes tempting for family members, case managers, and other concerned individuals to try to solve the hoarding and clutter problems by direct means, particularly when encouragement and referrals to treatment are not working. However, forced clean outs, coercion, threats, and similar methods are not only ineffective, but they inevitably lead to increased conflict, and in the worst outcomes, to mental health or other crises.

It is also important to note that someone with hoarding disorder, regardless of their insight into the problem, may have a different end goal in mind than their family members or others do. For example, they may not want their clutter to be gone, or to stop acquiring unneeded items. Instead, they may wish for their living spaces to be more comfortable or safer, without discarding anything. In other words, they simply may want to be able to live more comfortably *with* their clutter or to have more room for their things.

Rather than fighting about these different goals or endlessly discussing possible solutions to what are essentially different problems, finding areas of mutual agreement is essential. One place to start is with the idea that neither the person who hoards nor their loved ones want any harm to come to the individual. A safer living environment and good or improved health are goals that most people can agree on. Disagreement usually enters when deciding how those goals can and should be achieved—although sometimes there is also argument about what constitutes a "safer" home or "good" health. This is where the principle of harm reduction can be useful.

HARM REDUCTION

Harm reduction is a public health approach that was first developed in the mid 1990s to help slow or stop the spread of HIV and AIDS and other blood-borne diseases among injection drug users (Marlatt, 1996).

This approach arose from the recognition that it was costly, time intensive, and ultimately futile to try to stop injection drug use entirely.

From a population health perspective, minimizing the health hazards of intravenous drug use, for example, by providing clean needles and safe disposal sites for used needles, was a reasonable alternative goal, as it reduced the harmful impact of drug use, both to the individual, whose risk of infection was lowered, and to society as a whole.

Harm reduction approaches can also be used for individuals with problematic hoarding who refuse to seek treatment. Drs. Michael Tompkins and Tamara Hartl have pioneered the use of harm reduction for hoarding disorder, which is detailed in their book *Digging Out* (Tompkins, 2009). *Digging Out* is a practical, step-by-step guide for family members of individuals with HD. However, the principles outlined in it are useful for anyone who works with people who have hoarding disorder, including clinicians, case managers, and landlords.

The core principles of harm reduction for hoarding disorder are summarized in Table 11.1 and are then explained in more detail.

TABLE 11.1: CORE PRINCIPLES OF HARM REDUCTION FOR HOARDING DISORDER

- First, do no harm.
- Address the most critical problems first.
- Harm reduction is a collaborative effort.
- Have patience. Change is slow.
- Set realistic goals.
- The goal is safety, not elimination of the hoarding.

Source: Adapted from Adapted from Tompkins, M. A., & Hartl, T.A. (2009). Digging out: Helping your loved one manage clutter, hoarding, & compulsive acquiring. New Harbinger Publications.

FIRST, DO NO HARM

Superficially, this principle seems straightforward and obvious. However, in reality, it is not always easy to know how to help someone who denies that they need help. As discussed earlier in this section, coercion, threats, forced clean outs, and even begging are not effective. More importantly, these approaches can actually be harmful.

In the worst-case scenarios, forced clean outs, or clean outs done in secret when the person is away from home have led to acute decompensation and psychiatric hospitalization. In the best-case scenario, these approaches can lead to conflict, increased resistance from the individual with hoarding, and impaired or severed relationships. Maintaining a relationship with the person you are trying to help, and in particular, a relationship of trust, is essential for harm reduction to be effective.

ADDRESS THE MOST CRITICAL PROBLEMS FIRST

Sometimes, the hoarding disorder, with its resulting clutter and squalor, are not the most pressing problems. Other problems, sometimes caused by the hoarding and sometimes independent of the hoarding, may take precedence. Psychiatric or medical illness, dementia, or mild cognitive impairment, if present, may need to be addressed in order to even begin a harm reduction approach. Risk of eviction or risk of having a child or elder removed from the home may require intervention from legal or other specialists. Identifying and prioritizing these problems with the input and assistance of the person with hoarding is critical.

HARM REDUCTION IS A COLLABORATIVE EFFORT

It is important to remember that the person with hoarding disorder is an essential member of the team. Obtaining their input and buy-in for the proposed harm reduction plan is an important component of a successful approach. Working together to identify goals that you can agree on, to prioritize those goals, and to come up with a concrete plan and timeline is key. Involving the person with HD in every step of the process mini-mizes resistance and anxiety and improves compliance over time.

HAVE PATIENCE

Remember that hoarding disorder takes decades to develop, and it arises from genetic and other biological factors, not lack of willpower. Recall that if harm reduction is the chosen approach, then that means the person with HD is unwilling or unable to seek treatment or that ear-lier treatment has been ineffective. As is the case with many maladap-tive behaviors, change takes time. Progress will not only be slow—it will also be intermittent, with relapses and setbacks virtually guaranteed. Remember how hard it is to lose weight, quit smoking, exercise rou-tinely, or stick to any number of similar goals. Addressing hoarding will not be easier than addressing these problems; it is likely to be harder.

SET REALISTIC GOALS

Remember that the goal is not to stop the hoarding or to eliminate the clutter. Working to improve the safety and livability of the home, pre-vent or reduce the risk of eviction, or increase financial security are laudable goals, but how does one get there? The idea behind setting real-istic goals is the need for a series of concrete, specific, small, achievable steps toward those goals. Such steps should be measurable and doable. For example, clearing a pathway from the bedroom to the bathroom that is wide enough to navigate safely in limited lighting may be an agreed-upon goal. Identifying what items must be moved, where to place them, and when to move each one are the concrete steps toward that goal.

ELIMINATION OF HOARDING IS NOT THE GOAL

This is the most difficult principle of all to remember and adhere to for many people. The natural tendency of most clinicians and other providers is to want to cure a problem or an illness, and this principle flies in the face of that desire. It may help to remember that, as stated elsewhere in this book, hoarding is a chronic illness, and, as with other chronic illnesses, for most people the goal is maximizing health and safety rather than eliminating the disease.

This does not mean that, at a global level, researchers and clinicians should not strive to identify the causes and find effective treatments for hoarding disorder, with the ultimate goal of preventing or curing it. Instead, harm reduction is a realistic approach, on an individual level, to a complex and difficult problem. Fortunately, it is one that can be employed to improve lives and functioning in the short term, while science and knowledge continue to advance, and treatments continue to evolve and improve.

Helping a family member or friend with a serious problem for which they do not want help can feel frustrating and thankless. It is sometimes hard to remember that someone who suffers from problematic hoarding does not choose to live in squalor or deplete their savings with unnecessary purchases. As much as it may feel like a conscious choice at times, HD is a psychiatric illness in the same way that major depression, PTSD, and OCD are. Keeping in mind that HD is biological in origin can also help loved ones and others who care for and work with individuals with hoarding disorder maintain a sense of perspective and hope.

EPILOGUE

As outlined in this book, hoarding disorder is a complex illness that affects millions of people throughout the world. Once merely a subject for sensationalistic storytelling, HD gained legitimacy as a psychiatric disorder in 2013 with its inclusion in the DSM-5. The profound negative impact of hoarding disorder on individuals, families, and society at large is now much better understood, and our knowledge of the epidemiology, clinical manifestations, and underlying biology continues to evolve.

We now know that, although usually unrecognized, hoarding symptoms typically begin in adolescence or early adulthood, and tend to progressively worsen over time, such that noticeable clinical manifestations of HD appear in middle age, and older adults are disproportionally affected. The causes of hoarding are heterogeneous, and for the most part unknown. What is known is that one's susceptibility to HD is genetic. Specific environmental factors, such as trauma, as well as others as yet undiscovered, may also contribute to its development.

While some individuals experience only mild symptoms of hoarding, others manifest severe, and even life-threatening symptoms. Rates of co-occurring psychiatric and medical conditions are elevated among individuals with HD, and adversely impact quality of life for sufferers and for their loved ones. People with hoarding, whether mild or severe, are at particularly high risk for major depression, anxiety disorders, sleep problems, chronic pain, obesity, and cardiovascular disorders.

That said, hoarding disorder is a treatable condition. Treatment of co-occurring medical and psychiatric conditions can go a long way towards improving functioning. Evidence-based psychotherapeutic treatments, and to a lesser extent, medications, can reduce hoarding severity and improve quality of life, in some cases even leading to functional remission. Case management, peer-facilitated support groups or self-help options can be beneficial for those who do not have access to treatment with psychotherapy or medication. Family members and friends can also help, by providing support and accountability for those who are willing to accept it, and by working towards harm reduction and increased safety for those who are not.

Perhaps most importantly, scientific research into finding the causes, understanding the effects, and developing increasingly effective treatments for HD continue. Ongoing education, not only of the lay public and the medical community, as well as government and government agencies at local, state, and federal levels, is crucial for continued progress.

REFERENCES

ADA National Network. (2017). *An overview of the Americans With Disabilities Act* [Fact Sheet]. Retrieved from http://www.adainfo.us/adaoverview

Albin, R. L. (2002). Sham surgery controls: Intracerebral grafting of fetal tissue for Parkinson's disease and proposed criteria for use of sham surgery controls. *J Med Ethics, 28*(5), 322–325. doi:10.1136/jme.28.5.322

Alighieri, D. (1995*) The Divine Comedy: Inferno; Purgatorio; Paradiso.* Allen Mandelbaum (ed.). Everyman's Library. (Original work published 1472).

Alvarenga, P. G., Cesar, R. C., Leckman, J. F., Moriyama, T. S., Torres, A. R., Bloch, M. H., . . . do Rosario, M. C. (2015). Obsessive-compulsive symptom dimensions in a population-based, cross-sectional sample of school-aged children. *J Psychiatr Res, 62*, 108–114. doi:10.1016/j.jpsychires.2015.01.018

American Psychiatric Association. (2015). *Structured clinical interview for DSM-5 (SCID-5).* American Psychiatric Association. Publishing.

American Psychiatric Association. (1987). *Diagnostic and statistical manual of mental disorders* (3rd ed., revised).

American Psychiatric Association. (1994). *Diagnostic and statistical manual of mental disorders* (4th ed.).

American Psychiatric Association. (2013). *Diagnostic and statistical manual of mental disorders* (5th ed.).

American Psychological Association. (2020). What is cognitive behavioral therapy? [Guideline]. Retrieved 1/15/2020, from https://www.apa.org/ptsd -guideline/patients-and-families/cognitive-behavioral

An, S. K., Mataix-Cols, D., Lawrence, N. S., Wooderson, S., Giampietro, V., Speckens, A., . . . Phillips, M. L. (2009). To discard or not to discard: The neural basis of hoarding symptoms in obsessive-compulsive disorder. *Mol Psychiatry, 14*(3), 318–331. https://doi.org/10.1038/sj.mp.4002129

Anderson, S. W., Damasio, H., & Damasio, A. R. (2005). A neural basis for collecting behaviour in humans. *Brain, 128*(1), 201–212. https://doi.org/10 .1093/brain/awh329

Aranovich, G. J., Cavagnaro, D. R., Pitt, M. A., Myung, J. I., & Mathews, C. A. (2017). A model-based analysis of decision making under risk in obsessive-compulsive and hoarding disorders. *J Psychiatr Res, 90*, 126–132. https://doi.org/10 .1016/j.jpsychires.2017.02.017

Archer, C. A., Moran, K., Garza, K., Zakrzewski, J., Martin, A., Chou, C.-Y.,

Uhm, S.Y., Chan, J., Gause, M., Salazar, M., Plumadore, J., Smith, L.C., Komaiko, K., Howell, G., Vigil, O., Bain, D., Stark, S., Mackin, R.S., Eckfield, M., Vega, E., Tsoh, J.Y., Delucchi, K.L., Mathews, C.A. (2019). Relationship between symptom severity, psychiatric comorbidity, social/occupational impairment, and suicidality in hoarding disorder. *J Obsessive Compuls Relat Disord, 21*(April 2019), 158–164. https://doi.org/10.1016/j.jocrd.2018 .11.001

Ayers, C. R., Davidson, E. J., Dozier, M. E., & Twamley, E. W. (2019). Cognitive rehabilitation and exposure/sorting therapy for late-life hoarding: Effects on neuropsychological performance. *J Gerontol B Psychol Sci Soc Sci*. https:// doi.org/10.1093/geronb/gbz062

Ayers, C. R., Dozier, M. E., & Mayes, T. L. (2017). Psychometric evaluation of the saving inventory-revised in older adults. *Clin Gerontol, 40*(3), 191–196. https://doi.org/10.1080/07317115.2016.1267056

Ayers, C. R., Dozier, M. E., Pittman, J. O. E., Mayes, T. L., & Twamley, E. W. (2018). Comparing clinical characteristics and treatment outcomes between veterans and non-veterans with hoarding disorder. *Compr Psychiatry, 86*(October 2018), 1–5. https://doi.org/10.1016/j.comppsych.2018.07.005

Ayers, C. R., Dozier, M. E., Twamley, E. W., Saxena, S., Granholm, E., Mayes, T. L., & Wetherell, J. L. (2018). Cognitive rehabilitation and exposure/sorting therapy (CREST) for hoarding disorder in older adults: A randomized clinical trial. *J Clin Psychiatry, 79*(2). https://doi.org/10.4088/JCP.16m11072

Ayers, C. R., Dozier, M. E., Wetherell, J. L., Twamley, E. W., & Schiehser, D. M. (2016). Executive functioning in participants over age of 50 with hoarding disorder. *Am J Geriatr Psychiatry, 24*(5), 342–349. https://doi .org/10.1016/j.jagp.2015.10.009

Ayers, C. R., Iqbal, Y., & Strickland, K. (2014). Medical conditions in geriatric hoarding disorder patients. *Aging Ment Health, 18*(2), 148–151. https://doi .org/10.1080/13607863.2013.814105

Ayers, C. R., Ly, P., Howard, I., Mayes, T., Porter, B., & Iqbal, Y. (2014). Hoarding severity predicts functional disability in late-life hoarding disorder patients. *Int J Geriatr Psychiatry, 29*(7), 741–746. https://doi.org/10.1002/gps.4057

Ayers, C. R., Najmi, S., Mayes, T. L., & Dozier, M. E. (2015). Hoarding disorder in older adulthood. *Am J Geriatr Psychiatry, 23*(4), 416–422. https://doi .org/10.1016/j.jagp.2014.05.009

Ayers, C. R., Saxena, S., Espejo, E., Twamley, E. W., Granholm, E., & Wetherell, J. L. (2014). Novel treatment for geriatric hoarding disorder: An open trial of cognitive rehabilitation paired with behavior therapy. *Am J Geriatr Psychiatry, 22*(3), 248–252. doi:10.1016/j.jagp.2013.02.010

Ayers, C. R., Saxena, S., Golshan, S., & Wetherell, J. L. (2009). Age at onset and clinical features of late life compulsive hoarding. *Int J Geriatr Psychiatry, 25*(2), 142–149. https://doi.org/10.1002/gps.2310

Baldwin, P.A., Whitford, T.J., & Grisham, J.R. (2019). Emotion sensitivity of the error-related negativity in hoarding individuals. *J Psychopathol Behav Assess,* 41, 589–597.

Beattie, D. T., & Smith, J. A. (2008). Serotonin pharmacology in the gastrointestinal tract: A review. *Naunyn Schmiedebergs Arch Pharmacol, 377*(3), 181–203. https://doi.org/10.1007/s00210-008-0276-9

Bloch, M.H., Bartley, C.A., Zipperer, L. Jakubovski, E., Landeros-Weisenberger, A. Pittenger, C., Leckman, J.F. (2014) Meta-analysis: hoarding symptoms associated with poor tratment outcome in obsessive compulsive disorder. Mol Psych. *19*(9), 1025–1030.

Bogan, A. M., Koran, L. M., Chuong, H. W., Vapnik, T., & Bystritsky, A. (2005). Quetiapine augmentation in obsessive-compulsive disorder resistant to serotonin reuptake inhibitors: An open-label study. *J Clin Psychiatry, 66*(1), 73–79. https://doi.org/10.4088/jcp.v66n0110

Brain Health Registry. BrainHealthRegistry.org

Bratiotis, C., Sorrentino Schmalisch, C., & Steketee, G. (2011). *The hoarding handbook: A guide for human service professionals.* Oxford: Oxford University Press.

Brushlinsky, N. N., Ahrens, M., Sokolov, S.V., Wagner, P. (2018). World Fire Statistics. In I. A. o. F. a. R. S. Center of Fire Statistics (Ed.), (pp. 1–62).

Burton, C. L., Crosbie, J., Dupuis, A., Mathews, C. A., Soreni, N., Schachar, R., & Arnold, P. D. (2016). Clinical correlates of hoarding with and without comorbid obsessive-compulsive symptoms in a community pediatric sample. *J Am Acad Child Adolesc Psychiatry, 55*(2), 114–121, Article e112. https://doi.org/10.1016/j.jaac.2015.11.014

Buscher, T. P., Dyson, J., & Cowdell, F. (2014). The effects of hoarding disorder on families: An integrative review. *J Psychiatr Ment Health Nurs, 21*(6), 491–498. https://doi.org/10.1111/jpm.12098

Carbonella, J. Y., & Timpano, K. R. (2016). Examining the link between hoarding symptoms and cognitive flexibility deficits. *Behav Ther, 47*(2), 262–273. https://doi.org/10.1016/j.beth.2015.11.003

Carey, E. A., del Pozo de Bolger, A., Wootton, B.M. (2019). Psychometric properties of the Hoarding Disorder-Dimensional Scale. *Journal of Obsessive-Compulsive and Related Disorders, 21,* 91–96. https://doi.org/10.1016/j .jocrd.2019.01.001

Casey, C. M., Cook-Cottone, C., Beck-Joslyn, M. (2012). An overview of problematic eating and food-related behavior among foster children: Definitions, etiology, and intervention. *Child Adolesc Soc Work J, 29,* 307–322. https:// doi.org/10.1007/s10560-012-0262-4

Cath, D. C., Nizar, K., Boomsma, D., & Mathews, C. A. (2017). Age-specific prevalence of hoarding and obsessive compulsive disorder: A population-based study. *Am J Geriatr Psychiatry, 25*(3), 245–255. https://doi.org/10 .1016/j.jagp.2016.11.006

Chakraborty, V., Cherian, A. V., Math, S. B., Venkatasubramanian, G., Thennarasu, K., Mataix-Cols, D., & Reddy, Y. C. (2012). Clinically significant hoarding in obsessive-compulsive disorder: Results from an Indian study. *Compr Psychiatry, 53*(8), 1153–1160. https://doi.org/10.1016/j.comppsych .2012.05.006

Chou, C. Y., Mackin, R. S., Delucchi, K. L., & Mathews, C. A. (2018). Detail-oriented visual processing style: Its role in the relationships between early life adversity and hoarding-related dysfunctions. *Psychiatry Res, 267*, 30–36. https://doi.org/10.1016/j.psychres.2018.05.053

Chou, C. Y., Tsoh, J. Y., Shumway, M., Smith, L. C., Chan, J., Delucchi, K., . . . Mathews, C. A. (2019). Treating hoarding disorder with compassion-focused therapy: A pilot study examining treatment feasibility, acceptability, and exploring treatment effects. *Br J Clin Psychol.* https://doi.org/10.1111/bjc .12228

Chou, C. Y., Tsoh, J., Vigil, O., Bain, D., Uhm, S. Y., Howell, G., . . . Mathews, C. A. (2018). Contributions of self-criticism and shame to hoarding. *Psychiatry Res, 262*, 488–493. https://doi.org/10.1016/j.psychres.2017.09.030

Clark, A. N., Mankikar, G. D., & Gray, I. (1975). Diogenes syndrome. A clinical study of gross neglect in old age. *Lancet, 301*(7903), 366–368. https://doi .org/10.1016/S0140-6736(75)91280-5

Cromer, K. R., Schmidt, N.B., Murphy, D. L. (2007). Do traumatic events influence the clinical expression of compulsive hoarding? *Behav Res Ther, 45*, 2581–2592.

Damien, J., Colloca, L., Bellei-Rodriguez, C. E., & Marchand, S. (2018). Pain modulation: From conditioned pain modulation to placebo and nocebo effects in experimental and clinical pain. *Int Rev Neurobiol, 139*, 255–296. https://doi.org/10.1016/bs.irn.2018.07.024

Darke, S., & Duflou, J. (2017). Characteristics, circumstances and pathology of sudden or unnatural deaths of cases with evidence of pathological hoarding. *J Forensic Leg Med, 45*, 36–40.https://doi.org/10.1016/j.jflm.2016.11.004

DiMauro, J., Genova, M., Tolin, D. F., Kurtz, M. M. (2014). Cognitive remediation for neuropsychological impairment in hoarding disorder: A pilot study. *Journal of Obsessive-Compulsive and Related Disorders, 3*(2), 132–138.

Dozier, M. E., & Ayers, C. R. (2015). Validation of the clutter image rating in older adults with hoarding disorder. *Int Psychogeriatr, 27*(5), 769–776. https://doi.org/10.1017/S1041610214002403

Dozier, M. E., Porter, B., & Ayers, C. R. (2016). Age of onset and progression of hoarding symptoms in older adults with hoarding disorder. *Aging Ment Health, 20*(7), 736–742. https://doi.org/10.1080/13607863.2015.1033684

Drury, H., Ajmi, S., Fernandez de la Cruz, L., Nordsletten, A. E., & Mataix-Cols, D. (2014). Caregiver burden, family accommodation, health, and well-being in relatives of individuals with hoarding disorder. *J Affect Disord, 159*, 7–14. https://doi.org/10.1016/j.jad.2014.01.023

Dykens, E. M., Leckman, J. F., & Cassidy, S. B. (1996). Obsessions and compulsions in Prader-Willi syndrome. *J Child Psychol Psychiatry, 37*(8), 995–1002.

Dykens, E., & Shah, B. (2003). Psychiatric disorders in Prader-Willi syndrome: Epidemiology and management. *CNS Drugs, 17*(3), 167–178. https://doi.org/10.2165/00023210-200317030-00003

Eisen, J. L., Phillips, K. A., Baer, L., Beer, D. A., Atala, K. D., & Rasmussen, S. A. (1998). The Brown Assessment of Beliefs Scale: Reliability and validity. *Am J Psychiatry, 155*(1), 102–108.

Evans, A. H., Katzenschlager, R., Paviour, D., O'Sullivan, J. D., Appel, S., Lawrence, A. D., & Lees, A. J. (2004). Punding in Parkinson's disease: Its relation to the dopamine dysregulation syndrome. *Mov Disord, 19*(4), 397–405. https://doi.org/10.1002/mds.20045

Evans, D. W., Leckman, J. F., Carter, A., Reznick, J. S., Henshaw, D., King, R. A., & Pauls, D. (1997). Ritual, habit, and perfectionism: The prevalence and development of compulsive-like behavior in normal young children. *Child Dev, 68*(1), 58–68.

Finney, C. M., & Mendez, M. F. (2017). Diogenes syndrome in frontotemporal dementia. *Am J Alzheimers Dis Other Demen, 32*(7), 438–443. https://doi.org/10.1177/1533317517717012

Foa, E. B., Coles, M., Huppert, J. D., Pasupuleti, R. V., Franklin, M. E., & March, J. (2010). Development and validation of a child version of the obsessive compulsive inventory. *Behav Ther, 41*(1), 121–132. https://doi.org/10.1016/j.beth.2009.02.001

Fong, T. G., Jones, R. N., Rudolph, J. L., Yang, F. M., Tommet, D., Habtemariam, D., . . . Inouye, S. K. (2011). Development and validation of a brief cognitive assessment tool: The Sweet 16. *Arch Intern Med, 171*(5), 432–437. https://doi.org/10.1001/archinternmed.2010.423

Frank, H., Stewart, E., Walther, M., Benito, K., Freeman, J., Conelea, C., & Garci, A. (2014). Hoarding behavior among young children with obsessive-compulsive disorder. *J Obsessive Compuls Relat Disord, 3*(1), 6–11. https://doi.org/10.1016/j.jocrd.2013.11.001

Frost, R. O., & Gross, R. C. (1993). The hoarding of possessions. *Behav Res Ther, 31*(4), 367–381.

Frost, R. O., & Hartl, T. L. (1996). A cognitive-behavioral model of compulsive hoarding. *Behav Res Ther, 34*(4), 341–350.

Frost, R. O., Hristova, V., Steketee, G., & Tolin, D. F. (2013). Activities of daily living scale in hoarding disorder. *J Obsessive Compuls Relat Disord, 2*(2), 85–90. https://doi.org/10.1016/j.jocrd.2012.12.004

Frost, R. O., Kim, H. J., Morris, C., Bloss, C., Murray-Close, M., & Steketee, G. (1998). Hoarding, compulsive buying and reasons for saving. *Behav Res Ther, 36*(7–8), 657–664.

Frost, R. O., & Shows, D. L. (1993). The nature and measurement of compulsive indecisiveness. *Behav Res Ther, 31*(7), 683–692. https://doi.org/10.1016/0005-7967(93)90121-a

Frost, R. O., & Steketee, G. (2010). *Stuff: Compulsive hoarding and the meaning of things.* Mariner Books; Houghton Mifflin Harcourt Publishing Company.

Frost, R. O., Steketee, G., & Grisham, J. (2004). Measurement of compulsive hoarding: Saving inventory-revised. *Behav Res Ther, 42*(10), 1163–1182. https://doi.org/10.1016/j.brat.2003.07.006

Frost, R. O., Steketee, G., & Tolin, D. F. Comorbidity in hoarding disorder. *Depress Anxiety, 28*(10), 876–884. https://doi.org/10.1002/da.20861

Frost, R. O., Steketee, G., Tolin, D.F., Renaud, S. (2008). Development and validation of the clutter image rating. *J Psychopathol Behav Assess, 30*, 193–203.

Frost, R. O., Steketee, G., & Williams, L. (2000). Hoarding: A community health problem. *Health Soc Care Community, 8*(4), 229–234.

Fullana, M. A., Vilagut, G., Mataix-Cols, D., Adroher, N. D., Bruffaerts, R., Bunting, B., . . . Alonso, J. (2013). Is ADHD in childhood associated with lifetime hoarding symptoms? An epidemiological study. *Depress Anxiety.* https://doi.org/10.1002/da.22123

Gilbert, P. (2010). *Compassion focused therapy.* Routledge.

Grassi, G., Micheli, L., Di Cesare Mannelli, L., Compagno, E., Righi, L., Ghelardini, C., & Pallanti, S. (2016). Atomoxetine for hoarding disorder: A preclinical and clinical investigation. *J Psychiatr Res, 83*, 240–248. https://doi.org/10.1016/j.jpsychires.2016.09.012

Greaves, N., Prince, E., Evans, D. W., & Charman, T. (2006). Repetitive and ritualistic behaviour in children with Prader-Willi syndrome and children with autism. *J Intellect Disabil Res, 50*(2), 92–100. https://doi.org/10.1111/j.1365-2788.2005.00726.x

Grisham, J. R., & Baldwin, P. A. (2015). Neuropsychological and neurophysiological insights into hoarding disorder. *Neuropsychiatr Dis Treat, 11*, 951–962. https://doi.org/10.2147/NDT.S62084

Grisham, J. R., Brown, T. A., Savage, C. R., Steketee, G., & Barlow, D. H. (2007). Neuropsychological impairment associated with compulsive hoarding.

Behav Res Ther, 45(7), 1471–1483. https://doi.org/10.1016/j.brat.2006 .12.008

Grisham, J. R., Frost, R. O., Steketee, G., Kim, H. J., & Hood, S. (2006). Age of onset of compulsive hoarding. *J Anxiety Disord, 20*(5), 675–686. https://doi .org/10.1016/j.janxdis.2005.07.004

Grisham, J. R., Norberg, M. M., Williams, A. D., Certoma, S. P., & Kadib, R. (2010). Categorization and cognitive deficits in compulsive hoarding. *Behav Res Ther, 48*(9), 866–872. https://doi.org/10.1016/j.brat.2010.05.011

Hacker, L. E., Park, J. M., Timpano, K. R., Cavitt, M. A., Alvaro, J. L., Lewin, A. B., . . . Storch, E. A. (2016). Hoarding in children with ADHD. *J Atten Disord, 20*(7), 617–626. https://doi.org/10.1177/1087054712455845

Halliday, G., Banerjee, S., Philpot, M., & Macdonald, A. (2000). Community study of people who live in squalor. *Lancet, 355*(9207), 882–886. https://doi .org/10.1016/S0140-6736(99)06250-9

Harlow, J. M. (1868). Recovery from the passage of an iron bar through the head. *Publ Mass Med Soc, 2*, 329–347.

Harlow, J.M. (1851). A most remarkable case. *American Phrenological Journal and Repository of Science, Literature, and General Intelligence, 13*(4), 89.

Harris, J. (2010). *Household hoarding and residentile fires* [Paper]. International Congress For Applied Psychology, Melbourne, Australia. July 11–16, 2010.

Hartl, T. L., Duffany, S. R., Allen, G. J., Steketee, G., & Frost, R. O. (2005). Relationships among compulsive hoarding, trauma, and attention-deficit/ hyperactivity disorder. *Behav Res Ther, 43*(2), 269–276.

Hartl, T. L., Frost, R. O., Allen, G. J., Deckersbach, T., Steketee, G., Duffany, S. R., & Savage, C. R. (2004). Actual and perceived memory deficits in individuals with compulsive hoarding. *Depress Anxiety, 20*(2), 59–69.

Hasin, D. S., Sarvet, A. L., Meyers, J. L., Saha, T. D., Ruan, W. J., Stohl, M., & Grant, B. F. (2018). Epidemiology of adult *DSM-5* major depressive disorder and its specifiers in the United States. *JAMA Psychiatry, 75*(4), 336–346. https://doi.org/10.1001/jamapsychiatry.2017.4602

Hirschtritt, M. E., Bloch, M. H., & Mathews, C. A. (2017). Obsessive-compulsive disorder: advances in diagnosis and treatment. *JAMA, 317*(13), 1358–1367. https://doi.org/10.1001/jama.2017.2200

Hirschtritt, M. E., & Mathews, C.A. (2014). Genetics and family models of hoarding disorder. In R. O. Frost & G. Steketee (Eds.), *The Oxford handbook of hoarding and acquiring* (pp. 159–176). Oxford University Press.

Hoover, H. *The state papers and other public writings of Herbert Hoover, Volume 2.* William Starr Myers (Ed). 1934. Doubleday, Doran and Company.

Hough, C. M., Luks, T. L., Lai, K., Vigil, O., Guillory, S., Nongpiur, A., . . .

Mathews, C. A. (2016). Comparison of brain activation patterns during executive function tasks in hoarding disorder and non-hoarding OCD. *Psychiatry Res, 255*, 50–59. https://doi.org/10.1016/j.pscychresns.2016.07.007

Iervolino, A. C., Perroud, N., Fullana, M. A., Guipponi, M., Cherkas, L., Collier, D. A., & Mataix-Cols, D. (2009). Prevalence and heritability of compulsive hoarding: A twin study. *Am J Psychiatry, 166*(10), 1156–1161. https://doi.org/10.1176/appi.ajp.2009.08121789

Iervolino, A. C., Rijsdijk, F. V., Cherkas, L., Fullana, M. A., & Mataix-Cols, D. (2011). A multivariate twin study of obsessive-compulsive symptom dimensions. *Arch Gen Psychiatry, 68*(6), 637–644. https://doi.org/10.1001/archgenpsychiatry.2011.54

Ivanov, V. Z., Mataix-Cols, D., Serlachius, E., Brander, G. Elmquist, A., Enander, J., Rück, C. (2019). The developmental origins of hoarding disorder in adolescence: A longitudinal clinical interview study following an epidemiological survey. PsyArXiv https://doi.org/10.31234/osf.io/ns5wf

Ivanov, V. Z., Mataix-Cols, D., Serlachius, E., Lichtenstein, P., Anckarsater, H., Chang, Z., . . . Ruck, C. (2013). Prevalence, comorbidity and heritability of hoarding symptoms in adolescence: A population based twin study in 15-year olds. *PLOS ONE, 8*(7), Article e69140. https://doi.org/10.1371/journal.pone.0069140

Kaplan, A., Hollander, E. (2004) Comorbidity in compulsive hoarding: a case report. *CNS Spectr.* 9 (1):71-73.

Kellman-McFarlane, K., Stewart, B., Woody, S., Ayers, C., Dozier, M., Frost, R. O., . . . Welsted, A. (2019). Saving Inventory-Revised: Psychometric performance across the lifespan. *J Affect Disord, 252*, 358–364. https://doi.org/10.1016/j.jad.2019.04.007

Kelly, J. F. (2017). Is Alcoholics Anonymous religious, spiritual, neither? Findings from 25 years of mechanisms of behavior change research. *Addiction, 112*(6), 929–936. https://doi.org/10.1111/add.13590

Kelly, J. F., Stout, R. L., Magill, M., Tonigan, J. S., & Pagano, M. E. (2010). Mechanisms of behavior change in alcoholics anonymous: Does Alcoholics Anonymous lead to better alcohol use outcomes by reducing depression symptoms? *Addiction, 105*(4), 626–636. https://doi.org/10.1111/j.1360-0443.2009.02820.x

La Buissonniere-Ariza, V., Wood, J. J., Kendall, P. C., McBride, N. M., Cepeda, S. L., Small, B. J., . . . Storch, E. A. (2018). Presentation and correlates of hoarding behaviors in children with autism spectrum disorders and comorbid anxiety or obsessive-compulsive symptoms. *J Autism Dev Disord, 48*(12), 4167–4178. https://doi.org/10.1007/s10803-018-3645-3

Lai, M. C., Lombardo, M. V., & Baron-Cohen, S. (2014). Autism. *Lancet, 383*(9920), 896–910. https://doi.org/10.1016/S0140-6736(13)61539-1

Landau, D., Iervolino, A. C., Pertusa, A., Santo, S., Singh, S., & Mataix-Cols, D. (2011). Stressful life events and material deprivation in hoarding disorder. *J Anxiety Disord, 25*(2), 192–202. https://doi.org/10.1016/j.janxdis.2010.09.002

Lane, K. (2018, November 14). The dangers of cold weather. *Public Health Post.* https://www.publichealthpost.org/research/counting-cold-related-deaths -new-york-city

Lawlor, D. A., Davey Smith, G., & Ebrahim, S. (2004). Commentary: The hormone replacement-coronary heart disease conundrum—Is this the death of observational epidemiology? *Int J Epidemiol, 33*(3), 464–467. https://doi .org/10.1093/ije/dyh124

Leckman, J. F., & Bloch, M. H. (2008). A developmental and evolutionary perspective on obsessive-compulsive disorder: Whence and whither compulsive hoarding? *Am J Psychiatry, 165*(10), 1229–1233. https://doi.org/10.1176/ appi.ajp.2008.08060891

Lee, S. P., Ong, C., Sagayadevan, V., Ong, R., Abdin, E., Lim, S., . . . Subramaniam, M. (2016). Hoarding symptoms among psychiatric outpatients: Confirmatory factor analysis and psychometric properties of the Saving Inventory-Revised (SI-R). *BMC Psychiatry, 16*(1), 364. https://doi.org/10 .1186/s12888-016-1043-y

Leitch, D. (2019). *History and hoarding: Compulsive consumption through the ages.* Digital History–Histore Numérique. http://216.48.92.16/omeka2/ jmccutcheon/exhibits/show/the-great-depression-and-hoard

Li, F., Nasir, M., Olten, B., & Bloch, M. H. (2019). Meta-analysis of placebo response in adult antidepressant trials. *CNS Drugs.* https://doi.org/10.1007/ s40263-019-00662-y

Lim, S. Y., O'Sullivan, S. S., Kotschet, K., Gallagher, D. A., Lacey, C., Lawrence, A. D., . . . Evans, A. H. (2009). Dopamine dysregulation syndrome, impulse control disorders and punding after deep brain stimulation surgery for Parkinson's disease. *J Clin Neurosci, 16*(9), 1148–1152. https://doi.org/10 .1016/j.jocn.2008.12.010

Lucini, G., Monk, I., Szlatenyi, C. (2009). An analysis of fire incidents involving hoarded households. In W. P. Inst. (Ed.). Worcester, MA.Retrieved from https://web.cs.wpi.edu/~rek/Projects/MFB_D09.pdf

Luton Times and Advertiser (July 3, 1855).

Mackin, R. S., Arean, P. A., Delucchi, K. L., & Mathews, C. A. (2011). Cognitive functioning in individuals with severe compulsive hoarding behaviors and late life depression. *Int J Geriatr Psychiatry, 26*(3), 314–321. https:// doi.org/10.1002/gps.2531

Mackin, R. S., Vigil, O., Insel, P., Kivowitz, A., Kupferman, E., Hough, C. M., . . . Mathews, C. A. (2016). Patterns of clinically significant cognitive impairment in hoarding disorder. *Depress Anxiety, 33*(3), 211–218. https://doi.org/10.1002/da.22439

Macmillan, D., & Shaw, P. (1966). Senile breakdown in standards of personal and environmental cleanliness. *Br Med J, 2*(5521), 1032–1037.

Mark, J. J. (2014). Diogenes of Sinope. In *Ancient History Encyclopedia*: Ancient History Encyclopedia Foundation.

Marlatt, G. A. (1996). Harm reduction: Come as you are. *Addict Behav, 21*(6), 779–788. https://doi.org/10.1016/0306-4603(96)00042-1

Marx, M. S., & Cohen-Mansfield, J. Hoarding behavior in the elderly: A comparison between community-dwelling persons and nursing home residents. *Int Psychogeriatr, 15*(3), 289–306. https://doi.org/10.1017/S1041610203009542

Mataix-Cols, D., Billotti, D., Fernandez de la Cruz, L., & Nordsletten, A. E. (2012). The London field trial for hoarding disorder. *Psychol Med*, 1–11. https://doi.org/10.1017/S0033291712001560

Mataix-Cols, D., Nakatani, E., Micali, N., & Heyman, I. (2008). Structure of obsessive-compulsive symptoms in pediatric OCD. *J Am Acad Child Adolesc Psychiatry*.

Mataix-Cols, D., Wooderson, S., Lawrence, N., Brammer, M. J., Speckens, A., & Phillips, M. L. (2004). Distinct neural correlates of washing, checking, and hoarding symptom dimensions in obsessive-compulsive disorder. *Arch Gen Psychiatry, 61*(6), 564–576.

Mathews, C. A. (2014). Hoarding disorder: More than just a problem of too much stuff. *J Clin Psychiatry, 75*(8), 893–894. https://doi.org/10.4088/JCP.14ac09325

Mathews, C. A., Delucchi, K., Cath, D. C., Willemsen, G., & Boomsma, D. I. (2014). Partitioning the etiology of hoarding and obsessive-compulsive symptoms. *Psychol Med, 44*(13), 2867–2876. https://doi.org/10.1017/S003329 1714000269

Mathews, C. A., Mackin, R. S., Chou, C. Y., Uhm, S. Y., Bain, L. D., Stark, S. J., . . . Delucchi, K. (2018). Randomised clinical trial of community-based peer-led and psychologist-led group treatment for hoarding disorder. *BJPsych Open, 4*(4), 285–293. https://doi.org/10.1192/bjo.2018.30

Mathews, C. A., Perez, V. B., Roach, B. J., Fekri, S., Vigil, O., Kupferman, E., & Mathalon, D. H. (2016). Error-related brain activity dissociates hoarding disorder from obsessive-compulsive disorder. *Psychol Med, 46*(2), 367–379. https://doi.org/10.1017/S0033291715001889

Mathews, C. A., Uhm, S., Chan, J., Gause, M., Franklin, J., Plumadore, J., . . . Vega, E. (2016). Treating hoarding disorder in a real-world setting: Results from the Mental Health Association of San Francisco. *Psychiatry Res, 237*, 331–338. https://doi.org/10.1016/j.psychres.2016.01.019

Mayo Clinic. (2019, September 17). Selective serotonin reuptake inhibitors (SSRIs). Retrieved 12/20/2019,from https://www.mayoclinic.org/diseases-conditions/depression/in-depth/ssris/art-20044825-targetText=Selective%20serotonin%20reuptake%20inhibitors%20(SSRIs)%20are%20the%20most%20commonly%20prescribed,other%20types%20of%20antidepressants%20do

Merriam Webster Online Dictionary. Copyright 2019. Merriam-Webster, Inc. https://merriam-webster.com. Accessed 3-10-2020.

Millen, A. M., Levinson, A., Linkovski, O., Shuer, L., Thaler, T., Nick, G. A., . . . Rodriguez, C. I. (2020). Pilot study evaluating critical time intervention for individuals with hoarding disorder at risk for eviction. *Psychiatr Serv.* https://doi.org/10.1176/appi.ps.201900447

Miller, E. K., Freedman, D. J., & Wallis, J. D. (2002). The prefrontal cortex: Categories, concepts and cognition. *Philos Trans R Soc Lond B Biol Sci, 357*(1424), 1123–1136. https://doi.org/10.1098/rstb.2002.1099

Miller, W. R., & Rollnick, S. (2013). *Motivational interviewing: Helping people change* (3rd ed.). Guilford Press.

Monzani, B., Rijsdijk, F., Harris, J., & Mataix-Cols, D. (2014). The structure of genetic and environmental risk factors for dimensional representations of *DSM-5* obsessive-compulsive spectrum disorders. *JAMA Psychiatry, 71*(2), 182–189. https://doi.org/10.1001/jamapsychiatry.2013.3524

Morris, S. H., Jaffee, S. R., Goodwin, G. P., & Franklin, M. E. (2016). Hoarding in children and adolescents: A review. *Child Psychiatry Hum Dev, 47*(5), 740–750. https://doi.org/10.1007/s10578-015-0607-2

A most remarkable case. (1851). *American Phrenological Journal and Repository of Science, Literature, and General Intelligence, 13*(4), 89.

Moukhtarian, T. R., Cooper, R. E., Vassos, E., Moran, P., & Asherson, P. (2017). Effects of stimulants and atomoxetine on emotional lability in adults: A systematic review and meta-analysis. *Eur Psychiatry, 44*, 198–207. https://doi.org/10.1016/j.eurpsy.2017.05.021

Moulding, R., Nedeljkovic, M., Kyrios, M., Osborne, D., & Mogan, C. (2017). Short-term cognitive-behavioural group treatment for hoarding disorder: A naturalistic treatment outcome study. *Clin Psychol Psychother, 24*(1), 235–244. https://doi.org/10.1002/cpp.2001

Muller, R. T. (2013). Hoarding as a reaction to trauma. *Psychology Today.* Retrieved from https://www.psychologytoday.com/us/blog/talking-about-trauma/201306/hoarding-reaction-trauma

Muroff, J., Steketee, G., Bratiotis, C., & Ross, A. (2012). Group cognitive and behavioral therapy and bibliotherapy for hoarding: A pilot trial. *Depress Anxiety, 29*(7), 597–604. https://doi.org/10.1002/da.21923

Muroff, J., Steketee, G., Frost, R. O., & Tolin, D. F. (2014). Cognitive behavior therapy for hoarding disorder: Follow-up findings and predictors of outcome. *Depress Anxiety, 31*(12), 964–971. https://doi.org/10.1002/da.22222

Muroff, J., Steketee, G., Himle, J., & Frost, R. (2010). Delivery of internet treatment for compulsive hoarding (D.I.T.C.H.). *Behav Res Ther, 48*(1), 79–85. https://doi.org/10.1016/j.brat.2009.09.006

Muroff, J., Underwood, P., Steketee, G. (2014). *Group treatment for hoarding disorder: Therapist guide*. Oxford University Press.

NAPSA, N. A. P. S. A. (2019). Other safety concerns and self neglect. Retrieved from http://www.napsa-now.org/get-informed/other-safety-concerns-2/

National Center for Biotechnology Information. (2019). *Dopamine*, CID=681. Retrieved October 25, 2019, from PubChem Database https://pubchem.ncbi .nlm.nih.gov/compound/Dopamine

National Center for Biotechnology Information. (n.d.) *Norepinephrine*, CID=439260. Retrieved October 25, 2019 , from PubChem Database, https://pubchem.ncbi.nlm.nih.gov/compound/Norepinephrine

National Fire Protection Association. (2018). *Fire prevention week fire facts*. Retrieved from https://www.nfpa.org/public-education/campaigns/fire -prevention-week/fire-facts

National Institute of Mental Health, N. (2019. Mental health statistics.

Nordsletten, A. E. (2014). The Family Impact Scale for Hoarding (FISH): Measure development and initial validation. *Journal of Obsessive-Compulsive and Related Disorders, 3*, 29–34.

Nordsletten, A. E., Fernandez de la Cruz, L., Aluco, E., Alonso, P., Lopez-Sola, C., Menchon, J. M., . . . Mataix-Cols, D. (2018). A transcultural study of hoarding disorder: Insights from the United Kingdom, Spain, Japan, and Brazil. *Transcult Psychiatry, 55*(2), 261–285. https://doi.org/10 .1177/1363461518759203

Nordsletten, A. E., Fernandez de la Cruz, L., Billotti, D., & Mataix-Cols, D. (2013). Finders keepers: The features differentiating hoarding disorder from normative collecting. *Compr Psychiatry, 54*(3), 229–237. https://doi.org/10 .1016/j.comppsych.2012.07.063

Nordsletten, A. E., Fernandez de la Cruz, L., Pertusa, A., Reichenberg, A., Hotopf, M., Hatch, S. L., & Mataix-Cols, D. (2013). The Structured Interview for Hoarding Disorder (SIHD): Development, further validation, and pragmatic usage. *Journal of Obsessive-Compulsive and Related Disorders, 2*(3), 346–350. https://doi.org/10.1016/j.jocrd.2013.06.003

Nordsletten, A. E., & Mataix-Cols, D. (2012). Hoarding versus collecting: Where does pathology diverge from play? *Clin Psychol Rev, 32*(3), 165–176. https://doi.org/10.1016/j.cpr.2011.12.003

Nordsletten, A. E., Reichenberg, A., Hatch, S. L., de la Cruz, L. F., Pertusa, A., Hotopf, M., & Mataix-Cols, D. (2013). Epidemiology of hoarding disorder. *Br J Psychiatry, 203*(6), 445–452. https://doi.org/10.1192/bjp.bp.113.130195

Nutley, S.K., Camacho, M. R., Nosheny, R. L., Weiner, M., Delucchi, K. L., Mackin, R. S., Mathews, C. A. (2020). *Hoarding disorder is associated with increased risk of cardiovascular/ metabolic dysfunction, chronic pain, and sleep apnea.* Manuscript submitted for publication.

OED Online, Oxford University Press March 2020, www.oed.com/view/Entry/87398. Accessed 11 March 2020.

Pappas, D. A., Colpas, E.C., DeZulueta, J. A. (2012). *An analysis of hoarding fire incidents and MFB organisational response.* Digital Commons. https://digitalcommons.wpi.edu/iqp-all/2990

Park, J. M., Samuels, J. F., Grados, M. A., Riddle, M. A., Bienvenu, O. J., Goes, F. S., . . . Geller, D. A. (2016). ADHD and executive functioning deficits in OCD youths who hoard. *J Psychiatr Res, 82,* 141–148. https://doi.org/10.1016/j.jpsychires.2016.07.024

Park, L. S., Burton, C. L., Dupuis, A., Shan, J., Storch, E. A., Crosbie, J., . . . Arnold, P. D. (2016). The Toronto Obsessive-Compulsive Scale: Psychometrics of a dimensional measure of obsessive-compulsive traits. *J Am Acad Child Adolesc Psychiatry, 55*(4), 310–318, Article e314. https://doi.org/10.1016/j.jaac.2016.01.008

Perry, B. D. (2013). Bonding and attachment in maltreated children: Consequences of emotional neglect in childhood. Retrieved from https://childtrauma.org/wp-content/uploads/2013/11/Bonding_13.pdf

Pertusa, A., Fullana, M. A., Singh, S., Alonso, P., Menchon, J. M., & Mataix-Cols, D. (2008). Compulsive hoarding: OCD symptom, distinct clinical syndrome, or both? *Am J Psychiatry. 165,* 1289–1298. doi: 10.1176/appi.ajp.2008.07111730

Petronek, G.J. (1999). Hoarding of animals: An under-recognized public health problem in a difficult to study population. *Public Health Reports, 114,* 81–87.

Prescribers' Digital Reference (2020). Accessd March 24, 2020. Bleomycin. Retrieved from https://www.pdr.net/drug-summary/Bleomycin-bleomycin-sulfate-1444.362

Plassman, B. L., Langa, K. M., Fisher, G. G., Heeringa, S. G., Weir, D. R., Ofstedal, M. B., . . . Wallace, R. B. (2007). Prevalence of dementia in the United States: The aging, demographics, and memory study. *Neuroepidemiology, 29*(1–2), 125–132. https://doi.org/10.1159/000109998

Postlethwaite, A., Kellett, S., & Mataix-Cols, D. (2019). Prevalence of hoarding disorder: A systematic review and meta-analysis. *J Affect Disord, 256,* 309–316. https://doi.org/10.1016/j.jad.2019.06.004

American Foundation for Suicide Prevention. (2019). *Suicide statistics* [Fact Sheet]. Retrieved from https://afsp.org/about-suicide/suicide-statistics/ on November 11, 2019.

Pushkarskaya, H., Tolin, D. F., Henick, D., Levy, I., & Pittenger, C. (2018). Unbending mind: Individuals with hoarding disorder do not modify decision strategy in response to feedback under risk. *Psychiatry Res, 259*, 506–513. https://doi.org/10.1016/j.psychres.2017.11.001

Pushkarskaya, H., Tolin, D., Ruderman, L., Henick, D., Kelly, J. M., Pittenger, C., & Levy, I. (2017). Value-based decision making under uncertainty in hoarding and obsessive-compulsive disorders. *Psychiatry Res, 258*, 305–315. https://doi.org/10.1016/j.psychres.2017.08.058

Rasmussen, J. L., Steketee, G., Frost, R. O., Tolin, D. F., & Brown, T. A. (2013). Assessing squalor in hoarding: The Home Environment Index. *Community Ment Health J.* https://doi.org/10.1007/s10597-013-9665-8

Rees, C. S., Valentine, S., Anderson, R. A. (2018). The impact of parental hoarding on the lives of children: Interviews with adult offspring of parents with hoarding disorder. *Clinical Psychologist, 22*(3), 327–335. https://doi.org/10.1111/cp.12135

Rodriguez, C. I., Bender, J., Jr., Morrison, S., Mehendru, R., Tolin, D., & Simpson, H. B. (2013). Does extended release methylphenidate help adults with hoarding disorder? A case series. *J Clin Psychopharmacol, 33*(3), 444–447. https://doi.org/10.1097/JCP.0b013e318290115e

Rodriguez, C. I., Herman, D., Alcon, J., Chen, S., Tannen, A., Essock, S., & Simpson, H. B. (2012). Prevalence of hoarding disorder in individuals at potential risk of eviction in New York City: A pilot study. *J Nerv Ment Dis, 200*(1), 91–94. https://doi.org/10.1097/NMD.0b013e31823f678b

Rollnick, S., & Miller, W. R. (1995). What is motivational interviewing? *Behav Cogn Psychother, 23*, 325–334.

Royston, R., Oliver, C., Moss, J., Adams, D., Berg, K., Burbidge, C., . . . Waite, J. (2018). Brief report: Repetitive behaviour profiles in Williams syndrome—Cross syndrome comparisons with Prader-Willi and Down syndromes. *J Autism Dev Disord, 48*(1), 326–331. https://doi.org/10.1007/s10803-017-3319-6

Rylander, G. (1972). Psychoses and the punding and choreiform syndromes in addiction to central stimulant drugs. *Psychiatr Neurol Neurochir, 75*(3), 203–212.

Salthouse, T. A. (2009). When does age-related cognitive decline begin? *Neurobiol Aging, 30*(4), 507–514. https://doi.org/10.1016/j.neurobiolaging.2008.09.023

Samuels, J., Grados, M. A., Riddle, M. A., Bienvenu, O. J., Goes, F. S., Cullen, B., . . . Nestadt, G. (2014). Hoarding in children and adolescents with obsessive-compulsive disorder. *J Obsessive Compuls Relat Disord, 3*(4), 325–331. https://doi.org/10.1016/j.jocrd.2014.08.001

Samuels, J. F., Bienvenu, O. J., Grados, M. A., Cullen, B., Riddle, M. A., Liang, K. Y., . . . Nestadt, G. (2008). Prevalence and correlates of hoarding behavior in a community-based sample. *Behav Res Ther, 46*(7), 836–844. https://doi.org/10.1016/j.brat.2008.04.004

San Francisco Task Force on Compulsive Hoarding. (2009). *Beyond overwhelmed: The impact of compulsive hoarding and cluttering in San Francisco and recommendations to reduce negative impacts and improve care.* Mental Health Association of San Francisco.

Santiago, P. N., Ursano, R. J., Gray, C. L., Pynoos, R. S., Spiegel, D., Lewis-Fernandez, R., . . . Fullerton, C. S. (2013). A systematic review of PTSD prevalence and trajectories in *DSM-5* defined trauma exposed populations: Intentional and non-intentional traumatic events. *PLOS ONE, 8*(4), Article e59236. https://doi.org/10.1371/journal.pone.0059236

Saxena, S., Ayers, C. R., Dozier, M. E., & Maidment, K. M. (2015). The UCLA Hoarding Severity Scale: Development and validation. *J Affect Disord, 175*, 488–493. https://doi.org/10.1016/j.jad.2015.01.030

Saxena, S., Ayers, C. R., Maidment, K. M., Vapnik, T., Wetherell, J. L., & Bystritsky, A. (2011). Quality of life and functional impairment in compulsive hoarding. *J Psychiatr Res, 45*(4), 475–480. https://doi.org/10.1016/j.jpsychires.2010.08.007

Saxena, S. Brody, A.L., Maidment,K.M., Baxter, L.R. Jr. (2007). Paroxetine treatment of compulsive hoarding. *J Psychiatr Res, 41*(6), 481–487.

Saxena, S., Sumner, J. (2014). Venlafaxine extended-release treatment of hoarding disorder. *Int Clin Psychopharmacol.* 29 (5): 266-273.

Scahill, L., Dimitropoulos, A., McDougle, C. J., Aman, M. G., Feurer, I. D., McCracken, J. T., . . . Vitiello, B. (2014). Children's Yale-Brown Obsessive Compulsive Scale in autism spectrum disorder: Component structure and correlates of symptom checklist. *J Am Acad Child Adolesc Psychiatry, 53*(1), 97–107.e1. https://doi.org/10.1016/j.jaac.2013.09.018

Scahill, L., Riddle, M. A., McSwiggin-Hardin, M., Ort, S. I., King, R. A., Goodman, W. K., . . . Leckman, J. F. (1997). Children's Yale-Brown Obsessive Compulsive Scale:Reliability and validity. *J Am Acad Child Adolesc Psychiatry, 36*(6), 844–852.

Schorow, S. (2012). The dangers of too much stuff. *NFPA Journal.* https://www.nfpa.org/news-and-research/publications/nfpa-journal/2012/january-february-2012/features/the-dangers-of-too-much-stuff

Shakespeare, W. (2012*) Henry VI* Parts I, II, and III. Jonathan Bate and Eric Rasmussen (ed.).Modern Library Classics (Original work published 1623).

Sheehan, D. V., Lecrubier, Y., Sheehan, K. H., Amorim, P., Janavs, J., Weiller, E., . . . Dunbar, G. C. (1998). The Mini-International Neuropsychiatric Interview (M.I.N.I.): The development and validation of a structured diagnostic psychiatric interview for *DSM-IV* and ICD-10. *J Clin Psychiatry, 59*(Suppl 20), 22–33; Quiz, 34–57.

Sheehy, G. (1972, January 10). The Secret of Grey Gardens. *New York Magazine.*

Sheppard, B., Chavira, D., Azzam, A., Grados, M. A., Umana, P., Garrido, H., & Mathews, C. A. (2010). ADHD prevalence and association with hoarding behaviors in childhood-onset OCD. *Depress Anxiety, 27*(7), 667–674. https://doi.org/10.1002/da.20691

Shuer, L.J., Frost, R.O. Leading the Buried in Treasures Workshop: A Facilitator's

Manual. Smith College, 2011 (https://www.nationalcouncildocs.net/wp-content /uploads/2013/11/Shuer-Frost-2011-Buried-in-Treasures-Workshop.pdf).

Simmons, B. B., Hartmann, B., & Dejoseph, D. (2011). Evaluation of suspected dementia. *Am Fam Physician, 84*(8), 895–902.

Snowdon, J., & Halliday, G. (2011). A study of severe domestic squalor: 173 cases referred to an old age psychiatry service. *Int Psychogeriatr, 23*(2), 308–314. https://doi.org/10.1017/S1041610210000906

Snowdon, J., Halliday, G., & Hunt, G. E. (2013). Two types of squalor: Findings from a factor analysis of the Environmental Cleanliness and Clutter Scale (ECCS). *Int Psychogeriatr, 25*(7), 1191–1198. https://doi.org/10.1017/S10 4161021300032X

Solmi, M., Fornaro, M., Toyoshima, K., Carvalho, A. F., Kohler, C. A., Veronese, N., . . . Correll, C. U. (2019). Systematic review and exploratory meta-analysis of the efficacy, safety, and biological effects of psychostimulants and atomoxetine in patients with schizophrenia or schizoaffective disorder. *CNS Spectr, 24*(5), 479–495. https://doi.org/10.1017/S1092852918001050

Soreni, N., Cameron, D., Vorstenbosch, V., Duku, E., Rowa, K., Swinson, R., . . . McCabe, R. (2018). Psychometric evaluation of a revised scoring approach for the Children's Saving Inventory in a Canadian sample of youth with obsessive-compulsive disorder. *Child Psychiatry Hum Dev, 49*(6), 966–973. https://doi.org/10.1007/s10578-018-0811-y

South Wales Echo (February 3, 1898), page 3.

Spitzer, R. L., Williams, J. B., Kroenke, K., Linzer, M., deGruy, F. V., 3rd, Hahn, S. R., . . . Johnson, J. G. (1994). Utility of a new procedure for diagnosing mental disorders in primary care: The PRIME-MD 1000 study. *JAMA, 272*(22), 1749–1756. https://doi.org/10.1001/jama.1994.03520220043029

Stampfer, M. J., & Colditz, G. A. (1991). Estrogen replacement therapy and coronary heart disease: A quantitative assessment of the epidemiologic evidence. *Prev Med, 20*(1), 47–63. https://doi.org/10.1016/0091-7435(91)90006-p

Steketee, G., & Frost, R. (2003). Compulsive hoarding: Current status of the research. *Clin Psychol Rev, 23*(7), 905–927.

Steketee, G., & Frost, R.O. (2013). *Home Environment Index treatment for hoarding disorder.* Oxford University Press.

Steketee, G., & Frost, R.O. (2014a). *Treatment for hoarding disorder: Therapist guide.* Oxford University Press.

Steketee, G., & Frost, R.O. (2014b). *Treatment for hoarding disorder: Workbook* (2nd ed.). Oxford University Press.

Steketee, G., Frost, R.O., Kyrios, M. (2003). Cognitive aspects of compulsive hoarding. *Cogn Therapy Research, 27*(4), 463–479.

Stone, K. (2018). Most Commonly Prescribed Medications by Drug Class. Retrieved from https://www.thebalance.com/the-most-prescribed-medications-by-drug-class-2663215

Storch, E. A., Lack, C. W., Merlo, L. J., Geffken, G. R., Jacob, M. L., Murphy, T. K., & Goodman, W. K. (2007). Clinical features of children and adolescents with obsessive-compulsive disorder and hoarding symptoms. *Compr Psychiatry, 48*(4), 313–318.

Storch, E. A., Muroff, J., Lewin, A. B., Geller, D., Ross, A., McCarthy, K., . . . Steketee, G. (2011). Development and preliminary psychometric evaluation of the Children's Saving Inventory. *Child Psychiatry Hum Dev, 42*(2), 166–182. https://doi.org/10.1007/s10578-010-0207-0

Storch, E. A., Nadeau, J. M., Johnco, C., Timpano, K., McBride, N., Jane Mutch, P., . . . Murphy, T. K. (2016). Hoarding in youth with autism spectrum disorders and anxiety: Incidence, clinical correlates, and behavioral treatment response. *J Autism Dev Disord, 46*(5), 1602–1612. https://doi.org/10.1007/s10803-015-2687-z

Storch, E. A., Rahman, O., Park, J. M., Reid, J., Murphy, T. K., & Lewin, A. B. (2011). Compulsive hoarding in children. *J Clin Psychol, 67*(5), 507–516. https://doi.org/10.1002/jclp.20794

Substance Abuse and Mental Health Services Administration. (2014). *Results from the 2013 National Survey on Drug Use and Health: Summary of National Findings* Vol. NSDUH Series H-48, HHS Publication no. (SMA) 14-4863. Retrieved from http://www.samhsa.gov/data/sites/default/files/NSDUHresultsPDFWHTML2013/Web/NSDUHresults2013.htm-3.1

Summerfield, C., & Tsetsos, K. (2012). Building bridges between perceptual and economic decision-making: Neural and computational mechanisms. *Front Neurosci, 6*, 70. https://doi.org/10.3389/fnins.2012.00070

Rottingdean: The Asylum for Cats". (January 31, 1866). The Sussex Advertiser, pg. 3.

Szlatenyi, C. S., Lucini, G.L., Monk, I.M. (2009). *An analysis of fire incidents involving hoarding households.* Digital Commons. https://digitalcommons.wpi.edu/iqp-all/592

Testa, R., Pantelis, C., & Fontenelle, L. F. (2011). Hoarding behaviors in children with learning disabilities. *J Child Neurol, 26*(5), 574–579. https://doi.org/10.1177/0883073810387139

The Institute for Challenging Disorganization (2011). Clutter-Hoarding Scale: A Residential Observational Tool. St. Louis, MO. https://www.challengingdisorganization.org/clutter-hoarding-scale-

Thompson, C., Fernandez de la Cruz, L., Mataix-Cols, D., & Onwumere, J. (2017). A systematic review and quality assessment of psychological, pharmacological, and family-based interventions for hoarding disorder. *Asian J Psychiatr, 27*, 53–66. https://doi.org/10.1016/j.ajp.2017.02.020

Thompson-Hollands, J., Kerns, C. E., Pincus, D. B., & Comer, J. S. (2014). Parental accommodation of child anxiety and related symptoms: Range, impact, and correlates. *J Anxiety Disord, 28*(8), 765–773. https://doi.org/10.1016/j.janxdis.2014.09.007

Tolin, D. F., Frost, R. O., & Steketee, G. (2010). A brief interview for assessing compulsive hoarding: The Hoarding Rating Scale-Interview. *Psychiatry Res, 178*(1), 147–152. https://doi.org/10.1016/j.psychres.2009.05.001

Tolin, D. F., Frost, R. O., Steketee, G., & Fitch, K. E. (2008). Family burden of compulsive hoarding: Results of an internet survey. *Behav Res Ther, 46*(3), 334–344.

Tolin, D. F., Frost, R. O., Steketee, G., Gray, K. D., & Fitch, K. E. (2008). The economic and social burden of compulsive hoarding. *Psychiatry Res, 160*(2), 200–211.

Tolin, D. F., Frost, R. O., Steketee, G., & Muroff, J. (2015). Cognitive behavioral therapy for hoarding disorder: A meta-analysis. *Depress Anxiety, 32*(3), 158–166. https://doi.org/10.1002/da.22327

Tolin, D. F., Kiehl, K. A., Worhunsky, P., Book, G. A., & Maltby, N. (2009). An exploratory study of the neural mechanisms of decision making in compulsive hoarding. *Psychol Med, 39*(2), 325–336. https://doi.org/10.1017/S0033291708003371

Tolin, D. F., Meunier, S. A., Frost, R. O., & Steketee, G. (2010). Course of compulsive hoarding and its relationship to life events. *Depress Anxiety, 27*(9), 829–838. https://doi.org/10.1002/da.20684

Tolin, D. F., Meunier, S. A., Frost, R. O., & Steketee, G. (2011). Hoarding among patients seeking treatment for anxiety disorders. *J Anxiety Disord, 25*(1), 43–48. https://doi.org/10.1016/j.janxdis.2010.08.001

Tolin, D. F., Steketee,G., & Frost, R. O. (2007). *Buried in treasures: Help for compulsive acquiring, saving, and hoarding.* Oxford University Press.

Tolin, D. F., Stevens, M. C., Villavicencio, A. L., Norberg, M. M., Calhoun, V. D., Frost, R. O., . . . Pearlson, G. D. (2012). Neural mechanisms of decision making in hoarding disorder. *Arch Gen Psychiatry, 69*(8), 832–841. https://doi.org/10.1001/archgenpsychiatry.2011.1980

Tolin, D. F., & Villavicencio, A. (2011). Inattention, but not OCD, predicts the core features of hoarding disorder. *Behav Res Ther, 49*(2), 120–125. https://doi.org/10.1016/j.brat.2010.12.002

Tolin, D. F., Villavicencio, A., Umbach, A., & Kurtz, M. M. (2011). Neuropsychological functioning in hoarding disorder. *Psychiatry Res, 189*(3), 413–418. https://doi.org/10.1016/j.psychres.2011.06.022

Tompkins, M. A., & Hartl, T.A. (2009). *Digging out: Helping your loved one manage clutter, hoarding, & compulsive acquiring.* New Harbinger Publications.

Torres, A. R., Fontenelle, L. F., Ferrao, Y. A., do Rosario, M. C., Torresan, R. C., Miguel, E. C., & Shavitt, R. G. (2012). Clinical features of obsessive-compulsive disorder with hoarding symptoms: A multicenter study. *J Psychiatr Res, 46*(6), 724–732. https://doi.org/10.1016/j.jpsychires.2012.03.005

Torres, A. R., Fontenelle, L. F., Shavitt, R. G., Ferrao, Y. A., do Rosario, M. C., Storch, E. A., & Miguel, E. C. (2016). Comorbidity variation in patients with obsessive-compulsive disorder according to symptom dimensions: Results from a large multicentre clinical sample. *J Affect Disord, 190*, 508–516. https://doi.org/10.1016/j.jad.2015.10.051

Twamley, E. W., Vella, L., Burton, C. Z., Heaton, R. K., & Jeste, D. V. (2012). Compensatory cognitive training for psychosis: Effects in a randomized controlled trial. *J Clin Psychiatry, 73*(9), 1212–1219. https://doi.org/10.4088/JCP.12m07686

Uhm, S. Y., Tsoh, J. Y., Mackin, R. S., Gause, M., Chan, J., Franklin, J., . . . Mathews, C. A. (2016). Comparison of a peer facilitated support group to cognitive behavior therapy: Study protocol for a randomized controlled trial for hoarding disorder. *Contemp Clin Trials, 50*, 98–105. https://doi.org/10.1016/j.cct.2016.07.018

U.S. Department of Health and Human Services. (2014). *The health consequences of smoking: 50 years of progress.* A report of the surgeon general. https://www.ncbi.nlm.nih.gov/books/NBK179276/pdf/Bookshelf_NBK179276.pdf

U.S. Department of Justice, Federal Bureau of Investigation, Criminal Justice Information Services Division. (2016). New to NBIRS. https://ucr.fbi.gov/nibrs/2016/resource-pages/nibrs-2016-homepage_alt.pdf

van der Flier, W. M., & Scheltens, P. (2005). Epidemiology and risk factors of dementia. *J Neurol Neurosurg Psychiatry, 76*(2–7). https://doi.org/10.1136/jnnp.2005.082867

Vos, T., Flaxman, A. D., Naghavi, M., Lozano, R., Michaud, C., Ezzati, M., . . . Memish, Z. A. (2012). Years lived with disability (YLDs) for 1160 sequelae of 289 diseases and injuries 1990-2010: a systematic analysis for the Global Burden of Disease Study 2010. 380:2163-219doi: 6. 10.1016/S0140-6736(12)61729-2

Warner, C. B., Ottman, A. A., & Brown, J. N. (2018). The role of atomoxetine for Parkinson disease-related executive dysfunction: A systematic review. *J Clin Psychopharmacol, 38*(6), 627–631. https://doi.org/10.1097/JCP.0000000000000963

Weintraub, M. J., Brown, C. A., & Timpano, K. R. (2018). The relationship between schizotypal traits and hoarding symptoms: An examination of symptom specificity and the role of perceived cognitive failures. *J Affect Disord, 237*, 10–17. https://doi.org/10.1016/j.jad.2018.04.121

Weiss, K. J., & Khan, A. (2015). Hoarding, housing, and *DSM-5. J Am Acad Psychiatry Law, 43*(4), 492–498.

Wheaton, M., Timpano, K. R., Lasalle-Ricci, V. H., & Murphy, D. (2008). Characterizing the hoarding phenotype in individuals with OCD: Associations with comorbidity, severity and gender. *J Anxiety Disord, 22*(2), 243–252. https://doi.org/10.1016/j.janxdis.2007.01.015

Wilbram, M., Kellett, S., & Beail, N. (2008). Compulsive hoarding: A qualitative investigation of partner and carer perspectives. *Br J Clin Psychol, 47*(1), 59–73. https://doi.org/10.1348/014466507X240740

Wincze, J. P., Steketee, G., & Frost, R. O. (2007). Categorization in compulsive hoarding. *Behav Res Ther, 45*(1), 63–72.

Wolf, U., Rapoport, M. J., & Schweizer, T. A. (2009). Evaluating the affective component of the cerebellar cognitive affective syndrome. *J Neuropsychiatry Clin Neurosci, 21*(3), 245–253. doi:10.1176/appi.neuropsych.21.3.245

Woody, S. R., Kellman-McFarlane, K., & Welsted, A. (2014). Review of cognitive performance in hoarding disorder. *Clin Psychol Rev, 34*(4), 324–336. https://doi.org/10.1016/j.cpr.2014.04.002

Yamada, S., Nakao, T., Ikari, K., Kuwano, M., Murayama, K., Tomiyama, H., . . . Kanba, S. (2018). A unique increase in prefrontal gray matter volume in hoarding disorder compared to obsessive-compulsive disorder. *PLOS ONE, 13*(7), Article e0200814. https://doi.org/10.1371/journal.pone.0200814

Zakrzewski, J. J., Datta, S., Scherling, C., Nizar, K., Vigil, O., Rosen, H., & Mathews, C. A. (2018). Deficits in physiological and self-conscious emotional response to errors in hoarding disorder. *Psychiatry Res, 268*, 157–164. https://doi.org/10.1016/j.psychres.2018.07.012

Zakrzewski, J. J., Gillett, D.A., Vigil, O.R, Smith, L.C., Komaiko, K., Chou, C.-Y., Uhm, S.Y., Bain, L.D., Stark, S.J., Gause, M., Howell, G., Vega, E., Chan, J., Eckfield, M.B., Tsoh, J.Y., Delucchi, K., Mackin, R.S., Mathews, C.A. (2020). Visually mediated functioning improves following treatment of hoarding disorder. *Journal of Affective Disorders, 264,* 310–317.

Zaboski, B. A., II, Merritt, O. A., Schrack, A. P., Gayle, C., Gonzalez, M., Guerrero, L. A., . . . Mathews, C. A. (2019). Hoarding: A meta-analysis of age of onset. *Depress Anxiety, 36*(6), 552–564. https://doi.org/10.1002/da.22896

INDEX